Rocky Mountain

WARDEN

Rocky Mountain
WARDEN

Frank Calkins

ALFRED · A · KNOPF

New York

This book is for Rodello
A N D
for my mother and father

Man can climb to the highest summits but he cannot dwell there long.

GEORGE BERNARD SHAW

A C K N O W L E D G M E N T S

THE ORIGINAL IDEA FOR THIS BOOK WAS ANGUS CAMERON'S. THANK you, Angus, for that and much more. My friend Mike Hanson provided me with many ideas about the western range land we both cherish. Mike and I have not always agreed, but if all Forest Rangers were like Mike there would probably not be a chapter about sheep in this book. The librarians at the Teton County Library in Jackson Wyoming found every obscure reference book that I asked them for. That fine library in the log cabin never ceases to amaze and delight me. I would also like to thank Clare Conley, editor of *Field & Stream*, for granting me permission to here re-play a few incidents that originally appeared in that magazine.

My wife, Rodello, believed that I could write this book long before I ever did. She has made me mad at times, but she has never let me down. This book is ninety percent hers.

F. C.

February, 1970
Freedom, Wyoming

CONTENTS

Rocky Mountain

WARDEN

I / TAKING FRED'S PLACE

"No one wants you around unless they're hurt or in trouble."
—UTAH HIGHWAY PATROLMAN

I USED TO BELIEVE THAT ALL A WESTERNER NEEDED TO GET ON IN life was a horse, a dog, a razor, and a rifle. When I grew up and was hired as a warden by the Utah Fish and Game Department, I discovered the truth of my boyhood beliefs.

My first assignment was to the small town of Vernal, in the Uintah Basin of northeastern Utah. The first time I drove down the town's neon-jiggering main street, I had all the prerequisite equipment save the dog. Most of what I owned was packed into the back of my pickup truck or trailered behind it in a weathered horse van. Invisible among the wildlife texts, shotgun shells, and riding tack was an enormous set of ideals. I was bringing conservation to the heathen.

It was disconcerting, therefore, to be waved to and smiled at by some flashy young ladies whose car stopped beside mine at the town's single traffic light. I am afraid that I gave them a stony look, for who had ever glimpsed lust in the eyes of Aldo Leopold or dreamed of Gifford Pinchot embracing anything but a Douglas fir?

My new home was a stockmen's town and also a Mormon town; although it was not always both at the same time. Vernal is one of the few Mormon towns where you can see a Saint pause on the steps of his church and light a cigarette. It is also one of the few towns that boasts openly of having made a sucker of the United States Government. Vernal has always been a long way from a railroad and subject to high freight rates. When some of the first citizens decided to build a bank building, they were discouraged by the high cost of freighting in brick. "Why, it costs more to freight in a pound of bricks than it does to mail in a pound of clothes . . . say!" The complaint led to a remarkable idea, and the Bank of Vernal was mailed in, one package of bricks at a time.

I arrived in the town at night. It was late winter, and there was a ropey drift of old snow around the entrance of the motel. The clerk, who registered me and slid a key across the knotty-pine counter, asked, "You takin' Fred's place?"

[4

"Not exactly." I explained that I was taking Hinman's place; he had taken Huff's place; Clairon Huff had replaced the retired Fred Reynolds.

The room clerk was more interested in selling me a gastrolith from a basket labeled DINOSAUR GIZZARD ROCKS than he was in hearing a genealogy of the area's game wardens. He was also prepared to issue me a comic dinosaur-hunting license and give me professional advice on some oil and gas properties, or to direct me to the world's largest Gilsonite mine at Bonanza. But, like almost everyone else in the area, he didn't know what in hell Gilsonite was good for.

I had come like a thief in the night, and as far as a goodly portion of the citizenry were concerned, I was even less welcome. Someone in the restaurant said, "Jesus Christ! Another one! You guys must come by the dozen." And after such hearty welcomes, they were likely to give you their interpretations of the state game laws, interpretations that rarely coincided with what I had tried to memorize from my little pink-covered official booklet. Even the two mountains looming above town in the late winter moonlight seemed to offer a foreboding welcome. Taylor Mountain was named, I guessed, for either a deceased president of the Mormon Church or for an early stockman. To the east was Diamond Mountain, named in honor of the great mining swindle pulled off there in the last century.

After inspecting my room—the night before, I had rented a motel room that was so constructed as to prevent normal seating on the toilet when the bathroom door was shut—I went outside to my truck. I had been given directions for reaching the Vernal Game Farm where Bob Jensen, the regional game manager, lived with his family. Bob and his wife, Ruth, were eminently hospitable. Bob helped me unload my mare in one of the pastures, then spent the remainder of the evening giving me a run-down on the area.

Deer, elk, and antelope lived here. There were Canada geese along the Green River and ducks on every pond and rivulet in between. Pheasants lived from the town's edge to the end of the irrigated farm lands. Where the sage and greasewood began, the chukar partridges began, too. And above them, on flat-topped Diamond Mountain, sage grouse promenaded around beaver ponds that sometimes yielded huge rainbow trout. There were bighorn sheep still safe in their canyon redoubts along the Green River. Occasionally moose wandered south across the Uinta Divide from wild Daggett County. To the south, a goodly number of bears and mountain lions still hunted in the vast and mysterious Book Cliffs.

From the stories about him, which had almost become legends in the department's Salt Lake office, I half expected Fat Gardiner to tower out of the land like Paul Bunyan. But he did not. He was sitting quietly in a yellow-walled café with Bob Jensen when I went in for breakfast the next morning. Fat was in his thirties, lean and perpetually tanned. He was about my height, six feet, and when we shook hands I sensed in that cool grip the competence one finds in the hands of an artisan. There were wisps of gray in the black hair at his temples. His eyes were a vivid blue, and set into a face that was perhaps a hair too thin to make its owner a handsome man. Fat was just good-looking. The brim of his gray regulation Stetson had a non-regulation bronc-rider's curl. His tan uniform shirt was spotless and neatly pressed, although it lacked our green regulation necktie. He was wearing the Levis our department manual generally forbade. I liked Fat from the first.

Until I arrived he was responsible for two districts, which comprised about four thousand square miles. When I saw his pickup truck with its bashed-in door standing at the curb, I was ready to believe that Fat had driven it over every one of those miles—even the vertical ones. Knowing one's district is fundamental to being a competent game warden. Each of my several superiors in the game department had emphasized the necessity for getting along with Fat, and when they said "He knows the country," it was in tones of beatific admiration. There were few of them who had not had Fat Gardiner lead him to a trophy trout, prime buck deer, or majestic bull elk.

[6

We deferred exploration that first morning while Fat found an apartment for me. It was a trifle dank but all right for Vernal's latest bachelor priest of conservation, because it was in the basement under the home of the Baptist minister. It cost thirty-five dollars a month. After I had taken possession of the subterranean rooms we drove out to the game farm, where Fat appraised my mare. "She seems like a sensible old thing." Then he took me home to dinner, which is lunch in the west.

Fat lived in a modest home that he had built himself on his Dad's farm in Naples Ward. With its Johns-Manville siding, I could have said it looked like a "sensible thing," but I did not. When a man builds a home and begins raising a family of three boys on little more than two hundred a month, he doesn't go in for wainscoting and raw-silk wallpaper. Fat's wife, Russie, was a shy young woman from a wilderness ranch in the Book Cliffs. Their youngest son, Brud, was still at home, but the two older brothers were in grammar school. While Russie fried some meat, Fat took me outside to meet his bird dog, Poke, his brood mare, Dilsey, and her unnamed palamino colt. At the far end of Fat's paddock stood a magnificent sorrel horse. When he stepped over to accept Fat's offer of rolled oats, I realized why Fat had not praised my mare. His Joe was a lot of horse.

After dinner Fat drove me up onto the flanks of Diamond Mountain to check on the numerous deer wintering there. I saw every deer that Fat pointed out, and a few, a very few, that he did not see first. He told me about a pinch that Steve Radosevich had made over in Brown's Hole the previous hunting season. Steve had checked a hunter with a fine buck, but before waving the man on Steve noticed something peculiar about the carcass. When he bent to examine it he found an illegal Canada goose hidden inside the buck's body cavity.

"Look here," said Steve. The hunter looked and then frowned angrily.

"Why," he exclaimed, "that goose-eatin' son of a bitch!"

As we drove along, Fat recited a memorized list of local poachers. One had strong religious convictions but he nevertheless poached at every opportunity and seemed to spend his spare moments bedeviling the game department. Fat told me about men who would risk ruining new cars rather than have him catch them with illegal deer. Fat told me at what times and seasons the various poaching was likely to occur. He suggested that I watch for a sedan filled with local matrons: they occasionally collected pheasants by shooting from the car. Certain farmers shot pheasants from their bedroom windows, then retrieved them after dark. In August the corpses of young sage grouse were sometimes hidden beneath an auto's large hub caps. Pheasants were stuffed into wells for spare tires or under the car's seats. Sometimes deer were poached and then quartered and sneaked home under the hoods of automobiles. Overlimits of trout were likely to be hidden in rolled sleeping bags.

Turning from these subterfuges, Fat went on to explain the care and feeding of the Judge. "I try to see he gets a limit a' fish ever' summer an' maybe a piece of deer or elk in the fall. When you pick up a guy for mor'n one thing, make out a separate ticket on each violation. The Judge wants ever'thin' proper-like."

Back in town, we visited the Judge, who was friendly but properly judicial. Before we left he invited me and my wife over to see his new television set.

"I don't have a wife, Judge."

"Well, then," he said, "bring somebody else's wife over."

The Judge walked home for lunch each day, but before reaching there he invariably stopped for a glass of beer at one of the town's two beer parlors. The more pious in the community used to refer to "the Judge's drinking."

In an adjacent office I met the town's chief of police and learned that he was an avid fisherman and rather more of a gentleman than you might expect the chief of a small-town police force to be. The county sheriff was a better job of typecasting, although he had a reputation for being as stern in enforcing Mormon doctrine as he

[8

was in applying the ordinances of Uintah County. The highway patrolmen were about what I expected: tough, competent, and possessed of better hearts than most of the citizens I knew.

Across the street and down half a block was the Basin Loan Company. The benign occupant of that office was Jack Turner, a smiling avuncular man who was currently president and also a director of the Vernal Rod and Gun Club. A half block farther on I met Dale Jensen, a director of the gun club, owner of the Basin Laundry, and, I was to learn, a prince. Speed Haws was the third director of the club. He apparently alternated between a job in the post office and one drumming sewing machines. He gave me the impression of being a lifelong doubter of game departments.

As we went about the town, I became more and more impressed with Fat's remarkable grammar. He also tended to pronounce "God-damn son of a bitch" as one word. But when it was combined into sentences, his speech was colorful and delightfully descriptive. Who could be richer than someone "six foot in a bull's ass?" Who was more rude than one who was "plumb impudent," or less manly than the fellow described as "pissy-assed"? Fat had not gone far in school, nor had he acquired too much classical education while he was there. He could expound at length on the causes of lightning because a teacher had once shamed him into learning them. But mostly he talked and acted like the unpretentious ex-cowboy he was. He was a dead shot and a superb rider and roper, and as we drove through the countryside he spoke of "good" as opposed to "blind bridle outfits," which were ranches so uncaring of their stock and with such a paucity of tack that they used old, blinder-equipped, workhorse bridles on their riding stock.

Fat introduced me to a man who lived with his wife in a tiny spotless shack and kept a thousand-dollar stud horse in his corral. On our way there he had pointed out the home of a man who reputedly carried a hide-out gun in the crown of his tall Stetson.

The first days on my new job were quite an experience. I had suddenly embarked on a career that encompassed cowboys and

Indians, sheepherders, squaw men, traders, and trappers, in addition to several "pissy-assed sonsabitches." In time I learned to joke with the occupants of the county jail (never kid a man about his conviction). We stopped for coffee in drab cafés where blowsy waitresses grinned when Fat intimated that he possessed a salubrious wart that "would make 'em swallow their gum."

As March worried its way through fitful snowstorms, Fat visibly wearied of the Uintah Basin's brand of café society. His conversation dwelled more and more upon the Book Cliffs. So when the snow line began rising perceptibly on the Bolly peaks of the Uinta range to the north, Fat and I drove south into the Book Cliffs.

On our way we stopped at the little Indian town of Ouray. Like all the Indian settlements I had seen before, this one seemed to slump, to be down at the heels without giving a damn. The most impressive structure there is the state-owned bridge across the Green River, a murky stream that becomes even murkier below its confluence with the nearby White River. On one side of the settlement there are several decrepit log cabins patiently lined up across the highway from the weathered store. There are two bright Phillips gas pumps in front of the store, and their gaudiness is out of place in all that wind-whipped, dusty waste. The store is dark and gloomy despite the vast patio of shiny discarded bottle caps around its front.

Parking beside the "Regular" pump, Fat cranked the handle and began filling the pickup's tank with gas. He nodded toward a huge, vaguely yellow house that in stagecoach days had been a hotel, and explained that Wallace Tabee, a warden for the Ute Indian Tribe, now lived there. Lounging, scratching, and stretching on their chains behind the house were several rangy hounds; Wallace liked to run bear and mountain lions.

Inside the store a slightly worn but pleasant-faced white woman made out our gas ticket and sold us a slab of cheese. Her stock was of general staples—lantern mantles to enamelware and cream-style corn. On one side of the stove was a dry-goods department. It

[10

seemed to me that most of this section was devoted to the display of every sort of sombrero and straw cowboy hat in current manufacture.

As I looked out the store's filmed-over front window, an ancient Indian left one of the cabins and swung painfully across the street on crutches. He was a proper Indian, fringed and braided, wearing a filthy hat that was set off by a beautifully beaded band. The old man came into the store and flopped down on a bench beside the rusty pop cooler. I half opened my mouth to say hello, but the old man ignored us as one ignores the air—we didn't exist.

Then a fat young squaw came in with her cowboy-hatted little son. She made her selections slowly, bringing each one to the counter separately and placing it beside the old scrollwork cash register. While she shopped, her son also made selections, childish ones, which he placed on the counter beside his mother's. But, unlike a white mother, she didn't return them to the shelves; she bought them. The Ute man-child is rarely denied or corrected. Perhaps this is a custom that remains from the old days, when the Utes were ferocious warriors unused to entertaining second thoughts.

Ouray is desolate, but just yards beyond it are the cottonwood bottoms along the Green River. One is called Chepeta Grove for an Indian princess who was the daughter of Chief Ouray. I have seen some huge mule deer in these groves, but beyond them the land is sere, and the largest visible "game" are the ever-fleeing little antelope ground squirrels. Even in March auto tires churn up a spiral of dust in the drive across the expanse of brownish-gray bleakness. It is a hard, unforgiving land of flinty soils, dusty swales, and solitary buttes. Discarded beer cans and broken bottles border the dirt road, their labels spelling COORS to the end of the horizon.

A weathered, ramshackle sign appeared before us. Without consulting the gray, splintered board, Fat took the route marked WILLOW CREEK.

Willow Creek turned out to be very small. Its sluggish current carries a perpetual cargo of silt down a long hallway of pasture land that is crowded on each side by tawny, towering cliffs. Looking at those high rock walls with their layers of sedimentary rock, I began to understand why these were called the Book Cliffs; they looked like shelves filled with books. As we drove along I noticed that low spots in the road wore whitish halos of alkali, and when we hit the ruts in these places, the hardened mud had all the resilience of cement.

We passed one or two unhappy-looking ranches with some faded haystacks lumping the narrow meadow. Willis Stevens's home ranch is lodged in a big niche among the cliffs. A bunkhouse, some sheds, a corral, and a small bungalow nestle among the gray and leafless cottonwoods. The outbuildings are typical of a wilderness ranch: unpainted logs with clay chinking and dirt or tarpaper roofs. The bungalow, however, could have been found along many residential streets in America about 1935.

Standing in the bunkhouse door was a toothless old man. He was the only hand; he milked a cow twice daily, and between times pitched hay to the Herefords in the pasture. He waved us inside, then clumped around between the old wood range, on which he was brewing a pot of coffee, and the big, oilcloth-covered table, where he sat. Fat introduced us, then went back out to the truck and returned with a nearly empty bottle of whiskey. The old man grinned and poured most of what was left into his coffee mug. Fat and I divided the rest between the cups the old man had set out for us.

As he drank the old man become more agreeable. Oh, yes, there were lots of deer around, but he hadn't seen many chukars that winter. He asked Fat if they were good eating, and Fat assured him that they were. We learned that the cattle had wintered well and that Willis Stevens had gone off somewhere in the truck while his boy, Jim, had been gone since before daylight, "ridin' fer cattle." When he had brought us up to date the old man lit the kerosene lantern and filled the range with juniper. The resinous wood had a sharp, good smell. Before he shuffled out to milk the cow, the old man told us to bring in our bed rolls.

While Fat started supper I carried in our sleeping bags and put them on the scarred iron bedstead that our host had indicated. Across from it was another double bed. Between them was a home-made table littered with old magazines of the *Real West* and *Male!* genre. There were also ash trays made from cans, a jar containing some .22 cartridges, and another containing matches. Crumbling in the midst of this was a scarred and obviously impotent battery-powered radio.

Bits of mirror, horseshoe nails, spikes, files, and old clothing were fastened to or stuck into the log walls. A livestock commission had presented the ranch with its calendar, which bore a colorful Charlie Russell print. It was the only picture in the room.

I heard the old man return and set his bucket of milk to cool in a box just outside the bunkhouse door. Then he came in and hung his dirty and ragged denim coat on a nail. He covered it with his cap, then poured himself a cup of coffee. "Jim oughta' be in purty quick," he said.

It was pitch black outside when Jim came. He was a tall boy with a great frame he had not yet filled. He wore faded denims and flannel shirts over heavy, long underwear. "Hi, Fat," he grinned. He had good teeth set in a broad, handsome face. He shook hands with me, and my hand seemed to disappear in his huge, friendly fist. Jim was about nineteen, shy and utterly without guile.

After supper, we played penny-ante poker using kitchen matches for chips. Jim played a novice's game, and grinned rue-fully as he lost hand after hand. The old man crowed when he won, and scowled when he lost. At nine o'clock Jim said he was too sleepy to play any longer. Without waiting to be coaxed to keep the game alive, he stripped to his underwear and immediately fell asleep under the sheetless, dirty quilts. The old man counted his matches, cashed them, and happily announced that he was two dollars winners. He beamed and orally replayed all his winning

13]

hands. He hinted broadly that he would accept another drink if Fat had one. Fat said that he was sorry, and the old man shrugged and crawled into bed with Jim.

Fat and I unrolled our sleeping bags on top of the other bed and crawled into them. When he blew out the lamp the room fell into limpid blue darkness. I heard a mouse scurry somewhere, and outside a dog barked once. The old man began snoring wetly, and Jim bounced on the creaking springs. I thought of myself as a little boy, clipping Harold Von Schmidt illustrations from *Saturday Evening Post* westerns. The walls of my room had been covered with them, along with Remington's and Russell's. I would look at them and long to be a cowboy. That night in the log bunkhouse I decided that I had longed for the wrong occupation. I was content to be a game warden.

The wintry sun was spilling its first light into Willow Creek Canyon when we drove out of Stevens's pole gate. We saw a doe in the frosty meadow. She was watchful but unafraid, and Fat said that was a good sign—there was no poaching in the area. As we drove back down the creek small flocks of chukar partridges scattered before the pickup.

Fat turned up the rocky Buck Canyon road. "That old man's a boozer," he explained. "Willis brings 'em here to dry out. Then he lets 'em chore an' earn a little money afore he'll take 'em back to town." I asked about Jim. "When he finished high school," Fat said, "his dad offered him a choice—college or a trip around the world. Jim just asked to stay there on the Creek. He don't give a damn about anything but that ranch. He trusts ever'body, though—that'll cost him, someday." I thought about that nice, uncomplicated young man and hoped the world would take its time in disappointing Jim Stevens.

We came out of Buck Canyon and onto the top of a great ridge whose limits seemed to be the horizon. Fat turned right and drove toward P.R. Springs. He said they were small but they had the only reliable and easily obtainable water for miles. Sage, which had been spotty and haggard-looking, began to show up in robust abundance. Then the junipers gave way before the most elegant and extensive stands of deer browse I had ever seen. Fat said it grew this way for miles, and I began to understand Bob Jensen's enthusiasm about the area that first night at the game farm. The long, wide-topped ridges pushed out into unending blue sky, and between them deep canyons fell away into hazy depths. The ascent from Ouray had been so gradual that I was not prepared to suddenly find myself at nine thousand feet. There were deer tracks crossing the road at intervals. "When there's only two deer left," Fat said, "one will be in a zoo and t'other will be in the Book Cliffs." He was right; this was mule deer country—perhaps the best in the world.

Eventually, the ever-climbing road disappeared into an untracked mantle of grainy snow. "Nobody up here all spring," Fat said, turning the truck around. He drove us back down into the juniper belt. The sun was warm there and the ground was dry. We stopped in a little draw beside a downed tree. Its dry branches soon made us a fire, which Fat used to boil coffee and fry hamburgers. When the meat was cooked we made sandwiches and filled out the meal with cheese and pickles.

While we ate, I looked out at the quiet land. Not so much as a signpost intruded upon the solitude. "You can drive for two hundred and fifty miles up here," Fat said, "an' never take the same road twice or see another car." No map of this seemingly limitless land was generally available, and I thought, "So be it."

There was no sign of men except the drying carcass of a fox the government hunters had poisoned. But this was the cowman's kingdom, and we were not allowed to protect foxes, so we turned toward Vernal. It was a long drive, but eventually we passed down Evacuation Creek (named for its laxative properties) and came to the great Gilsonite mine at Bonanza. It was a seemingly haphazard collection of towers, piping, and huge black hoppers, a smudge on the memory of a wilderness.

Near the tiny community of Jensen, a weathered rancher waved us down to complain about beaver trouble. I did not know it at the time, but this meeting prefaced an antipathy I was to have toward beaver which persists to this day. The Green River, which flows past Jensen, is a beaver's paradise. Abundant cottonwoods and willows furnish choice food, and the high, sandy riverbanks afford excellent tunneling sites. We call these tunneling animals "bank beaver" to distinguish them from the lodge-building variety. A bank beaver's excavations often extend twenty feet into the stream bank. After a time these tunnels are liable to collapse, creating traps for livestock or ruining cropland.

Unfortunately, no beaver has yet learned to differentiate between a natural stream and an irrigation ditch. Many a wandering beaver has come upon a farmer's headgate and decided to improve that dam with one of his own. Sometimes the unwanted dam could be broken open or dynamited, and its builder would move away. But far too often the beaver would rebuild his dam overnight and then be made to pay for his industry with his life. By trapping nuisance beaver in the early spring, we not only removed the nuisance and got a prime pelt for the state of Utah, we also saved ourselves some headaches later when farmers began to irrigate.

Trapping beaver is fairly easy. All that is usually necessary is to make a hole in the dam, set a trap there, and collect the unhappy creature the following morning. Unless the trap is skillfully set to catch the beaver by the hind foot, he is liable to wring off his front foot and escape. To prevent this, trappers often use drowning sets— a heavy stone is fastened to the trap wire in such a way that when the caught animal struggles, the stone slides down the wire into deep water. The stone holds the beaver there until he drowns.

Traps are also set in the water at the foot of slides, and sometimes along the beavers' travel ways. Some fresh mud smeared on a slide or a few drops of castor essence, judiciously placed, often improves the set's effectiveness. When the beaver is to be "transplanted" rather than killed, a live trap is set. This trap looks like a large piece of folded chain-link fence. It is set by unfolding its two

[16

halves. When a beaver crawls through it, the trap closes on him like a book.

Unfortunately for the warden-trapper, all beaver aren't so easily removed. The I.Q. of a beaver that has gotten out of a trap zooms up about 50 points—to about 51½. I have had these fellows spring my carefully set traps by pushing sticks into them, or they will slide the set trap onto their dam site and bury it under sticks and mud. They will also simply walk around a trap. If you litter their pond with traps, they may move and cause new and more aggravating troubles somewhere else. These aggravations include making their ponds a half-inch over your hip-boot tops, and weaving flesh-raking barbed wire into their latest project. I have even heard of beavers that used unexploded sticks of dynamite from dam blastings to build new dams.

What is more, God never meant the beaver to be skinned. I can skin a seven-hundred-pound elk in a third of the time it takes me to skin a forty-pound beaver. The nearest I can come to describing the process is to suggest that you skin a football that is two-thirds inflated—without puncturing the bladder. Every inch of hide must be cut away from the carcass; it can't be pulled off, and no fat should be allowed to come away with the pelt. A green skin is very difficult to flesh once it's off the beaver, and if this fat is allowed to remain on the hide, it "burns," subtracting greatly from the value.

Some ranchers can't abide a beaver on their property, even if it is doing no harm. Once scarce and therefore bringing high fur prices, the Utah beaver increased to the point of being commonplace and hardly worth trapping. As a result, the game wardens or a state trapper had to remove the animals. Usually I could get the offending beavers and stop the ranchers' complaints, but one fellow had a strange notion of beaver control. In essence, he wanted me to trap just enough beaver from his place to allow the survivors to irrigate his meadow once a week—except when he was mowing hay there. I failed to do this, and the first letter of complaint was filed in my dossier at headquarters.

A few other landowners complained about beavers merely to get attention or to alleviate their loneliness. At one isolated ranch the lonely woman who lived there confided, "I ain't had any for so long that I bet it's haired over."

I was a minion of the law all that spring before making my first arrest. My first "victim" was a fellow who had been fishing without a license.

"I wasn't fishin'," he said.

"I'm sorry," I replied, "but I watched you fish for twenty minutes before I came over."

"Well, for Chrissakes! If you was watchin' so long, why din'tcha honk or wave so I'da knowed you was around?"

At first, most of the people I arrested had already been picked up more times than I had issued citations. Once I erred in indicating where a fellow should sign his summons, and he very kindly corrected my error and placed his signature on the proper line. I did not enjoy arresting people, although some of the officers did.

One of these was patrolling a stream with another department employee prior to the opening of fishing season. Some anglers simply can't wait those last few days, and this warden thought he'd found one when he spied a car partly hidden in some streamside bushes. "There's a sonofabitch in there fishing!" he cried happily. As he drew up beside the suspect sedan, a head appeared, furtively peeping over the hood at the officers. "Aw right, you bastard, come outta' there."

A dapper little fellow obeyed the warden's order, and although he was badly frightened by the warden's accusations and abusive language, he stoutly denied fishing. The warden refused to believe him and brushed the man aside to jerk open the sedan's back door. "Aha, you lyin' bastard! What's this?" The officer had grabbed a long, cylindrical object wrapped in newspaper from the back seat.

"Honest, I haven't been fishing. That isn't a fish."

The warden ignored the protests and ripped open the package. What he found there set him raging in furious disbelief. His blush-

[18

ing suspect said he thought it was illegal to defecate on the water-shed, so he had used the paper and was taking it home for disposal. The same warden was famed for his profanity. Nevertheless, the announcer at a local radio station decided to interview him after the first day of either-sex deer hunting. Biologists had worked long and hard to convince the public that this form of herd reduction was justified. The winter ranges were badly overbrowsed, and the deer losses caused by starvation were tragically high. Nevertheless, this warden told his listening audience, "This doe hunting is the damndest slaughter in history. If it isn't stopped quick, there won't be a deer left inside of two years." He made his point, but he left the game department soon afterward.

Some game departments are torn by dissension between their biological and enforcement divisions. In Utah, though, the wardens did much of the biological work in cooperation with a regional game manager. Many of these biologists, including Bob Jensen, were former wardens themselves, so we usually got along well. Each spring the wardens set aside their enforcement work to make a series of rides over the winter big-game ranges. We spent a month or more at it, trying to see all the important deer wintering areas in our district. And while the rides were valuable to us, they were de-signed principally for the hunting public. The biological staff felt that if laymen understood what conditions on winter ranges were like after a season of use, they might be more likely to support the department's management programs. In addition to sportsmen, the department invited forest rangers, ranchers, and men from the Bureau of Land Management to participate in the rides. Unfortun-ately, many of the rides were often made only by the professionals, because laymen simply wouldn't go with us. While on the rides, we attempted to judge the amount of use the forage had had, and we counted all the deer and elk seen.

Often the local newspapers would seize upon this information as the full story about deer populations in that locality. A single year's rides certainly did not produce enough information to base a hunting season on. As a "new boy," I hadn't much to say after my first season of riding, but I was able to get an over-all opinion of range conditions.

I also helped Fat and Bob Jensen "read" transects and count deer-pellet groups. A transect is an arbitrarily selected line across a section of winter range. The branches of important food plants along this line are tagged and photographed. Each fall the annual growth of the tagged branch is measured. The following spring, after the game has nibbled it, the branch is remeasured. When the spring measurements are subtracted from the fall measurements, the biologist knows the percentage of use on browse plants along his transects; hopefully, he also has a reliable estimate of the amount of use on the winter range. In general, western range plants decline and finally die if 50 percent or more of their new growth is eaten annually.

The work was often made more interesting by the discovery of Indian artifacts, geodes, or gastroliths along the transect. In fact, Fat had marked one of the transects with a cairn topped with a *metate* or, as Fat called it, "an Indian grindin' rock." One afternoon, when we were counting deer-pellet groups, we found a beautiful arrowhead along our transect.

People are inclined to get hilarious about our counts of deer crap. Actually, it is a rather ingenious tool developed by a biologist for gauging deer numbers. When a deer empties his intestines the fecal material emerges in pellet form, and unless the deer is walking or running, these pellets fall in a group. We counted the pellet groups, not the pellets themselves. In Utah's dry climate, however, pellets persist from one season to the next, and the ubiquitous sheep droppings are identical to those of deer. So Fat and I spent considerable time discussing in a learned manner the quality of the crap literally in hand. I suppose that at such times we looked like two fools standing in the sagebrush examining small olives between thumb and forefinger.

A long steel rod fastened to a measured chain is used in counting pellet groups. The rod point is punched down at intervals along the transect, and all pellet groups within the circle described by the chain are counted. The result is found by simple algebra; a deer relieves himself about thirteen times in twenty-four hours and the area within the chain's circle is a known constant. So when the problem is set down and computed, the answer is the number of deer-days' use per acre. It might be one deer using that acre for twenty days or twenty deer using it for one day, but, like the browse measuring, it gives us another idea of what the deer have been doing on their all-important winter range. Our game biologists, for example, felt that thirty days of deer use on an acre of winter range was about the maximum desirable for a season.

Of course, these methods give indications only of what a deer herd is doing. We also made sex-ratio counts, trend counts, and kill counts. If these various counts are made accurately, and the samples are large enough and unbiased, it is amazing how closely a statistician can estimate an entire herd's size. The methods used are similar to the ones pollsters and TV networks use in telling us in advance with whom we're stuck for President.

I have also helped to weigh dead deer, for the body weights of hunter-killed animals are an excellent basis for estimating the condition of the range the animals lived on. But one job that I balked at was scooping out deer's eyeballs with a teaspoon and then preserving them for later analysis. A live deer can be "aged" very accurately by examining his teeth until he's about three and a half years old. After that, the examiner must judge age by the wear on the teeth. On overbrowsed range it's easy to make errors, because the animals' teeth wear so much faster on the coarse growth available to them. Biologists have found that the lens in a deer's eye thickens over the years at a predictable rate. So the eyes are scooped out and their lenses measured microscopically to determine the animal's age. Teeth also may be removed from dead animals, then sectioned and examined under magnification; a tooth forms annual rings similar to those found in trees or on fish scales.

I think that wildlife management is terribly susceptible to fads in research. At one time all incipient biologists were turning in theses and dissertations on the life histories of animals and birds. Then they shifted to a study of food habits, and after that, population dynamics. When I entered the business, everyone was going bug-eyed subjecting the collected data to statistical analysis; unless you mastered the chi-square test, you weren't worth much as a game man. Now, thanks to Tinbergen, Lorenz, and other behaviorists, everyone interested in game biology is spending his time psychoanalyzing some species of bird or animal. One of my professors at Utah State went off to England to study the behavior of the blue tit!

Whatever the popular phase of game research, however, a warden's time is spent counting, recounting, and then re-recounting some wild population, or the ratio of their sexes, or even (as with the pellets) their signs. In the early spring we counted sage grouse on their strutting grounds. These large birds (the males may weigh five pounds) collect on the same spots year after year, decade after decade. The mature males puff and posture with their spiky tails fanned and the great white ruffs around their necks expanded. The females, smaller and less splendidly dressed, scurry through the sage to emerge shyly on the strutting ground, where the resplendent males have their will with them.

I also have counted beaver houses and creaked out of bed in many, many pre-dawn mornings to go out to count the crows of cock pheasants. I counted Canada geese on their muskrat-house nests. Each pair of adults averages five goslings, and before the hunting season, I learned to count the flocks of geese I saw and divide that number by seven. The result told me how many goose families I had seen in the flock, because a goose family stays together. Later, after counting the rooster and his harem, we counted hens and their chicks, and we counted sage-grouse broods, and then the progeny of the sometimes prolific chukar partridge. Fat counted goslings on the Green River from a raft, often while I was crisscrossing the Bonanza Desert in an airplane, counting antelope.

TAKING FRED'S PLACE

I counted farm ponds from the air, and when the season opened we counted fishermen on streams and the contents of their creels. I have counted the nymphs and larvae scraped up from a square yard of stream bottom. The tallies seemed endless: suckers and other rough fish netted each hour in lakes and reservoirs, the coos of mourning doves and the amount of property damage hunters did (it was not a fraction of what some newspapers liked to indicate). The Forest Service asked us to count the number of fishermen's horses going into the Uinta Mountain's high lakes. During my first fall, I even found myself collecting elk tails—the vertebrae grow at a predictable rate, so measurement can determine the animal's age. I skinned the first of the tails for this collection before putting them into the formalin. But my collection soon had the appearance of a bloodthirsty pervert's slashings, so later tails were pickled, hide and all. It was amusing to see the expressions on hunters' faces when they entered my trailer and saw those jars of tails on the table.

One thing made all the counting and collecting worthwhile— seeing the wildlife. On the Book Cliff's McCook Ridge, a half-hour's drive at twilight invariably revealed seventy-five to one hundred deer. Few of the diversions in cities are so thrilling as the sight of a buck antelope rounding up his harem at thirty to forty miles an hour. No skydiver or jet-powered aerobat can top the mating flight of a pair of hawks. And I doubt that Bernhardt playing *Camille* was ever more desperately stricken than a female mallard luring you away from her brood. Courage is personified by the often-maligned magpie couple protecting their clumsy fledglings.

One of Fat's favorite object lessons concerned the young game warden who came with his wife to a new town. The young man was hurt because he had not been asked to join the Lions Club, and his young wife sat tearfully beside a telephone that never rang unless there was some sort of trouble for her husband. I think Fat told that story to prime me for the fact that the local game warden ranks socially with the dog catcher and the animal by-products man. When I was at home for an evening I sat groggily in a battered rocker staring at the lung-colored walls, too weary to open the Book of the Month or the *Atlantic Monthly* I'd subscribed to. I couldn't afford to join the local social club, and to show up in one of Vernal's beer parlors was to invite an argument. My basement rooms grew dingy, and as the weather improved I contrived to spend as much time as possible away in the hills.

I have never known a mood so blue or an hour so melancholy that it could not be brightened or even cured by watching some wildlife. I feel better after I have seen a deer. A fat ground squirrel sitting in a sunlit meadow does more for me spiritually than a thousand sermons. Those first lonely months, I sometimes felt that I was accomplishing very little for my cherished conservation, but I realize now that the wildlife I spent my time with alleviated my loneliness and probably helped to anchor my sanity.

I often wish that everyone who aspires to arm himself with a rod or gun could first serve a year as a game warden. Then, perhaps, the only thing left to arrest would be the ruination of the land under the name of "progress."

II / NO SUCH THING AS A GOOD BOY

"Em and I were talking about the people we knew
the other day, and out of all of 'em, we could
only think of a half dozen who were human beings."

—AL NIELSEN

ON SATURDAY AND SUNDAY AFTERNOONS, FAT OFTEN INTER-rupted my education in order to take his three sons along on patrols. Ted was the oldest, a good-looking, active boy of eleven. Next came Lee, a couple of years younger, the freckled family scholar, and then little Brud. He was about four, blond, and too cute for his own good. Fat doted on him. Everything Fat did, Brud and his two brothers expected to do, too. Ted stretched himself into a shooting position while his dad steadied a man-sized .22 rifle for him. Lee tugged mightily on his dad's bow and, with some assistance, saw the arrow strike fairly near his target. Brud rode in front of his dad on Joe, the sorrel horse, or sometimes alone while Fat led the horse.

At lunchtime they stopped in some glade or beside a mountain stream, and the whole troop debouched from the confines of the pickup. Packages of hamburger or wieners and a loaf of bread or buns were produced from the grub box and quickly became sandwiches while the boys played or fished. From long practice Fat was able to whip up an interesting meal while settling arguments, baiting hooks, and answering questions that varied from the effective range of his "big" rifle to what old Joe would do if they put the dog, Poke, on his back.

Sometimes in the midst of this Brud would have to relieve himself. It was a problem at first, because Brud had been toilet trained. He tearfully complained that he could not go outdoors. Fat would tell him that it was perfectly all right and no one would watch him.

"But, Daddy, I can't go on the ground."

"Yes, you can. Now go ahead."

"I can't pee on the ground!"

"Yes, you can, you pee right there on the ground." Finally sighting through his tears and still protesting, the little boy gave himself up to what in his world of flushing toilets seemed a barbarous act.

Shortly before the June 1 opening of the fishing season, we planted trout in Brush Creek. They were fine-looking rainbows, and Fat handled them with unusual care. Most of the truckload of fish were scattered along the creek, a dipnetful at a time. At a bend in the stream, where there was a grassy bank and overhanging willows, Fat sweetened the eddying pool with some particularly fine fish. The next Saturday, the opening day of the fishing season, I saw Fat and his boys in that same bend of the creek. Each boy had a rod in his hand and a big grin on his face. It was one day when being the game warden's kid really paid off.

I am rigidly against "Huck Finn Days" and "Trout-a-ramas" for kids, because they too easily become first lessons in greed and dishonesty. But I think a sensibly stocked and safe section of stream, or a pond reserved for youngsters, is worth many times the cost of stocking and policing it. Outside of Vernal an amiably flowing section of canal had been reserved for anglers twelve years and under. After their first flush of seasonal interest, most of the kids gave up fishing. But a few could be found there almost all summer. Sometimes they'd have an unusually nice trout, but at other times they might fish all afternoon for a seven-incher, or for nothing at all. I would sometimes drive along the canal and find a kid who'd gotten soaked to the waist recovering the lure that he'd spent a week's allowance to buy. It seemed to me that the kids who fished that quiet canal by themselves or with other youngsters got the most from it, not in fish but in fundamental esthetics and natural history. When a father took his kid to the canal, the man was likely to end up holding the rod while his son became more and more disinterested. The surest way to cure this kind of dad was to glide up quietly behind him and ask, "You're awfully big for twelve, aren't you?"

My own father lost his interest in fishing about the time mine began to develop. But he made it possible for me to fish, and turned over to me what I considered a bonanza in fishing tackle. I got good bamboo bait-casting and steelhead drifting rods. There were cane fly rods in canvas cases, each joint of the rod nestling safely in its niche in a long wooden holder that slipped into the case.

My first real fishing trip—one on which we camped out—was to Fish Lake with Rex Hanson. Rex is an attorney and one of my Father's best friends. It was his habit to take two or three days in early June and go to south-central Utah, where beautiful Fish Lake rests on a high plateau. Rex took me, his small son Tim, and an old friend of his named Dan.

Before daybreak on the opening morning the three adults waded out into the lake. The water was so cold that I still remember the delicious agony it produced in my joints. I remember the wonderful fishing even better. We were all using bait-casting outfits and big shoehorn spoons. A long cast would drop the lure over a dense bank of aquatic plants. The rainbows lurked there, eagerly grabbing the tantalizing spoon as it fluttered by them. Then, with a prodigious effort, the hooked fish came kicking from the water and rattled the spoon in his jaw. If he couldn't shake it free, he burned your thumb as it braked the reel's swiftly unwinding spool.

In what seemed to be no time I had caught my first limit of trout, big ones. Rex and Dan caught limits, too, and they were cleaning their catch when I came along with mine. We were delighted with our good luck, but also beginning to feel the lack of breakfast, which we'd postponed.

"I could eat a couple of these biggest ones all by myself." Dan grinned at me. "I'll bet I can eat more than you can. Go up in the tent and put my big frying pan on Rex's gas stove. Get it good an' hot."

I turned to go as I heard Dan say, "While you cook some of these, I'll go back and get a limit to take home to the folks." Rex didn't say anything, and neither did I, but my sense of rapture vanished. Dan was not entitled to catch any more fish: he had his day's limit.

While he waded back into the lake, I carried part of our catch back to camp. Putting them aside, I pumped up Rex's Coleman stove and lit it. The fierce blue flame instantly melted a hole through the icy morning air. Then I got Dan's big cast-iron frying pan and set it on the flame. The blue jet of fire roared at its bottom for a moment, then, *ping!* A big crack leaped three-quarters of the way across the pan's bottom. It was ruined.

I showed it to Rex, who examined the damage and then called to Dan. "Your pan split. We can't cook breakfast here; we'll have to go down to the lodge. Come on in!"

Dan returned grumbling and without any more trout. But said no more after Rex reminded him that he had given the orders to get the pan "good an' hot." I can't remember enjoying a plate of greasy bacon and eggs more than those I had at the lodge that day.

Bruce Jensen, the warden stationed west of Vernal in the little mountain settlement of Tabiona, told a similar story that summer. He'd checked on a man and his son camped beside a stream and found their ice chest packed with two limits of trout. The father was expansive about his fishing skill, and Bruce patiently heard him out. Then, as the warden turned to go, the man's son blurted out, "What about those other fish in the car, Dad?"

While most of the community appeared to regard its game wardens as social eunuchs, the kids held us in awe. To them we were unfailing shots and fishing magicians. We were the wonderous fellows who went in and out of Never Never Land every day of the week. It was fun to pick up a farm kid and give him a ride home. He would sit there on the seat very straight, with his legs sticking out because they were too short to reach the floor. He was a little frightened, because he had heard many times from his father and older brothers what had happened "that time the game warden came around." But he was also proud to be sitting there beside the game warden. "God, you guys! He keeps a big pistol right on the seat beside him!"

The friendliness wasn't entirely altruistic. A young enemy with a .22 rifle can deal a game warden all sorts of misery. If I passed a farm kid pegging along the road in the opposite direction, I always waved. Not an elaborate wave, but the sort of man-to-man salute heroes render one another when passing on the battlefield. The kids were malleable, and if they corrected their dads on a point in the game code, it was remembered much longer than if the warden had done it.

Every boy enters a cruel, bloodthirsty stage in his life, and some eventually pass through it. But while there, a boy has no pity for a gasping, dirt-covered trout. Fortunately, he cannot catch too many, and there may not be a display of innocent cruelty for days at a time. A boy is a lot more interesting during a hunting season. He usually shoots what he does manage to hit a lot more times than is necessary, so his killing of game, while messy, usually is humane.

In the fall I had two favorite kinds of hunters. One group were the trophy hunters; men who stayed the season and brought out huge bucks or nothing at all. And I liked the boys. Specifically, I liked the boys who came out with their dads or grandfathers. They were the quiet kids who lugged the wood and water. During bird season they carried the game and cleaned the guns in the evening. They didn't whine at their chores, and they ate what was put in front of them. Their reward, of course, was to get to go again.

I liked the kind of boy who got out of the car and came to stand proudly beside me while I checked his first buck. Unless his delighted father got out, too, and spilled the beans about this being his son's first buck, I treated the boy as if he were a veteran hunter. "You got one, huh?"

Depending upon the sort of boy he was, the youngster would say, "Yessir, a *four*-pointer," or, trying to act the part of the old hunter, only, "Yeah," when I knew he was bursting with pride.

"Well, now," I'd say, examining the deer, "you did get one! You know, this is the nicest buck I've checked today."

A game warden said that to me once. He said it with a straight face while admiring what was undoubtedly the most evil-smelling, poorly dressed, and rock-abraded deer carcass in Tooele County. But he told the truth—a boy's first buck is generally the best one he will ever kill.

I saw a reflection of myself in such boys. If a man is around them very long, it becomes natural to want to improve upon that reflection and make the boy a perfected image of yourself. Judging from the number of shitheels abroad these days, it must be an easily botched project. Nevertheless there is immeasurable satisfaction in taking a boy (especially a "problem" boy) and helping to make a human being of him—one who won't cheat on limits, get his thrills shooting does, mess up a nice girl, fish with worms, or petition his government by throwing excrement at a cop.

Some of my early protests were against high school. I avoided class as often as possible and practiced yoga-style detachment when avoidance was no longer possible. I shocked my Mormon teachers (except Miss Reynolds, who was the best Saint of them all) by smelling of tobacco and drinking beer at class outings. Finally, my chemistry and Spanish teachers met and decided to put a rein on me. If I didn't get to work, they decided, I would not be graduated that spring. They said this and described my dreary performance to my mother and father at a parent-teachers meeting. When they came home that night, mother was weeping and my father was tight-lipped.

After mother went to bed he came to my room for a brief confrontation. He was pretty smart about it, too. He reminded me of the hunting trips and all the other attentions I'd had lavished upon me. Were these things the reason I had made mother so unhappy? If they were, my father suggested, they could be eliminated. He also suggested that I do some thinking. Then he went to bed—with an aching heart, I am sure.

Late in the afternoon of the following day, a day I had spent in school, mother called me into our dining room. A long brown carton lay on the table. "Your Dad brought this home for you," she said.

I opened the carton and there, gleaming deep blue and walnut brown, was a Winchester Model 12 shotgun. I was graduated from high school without any honors but on schedule.

It wasn't bribery, because my father was a great bird hunter, and he took me and the new Winchester on all his trips. He was looking after his investment, I guess.

I didn't realize how necessary it is to look after such investments the day I found two boys spearing carp in the state-owned marsh near Jensen. As I drove up they tried to run but there was no place to run to; all I had to do was wait for them to tire and come ashore. "Get any fish?" I asked when the sullen-faced boys walked up to where I was waiting.

"We wasn't fishin'," said the larger of the pair, a muscular boy of about eighteen.

I didn't say he was lying, I just acted as if I hadn't heard him and said, "We're tickled to death to have people come here and help get rid of the carp. They raise hell with the marsh."

The boys stared at me in surprise. They had been all set to catch some more hell from another cop and here I was thanking them! I could see that here was a chance to spread some of my long-holstered ideals around. But neither boy had a fishing license, and one was required to spear any kind of fish. I explained this and also why I was required to cite the older boy for not having a license. I told the younger one to buy a license within the next couple of weeks and then show it to me. I told the older boy, who when he worked was an oilfield roughneck, that any fine he paid went into a wildlife fund. This didn't seem so useless as simply giving money to the judge.

We talked for a couple of hours and after that I gave the boys a ride into town. They thanked me and asked if they might ride around with me some day. "Sure," I said, "just give me a call."

They didn't call, but the older boy paid his modest fine promptly and the younger one stopped me on the street a few days later to display his fishing license. Although the boys never called, they always gave me big grins and waves when we passed. I began to believe that my two-hour sermon on the marsh was all that had been necessary to straighten them out.

One Sunday morning I dropped into the police office in the

courthouse basement. One of the state patrolmen was leaning back in a swivel chair, his feet on the desk. "You knew that Morris kid, didn't you?"

"I pinched him a few weeks ago, but he's all right if you give him a break."

"Not anymore," the patrolman said, "he got killed breaking jail over in Colorado last night."

You can learn just about anything in a courthouse—from whose wife is sleeping with whose husband to inside dope on the latest mineral developments. When the courthouse regulars weren't gossiping, they were often "jobbing" each other.

One of the place's regulars described a dude hunter. Some of the local men took this fellow to their camp for his first deer hunt. That night he asked about toilet facilities and was shocked to see the bathroom indicated by a generous wave of an arm. After he stumbled back from the darkness, the young fellow asked one of his hosts, "Have I got anything brown on my face?"

The man looked him over. "Say," he said in surprised understanding, "did you really shit and fall in it?"

Another man returned to the city praising his hunt but lamenting because he had missed his only shot at a buck. One of his audience opined that the lad's rifle or ammunition might be to blame. "Bring in your gun and shells," he said.

When the young fellow produced them the man examined the rifle, working its action and peering knowingly down the barrel. "The rifling in this barrel has a right-hand twist. Let's see your shells." The man studied the cartridges and the box they had come in. Finally he said, "Here's your trouble. These here shells is for a left-hand twist barrel. No wonder you couldn't hit nothin'." The poor kid spent the next half hour trying to persuade the clerk in the hardware store that he had sold him the wrong ammunition.

In today's service-oriented society, many parents hope that if they enroll their artless kids in a Boy Scout troop the boys will undergo a mountain metamorphosis and either learn to hate the woods or emerge therefrom as polite replicas of Baden-Powell. It won't work. Nor would such notions have worked in the days when the deliverer of Mafeking got his inspiration about forming the scouting movement. He envisioned semi-autonomous and reasonably sedate troops of six or seven boys marching off on expeditions with one older youth. Nowadays a Scout troop is likely to have twenty members plus a master and assistant master, who take their marching orders from the local religious hegemony.

As Scouting grew to its currently colossal proportions, a marvelous press grew with it. But, contrary to what you hear, Scouting does not invariably build men and there are ex-Scouts in state prisons. Nevertheless, all game department employees were expected to cooperate with the Boy and Girl Scouts. But after some unhappy attempts at cooperation, I began avoiding them assiduously.

I have met boys sagging under the weight of merit badges who weren't competent even as boys. Too many leaders pass out awards with the generosity of religious fanatics passing out tracts. I knew one leader who passed two kids as responsible marksmen; on their way home, one of the boys shot the other. A biologist friend used to send his conservation-badge aspirants out to collect a few common aquatic insects. He felt that the boys should understand more about a trout's food requirements than what they had learned watching hatchery trout gobble food pellets. Some of the boys groaned, and the biologist noticed that they never came back again. Checking, he learned the reason: a shoe salesman was passing out the identical badges free just to be a good fellow and establish a clientele in the bargain. He was similar to the Scoutmaster I met by a lake one day in Naturalist Basin. He had gathered some of his troop around him on the shore, and pointed to bright-green algae in the water, saying, "These here things is fish eggs."

The incompetence of too many in the Scouting hierarchy becomes bloodily apparent each season when Scouts are killed, maimed, or lost in the wilds. Some Scouting professionals have risen in the organization without knowing how to pitch a tent, let alone saddle a horse. Most of the field trips I have observed are just a means of getting the neighborhood good guy to mind the kids for a few days. One father boasted to me that his son was the only boy in his troop who could catch fish from the lake where the boys were camped. "Fed the whole gang," said the proud father, forgetting that his son had broken the game laws to provide all those fish. His transgression was minor, however, in comparison with the seventeen hundred pounds of rainbow trout a professional Scouter and his small band bragged about killing during a five-day outing in Canada. Perhaps the sorriest example of an outing was the group I met coming up a Uinta Mountain trail. The two Scout leaders were buoyantly unconcerned about the cruelly overloaded pack horse they led. Nor were they any more concerned about the imminent night. Their troop was an amalgam of ages, from husky louts with cigarettes in their pockets to tiny boys awash with sweat and aswarm with mosquitos. The smaller the boy, the farther back he was from his leaders. I found the smallest boy a half-mile back down the trail. He was struggling to keep up, and naturally frightened. I didn't have the heart to tell him his masters had resolved to hike another seven miles that night.

Another time a Scout leader called and asked me to help his boys accomplish their conservation project. I suggested we take them to an abused plot of ground and spend a day there planting trees. The man readily agreed, and so I met him the next Saturday with a pickupload of tree slips. I also met the boys, swarms of them arriving by car, truck, and even bus.

After an hour or so of pandemonium we got most of the boys collected in a semicircle. I took a tree slip and demonstrated the ease with which it could be planted. "Is that what we're gonna' do?" one groaned. "Nobody told us to bring a shovel." As a result I ended up digging nearly all the holes while some of the boys planted trees. When we had finished and after I had muttered, "Jesus Christ!" enough times to ensure a Second Coming, I announced, "Now we'll assign teams to water and look after these trees until they get started."

The *"Huh?"* was universal. I was told in no uncertain terms that this was their project and now they had done it, the scraggly little trees could go to hell, because next week the Scouts were due in the mountains, where, judging from past experience, they would deface other, larger trees.

It may be true that "there is no such thing as a bad boy," but if this is so, it is equally true that there is no such thing as a good boy. I think there are just boys, and that the adjectives used to describe them correctly are variable. There are very few boys who aren't improved by what Fat called "a tunin'," and there are equally few who amount to much after a childhood of constant cuffing.

Not all boys are as lucky as I was. I defected from the Scouts at an early age, and it was my great good fortune never to have been sent to camp: I was taken. My presence there was at least part of the reason why my father never brought a deer back from our hunting trips—he was too busy looking after me. I was taken on deer-hunting trips before I was taken to school. In those first years we lived in Oregon, and deer were almost as scarce as deer hunters. What game there was had a supremely easy time eluding the hunters.

I remember the morning I followed my father to the edge of a small clearing. He pointed out some alert does and fawns standing at the clearing's farther end. While we watched them the deer exploded into high-trajectory bounds that quickly carried them into the timber. Despite his admonitions that I remain silent in the woods, I exclaimed, "Oh, Daddy; they've got springs in their legs!"

I couldn't have been very old then, because after we returned from our wonderful, unsuccessful hunting trip, I lay on my bed in the darkness and bawled because it was over. Then my father came down the hall, climbed into bed with me, and promised we would go again next October. He said I shouldn't cry, because mother was so happy to have me home again. At such times my mother seemed terribly selfish.

The trip to the deer camp was fully half the fun, because it was filled with a year's expectations and unaccustomed supplies of Coca-Cola and Hershey bars. A couple of years we stopped in the little eastern Oregon towns of John Day or Burns. My father would see the local forest ranger, who would give us the key to the ranger station at Calamity Creek or some other outpost with an equally romantic name. All that was expected in return was that we keep the place clean and fill the woodbox before we left.

Piled neatly beside those back-country woodboxes I often found copies of *Dime Western* and *Ten-Story Western.* When he was with us, my Uncle Ransom read to me from those wonderful pulps. And when he was not there, I read them to myself. American letters have never been quite so vivid since the demise of the pulp western. But as good as the stories were, they never quite matched the excellence of the exciting covers, done in sun-bright reds, yellows, and blues.

It was impossible to imagine then the hordes of hunters who would invade the silent woods within the next decade or so. It is almost as difficult nowadays to recall the splendid solitude of those fall days. If we had camp neighbors, they were likely to be Mike Leupold and his handsome wife. They carried fine rifles mounted with the first telescopic sights I ever saw. I realize now that they were cumbersome German sights, unreliable despite their high cost. Mike's firm manufactured compasses and surveying instruments. He is dead now but the company that bears his name today makes scopes that are world-famous and not at all cumbersome.

That quiet green world seemed limitless to me. Just to hike around the perimeter of the wooded horse pasture below the ranger station was an afternoon's adventure. It would be an even greater thrill if I could do it today, because I never saw even a single beer can.

We all wore red felt hats, but they were more to identify us as deer hunters than to warn away other hunters—there were none to warn away. Rain and the resultant gumbo roads were the dangers my father feared. Our Ford sedan was reliable, but it couldn't get us and our homemade trailer out of the woods if it rained hard. Model A's were better back-country cars, but many of them were still too new and precious to be used there.

There was a small spring in the meadow below the ranger station. Someone reported seeing a huge trout finning there when he went for a bucket of water. I always meant to go look for it, but I never did. Bob Sulser, our neighbor across the street at home, was always bringing home huge trout. And if you really wanted a big fish, any Siwash Indian would sell you a fine salmon, bright from the sea, for a dollar. I regret that as wonderful as those times were, I took too many of them for granted.

Sometimes before we could start our next pulp story, Ransom would have to go out and gather wood. He usually took me along, and before entering the forest he often would post me on its edge with his Winchester .32 Special. As sentry, I was to sound the alarm, then hold off any Indians who might try to sneak up on us. Ransom took the cartridge from the rifle's chamber, but I could see a sliver of one gleaming brassily under the loading gate. Ransom wore blue jeans just like the cowboys in the pulps did, and he held them up with a belt of horsehair woven by convicts. If those Indians had ever dared to appear, we could have shown them a thing or two!

When the wood was gathered and the stories read, my father or Ransom would sometimes uncase and assemble an octagon-barreled .22-rifle. It was a take-down Remington pump with a tubular magazine that seemed to hold a king's ransom in cartridges. With this gun under his arm, we would go out to stalk blue jays. These noisy, beautiful birds, I was told, ate the eggs of other birds. They were extremely wary, and their wildness somehow added to their predatory dimensions. But when the rare moment came and we had slipped to within range, then stealthily raised the rifle and aimed at a sitting bird, there was often no report. Just a metallic *click!* because unless it was fresh Remington's Palma and Winchester's Lesmok ammunition often failed. We never killed a jay, "but we sure would have got that one if the gun had shot."

One fall I developed a torrential head cold just before the deer season. Even I could understand why I had to stay home. But I watched with a breaking heart while my father methodically collected and checked off each exciting item of gear. I was so eager that even the pots and pans used exclusively on hunting trips had magical properties. Finally everything was packed into the little red trailer and roped down under canvas. Shortly before I went to bed that night my father said, "You know, I had a head cold like yours once. But I went hunting anyway and the smell of the pines seemed to cure it. Do you think you'd like to go?"

As I recall, that was the year we saw a brand-new .22 in a general-store window and walked right in and bought it. Such things to a boy in October beat all hell out of being a Boy Scout any time. At least they did when I was a boy.

III / THE PIG WAS
A HORSE

*"It's worth ridin' the old bastard all day just
to see him buck an' hear him fart when I turn
him out."*

—COTTON BOB JENSEN

S PRING RITES IN THE UINTAH BASIN OFTEN INCLUDE HANGING over the top pole of a horse corral and speculating on the ultimate color of the pretty little colt frisking there. When the Basin man is done with looking he may stop in the saddle shop on his way home to see how that new saddle is coming. If he already has that, he'll price a bridle or just stand around for a while, smelling the new leather and running a forefinger thoughtfully over the seats of the second-hand saddles. The shop atmosphere is something like a barbershop's. The main exceptions are that there are no magazines save *The Western Horseman*, the conversation is all horses and tack, and no woman comes in to wait with her shaggy-headed son and unknowingly stifle conversational swearing.

To watch a saddlemaker at work, cutting the thick brown skirting and fitting it into place with scarcely a measurement and never a pause, is a constant wonder to me. A good saddlemaker really has two skills: besides his craft, he knows how to fashion his customers' ideas into leather goods. There are few things I enjoy more than going into a saddlemaker's and with him figuring out a new holster, rifle scabbard, or bridle.

I have never developed enough interest in horses, however, to join the cult of their fanciers. I used to get terribly bored when Fat took me off to while away an afternoon talking horses with some rancher. The time wasn't entirely wasted, though, because we never had complaints of deer or beaver depredations from Fat's horse-fan friends. And I had not realized how much my owning a horse had impressed Fat. Long after I became settled he told me, "You was the first one the office sent out here that wasn't plumb halpless."

I could shoe a horse, throw a diamond hitch (even if it was sometimes only an industrial diamond), and put a deer carcass on a horse so it would stay there. Frank Fletcher, another friend of my father's, taught me a lot of it. Nibs Watt, a journeyman

Montana cowboy turned game warden, taught me some more. And, finally, there was the Pig; she was a mare and she taught me all she knew.

In a way she was foaled during a mid-watch on board the USS *Suisun*, an auxiliary vessel of the *Reluctant* class. Perhaps it was one night when the sea was an infinite black mirror and we seemed to be motionless in the center of it. I was perched on the splinter shield that surrounded the bridge's starboard wing, with my feet propped in a most un-seamanlike manner against the gyro-repeater's binnacle. Inside the wheelhouse the watch steered, sipped coffee, and listened to San Francisco on an illicit radio patch. Periodically the quartermaster leaning on the chart table rolled from one elbow to the other and noted, "Steaming as before" in his log. It must have been on this kind of night that I decided I wanted a horse.

The *"Sue"* was a lucky ship. We had a horseshoe welded to our mast. Scuttlebutt said the shoe had come aboard lodged on an anchor fluke when the anchor was weighed in some forgotten Pacific harbor. So when I sent a hundred dollars home (which was then Utah) and asked that Frank Fletcher buy me a horse with it, it was in the tacit belief that the long months would finally pass and I would come home from the sea.

When that time came, it seemed unreal. My plane banked over the moonlit marshes of Great Salt Lake, but it wasn't until the wheels bumped down that I honestly believed that I was home at last.

By the time my mother had stopped patting my arm and saying, "Gee, it's good to have you home, honey," we almost were home. But instead of going there, my father turned his car into the Fletchers's darkened driveway. Frank had a corral at the back of his lot where he kept horses.

"They're asleep," Mother said, "don't bother them tonight." But my father ignored her and got Frank out of bed. He came out blinking and ineffectually trying to smooth his sparse fronds of graying hair. He was wearing a canary-yellow bathrobe and cowboy boots. It was a warm night.

"Welcome home!" Frank shook my hand with warmth. "The Pig's down in the corral. Come on!" With his bathrobe flapping against his bare legs, Frank led us around his house and down to where there were rustling and munching sounds amidst the manure smell of horses. Frank ducked through the corral poles. "Whoa, now," he said, "here she is." He was leading an immense form out of the deeper shadows. "Want to ride her? She's gentle as a kitten."

I should have celebrated my last appearance in dress blues by scrambling aboard that great back, but I demurred. I think I was a little startled at just how much horse one hundred dollars would buy. But Frank wasn't dismayed; he only wanted me to be happy with my purchase. To prove his words, he swung himself onto her back and steered her around the corral. There is something remarkable about a man riding a horse in his bathrobe and cowboy boots—not the stuff of heroic statuary, but unforgettable all the same.

About the only other possession a man can own that requires so much auxiliary paraphernalia as a horse is a wife. But for a man it is a lot more fun to buy riding tack than it is to select rings and housewares. I bought most of my tack from J. W. Jenkins & Son in Salt Lake City. The old store was narrow, high-ceilinged, and dimly lit. The air inside was tangy with the aroma of good leather. The walls were hung with bridles, halters, lariats, reins, blacksnake whips, hackamores, and a hundred other equestrian items. Half the floor space was covered with little sawbucks supporting saddles. The rest was given over to a long glass counter that displayed everything from fly-tying material to silver-mounted bits and saucer-sized belt buckles ornamented by the likenesses of ruby-eyed steers. Behind the counter was a gun rack and glass-doored cabinets filled with snaps, buckles, and scores more work-a-day items for the horseman.

Down at the end of the counter was a dark, almost black, roll-top desk, and here sat Mr. Jenkins (father or son, I never learned which). Mr. Jenkins was balding and had a nasal voice that seemed to bubble out of a gravelly throat. He wore glasses and grinned a lot. But he never slapped your back or hooked his thumbs in his belt and talked "horsey."

After I stated my business he led me to a mahogany-colored saddle. "Sheepman traded this on a new one. We just got it cleaned and on the floor today." It was a Frazier saddle made in Pueblo, Colorado, and I asked if it was a good make. "Frazier used to make as good a saddle as you could buy. But he was a poor businessman and couldn't keep good help. He made a few saddles that weren't good. This is a good one." Mr. Jenkins turned the manila price tag up so I could read it. "Seventy-five dollars."

I didn't care for the carving—big, floppy-looking flowers—but the saddle appeared to be well-made and was not very worn. But, being fresh from the Orient's bazaars, I haggled. "Sixty-seven fifty?"

Mr. Jenkins grinned. He always wore an old brownish sweater and now shrugged its tabby-colored shoulders. "Nooo, this saddle is worth what I'm asking. I just have one price, and I try to be fair."

I paid Mr. Jenkins what he asked. I still have that saddle, and it is everything he said it would be. It was full double-rigged when I got it, which means the front cinch circles close behind the horse's withers while the back one forms a sort of loose anchor aft of the animal's barrel. Later I had this changed to three-quarter double-rigging.

When I saw her in daylight, I found the Pig was a bay mare with a black mane and tail, a small blaze, and one white stocking. Her color was as proletarian as her ancestry, which was "rang," a corruption of "mustang." She was about ten years old, and one hundred pounds overweight.

She had gotten her name when Mother saw her push Frank's horse away from the manger. "Don't be such a pig!" The name stuck, despite Mother's substitution of "Dobbie." Pig really suited her better, for she was that horseman's delight, "an easy keeper"

45]

or "thrifty." I have camped with that mare on sheep-gutted mountain meadows and watched her fatten by rustling around and inside the willow bushes for spears of grass the voracious woollies had missed. On good grass the Pig became an equine baling machine and could stuff herself full in a couple of hours.

She was a trifle long-headed and "puddle-footed," too. No one had worked on her gait, and she sort of ambled until I went to Montana on a fisheries job. Once there, Nibs Watt speeded her up both by riding her and by showing me how to do a better job of shoeing. Nibs didn't just ride a horse, he amalgamated himself with it until you could believe he was a centaur. There were several state-owned jugheads at the Great Falls fish and game headquarters. All of them had bad faults, nasty dispositions, or both. Each time Nibs had to make a mounted field trip, he took a different one of these plugs, and he returned with a schooled and well-mannered animal that was worth up to three times what the state had paid for it.

Another cowhand once advised me, "If you're ever broke in a strange town, go to a whorehouse. The girls will feed you and sleep you 'til you find a job—they won't sleep with you, though, until you've got some money." I never had occasion to test this advice but if that fellow knew as much about whores as he did about horses, I can guarantee it.

Speaking of whores, I should tell about one in particular. She operated out of her own suite of rooms in a small-town hotel. She was very pretty in a girl-next-door sort of way, and her trade was large. I frequently glimpsed the young lady strolling along the sidewalk. Her street behavior was not lewd, although her line of work had made her locally notorious.

One day I picked up a newspaper and saw a cheesecake picture of the smiling whore on the front page; she had been chosen queen of a sportsmen's contest. When the competition ended, she was again pictured on the front page, kissing the winner.

Unlike that dubious queen, the Pig only had one feminine

charm. She whinnied warmly when I went out to see her. I liked to think it was affection sometimes and not always appetite, but whatever it was, the Pig was easy to catch. That is a virtue of the greatest magnitude.

Bruce Jensen, the Tabiona warden, had a horse called Whitey. He was almost impossible to catch. He was a fast horse, and the moment he saw anyone coming in his direction he began taking evasive action. When Bruce wanted to get Whitey up for the spring range rides, he'd have to start chasing the horse a couple of days before the first ride. At the end of that time Whitey probably thought his full name was, "Whitey-whoa-you-son-of-a-bitch!"

After the first capture of the spring, Bruce would feed Whitey and give him a good currying. Whitey liked that. Later, if you hid some baler twine in your hip pocket and went out toward the horse with a curry comb in your hand, there was a chance of easing up beside him. Then, with the gentleness of a man treating his piles, you curried up toward Whitey's head. When you were standing beside his neck you quietly slipped your arm around it. Then with your other hand you drew the twine from your pocket and passed it around the horse's neck. It was as good as a hawser, for Whitey played the game: once caught he was yours—until the next time.

Some day when traffic, the kids, and your wife have pushed you to the point of screaming frustration, think of having to catch a Whitey. Imagine walking up near him, of finally getting close, of holding your temper and not yelling, and of saying nice, earnest words you don't mean. Then think of slipping your arm out to catch the horse and having him suddenly whirl, fart loudly in your face, and run to the far fence.

The Pig didn't do that, and she practically bounded into the trailer when I wanted to take her somewhere. But, too often to be pure coincidence, she would defecate on the tailgate hinge, binding it, just as I was about to shut the tailgate. Also, when I was shoeing her, the Pig would begin to lean on me. She did it very slowly, an ounce at a time, until I woke up to the fact that I was holding up the whole damn horse.

But the Pig was a good traveler, and I didn't hesitate to take her to Montana with me. We spent a month on the Judith Game Range in the Pig-Eye Basin. Years before, the artist Charlie Russell had "batched" with the hunter Jake Hoover in this lovely region of pines and grassy parks. The tiny cow town of Utica looked much the way it had when Russell painted it nearly forty years earlier. "B. Gray's Saloon," shown in the painting *A Quiet Day in Utica,* had been replaced by a larger one, but that's about all. The Saturday night dances still attracted customers from miles around; teeth were still knocked out, and two old-timers—brothers—still showed up in rusty black suits and shoulder holsters. They never danced, they never took off their hats, and they were never bothered.

My job was to make biological collections and do some creel census on the Judith River, but there were big dollops of time when I had nothing to do. So I would saddle the Pig and start off in a new direction almost every day. It was a wonderful country to ride through. Homesteaders had tried to farm the natural parks and failed in the late 'twenties, and now their fences were gone and the fields grown back to native grasses. As the Pig hardened in, I would gallop her for increasing miles across the uncluttered, uninhabited grasslands.

There is a buoyant, visceral elation in running a horse. The farther you go, the higher the excitement rises in your throat, and you either rein in or continue until the drumming euphoria makes you yell. I suppose there is a Freudian implication in this exhilarating sense of motion; but as a rustic once asked, "Who the hell is this here Frood?"

I often carried my fishing rod on these rides and fished in the murmuring little Judith River. Captain William Clark had named the stream for his sweetheart about 1805. But, like all sweethearts, it had its ups and downs. It would become turbid after a rain shower, and on such days I often rode up to the "English Mine" and hunted sapphires on the old dumps there. The largest I ever found was about the size of Number 4 birdshot. The most fun, however, was to have a welder melt an old blue Bromo-Seltzer bottle with his torch and then watch the tourists when they found a "sapphire" the size of a walnut.

Riding east of Vernal, the treasures I found most often were gastroliths. These relics of the dinosaurs were also best hunted after a rain. I found them glistening in the barren, reddish soil, often on the banks of gullies. The unusual patterns and colors of the baseball-sized rocks made them easy to see. Some Mormons believe that such rocks, and indeed all fossils, are scrap from other worlds that God used to build this one. I gave all my gastroliths away, some to good Saints who frowned and shook their heads when I explained that the rock in their hands had been polished in a dinosaur's gullet and was millions of years old.

It is probably true that each generation adopts its own set of facts so that it may believe what it wanted to in the first place. Maybe the round rocks did come zinging through the ether not quite five thousand years ago. Fat and I used to visit a trapper whose wife was "religious." She belonged to some obscure sect of fundamentalists and didn't greet us with a "How are you?" Instead, she always asked, "Well, have you repented yet?"

Fat used to duck his head, avoiding her inquisitorial eye, and say, "I'm aworkin' on it." And I kept silent, being one of those who keeps his eyes open when everyone else has his scrunched tight during grace.

I do not think that horses have enough intelligence to be reverent, yet I have ridden the Pig out on some point where a magnificent vista lay spread before us and felt that she appreciated it, too. I know she liked to help round up the hard-to-catch horses, because I could feel her enthusiasm in my legs.

Once, in early spring, I was riding some deer winter-range. The snow had melted but the soil was still full of water. The Pig was sure-footed, though, so I was paying more attention to the browse plants than I was to the ground. I turned the mare up the side of a ridge, and suddenly we were in trouble. Her back legs were sinking into the gumbo, and as they sank my weight and the weight of her own forequarters were tipping her over backward. I leaped from the saddle. When I landed my feet slipped in the mud and I went down on my hands and knees. The Pig's front hooves were flurry-ing in her effort to stand, and one of them struck me on the fore-head. I saw a white flash and then a red one. Blood was pouring from the cut and cascading off my nose. And through this gory haze I could see the Pig looking down at me. There was such palpable concern in her expression that I knew she was asking if I was all right. I was.

Another time I was leading the Pig around the horse trailer and got her too near a fender. The sharp metal edge slit a three-inch gash in her hind leg. I was relieved to see, after the bleeding stopped, that the cut had not gone into the muscle. But the hide was hanging down and I knew that if I allowed the wound to heal by itself, it would leave an ugly blemish. So I borrowed a needle and thread and stitched the cut myself. To my vast satisfaction, it healed perfectly without leaving a scar.

Not all horses would have permitted that operation; many of them go crazy if anything gets near their legs. Once Frank Fletcher and I were packing into the Uinta Mountains for some high-lake trout fishing. On a precipitous section of the trail, the top strap of Frank's rod scabbard came off the saddle horn, allowing the case to dangle beside the horse's front legs. The horse immediately began trembling, and then tried crow-hopping on the narrow trail. Only his luck and skill saved Frank from being pitched into the canyon below. With a mixture of firmness and sweet talk, he steadied the panicky animal until he could reach down and recover the pendulous scabbard. As soon as he had refastened it, the horse was serene again.

As gentle and easily caught as she was, I had been warned to never let even the docile Pig get completely out of my control. The best of horses will abandon you without a second thought. On pack trips I either hobbled her or tied her in the timber away from the insects. When we "nooned" I often unsaddled her and let her graze trailing her reins. She stepped on them often enough to discourage her from wandering too far. On trips into Jones Hole I traveled light and seldom stayed more than three days, so I used this latter means of restraint.

To my knowledge there was no stream of any size left in Utah that hadn't been dammed, diverted, or pissed in by the community, except Jones Creek. It rises from springs in a canyon at the foot of Diamond Mountain. It is not a big stream, but there are deep pools, riffles, and sparkling bends all enhanced by the accompaniment of rushing sibilance that continues for ten canyon miles. On rare occasions thunder clouds coalesce over the canyon and send a muddy flood flashing down the creek. Most of the time, however, the creek runs clear and constant from one January to the next. A large cabin, almost a house, had been built by the Park Service at the Creek's confluence with the Green River. Up-creek from there was a tiny cabin that the Park Service let us use. From time to time fishermen had held trout up to the door jamb and marked their length there. They must have been beauties, reaching from the door latch almost to the floor.

One day Fat came riding up the creek to find a fisherman, his rod bent almost double, struggling with a great fish. The trout was winning and the fellow begged Fat to help him. Naturally, Fat obliged and shortly had the lunker played out and panting on the bank. "He was really a big one," Fat said, "an' so fat he couldn't a' swum out of that hole ifn' he'd wanted to. When that guy gutted him the stomach was full of white grubs. I was really jealous of that fish 'till I rode up the crick a little further. There was an ol' dead steer layin' in the water an' crawlin' with maggots."

Although it was in my district, Jones Hole was dear to Fat. Before opening day of the trout season he asked if I minded letting him check the stream that first day. Some intrepid anglers made the journey in there on first days, but mostly Fat wanted to put his sons on horses and give them a look at paradise. I didn't mind, but unless you are a kid or a dad, Jones Creek should be fished in solitude.

There are only three routes into it. One leads over Diamond Mountain and then down a jeep-rutted canyon track to the trail head. From there it is a long, hard walk. It is also possible to reach the creek by floating down the Green River from Brown's Park or Steamboat, then beaching at the mouth of Jones Creek. This is the longest route but also the most scenic and exciting. The third route is by horseback from Island Park, then up over the dry, juniper-dotted foothills to the wall of blazing yellow rock about eight miles away. The trail rises most of the way to that yellow rock and then plunges in steep, vicious switchbacks to the verdant little stream bottom. As a man goes down, the sheer, burning cliffs rise higher and higher above him until the day becomes only a narrow slot.

Island Park is in a widening and softening of the otherwise hard and steep Green River Canyon. Ranching had been tried there; water was pumped from the river and poured over the sandy meadow that lay in front of the now quiet ranch house. Usually there was a big white horse in the field, an incongruous bit of domesticity in a land inching back to wilderness. The game department had bought the ranch, and when the contract was signed it carried a provision that the rancher's old horse could remain there as long as it lived.

Not long after he sold his overgrazed range, the rancher died. You could see from his fences, however, that he had loved horses. He had unlaid heavy cable and then strung the strands from post to post. It took work, but such a fence will not rip a horse or flighty colt the way barbed wire does.

In the dooryard, just outside the fence that separated it from the squat, gray ranch house, stood a tremendous cottonwood tree.

Rhy Hyatt, the regional warden supervisor, and I measured it with a fish line once; was it twenty-nine feet around? I don't remember. But I do recall its being recognized as the largest cottonwood in Utah, and so far as I am concerned it is the biggest cottonwood anywhere. At intervals around the tree, spikes had been driven so that cowboys could hang their saddles. Seven or eight saddles might have swung there and left ample room for their owners to hunker beside them in the shade.

The empty house was as dark inside as its gloomy exterior led one to expect. It had ended as an old man's house, sad and sagging, mouldering and mousey-smelling, with yellow rags stuffed into a broken pane of glass. Vandals had been at the doors and treasure hunters had ransacked it. The pump by the kitchen sink clattered if the handle was lifted, but no water came forth. There is a breed of antique hunter abroad nowadays who would make her husband steal that old pump so she could spray it gold and mount it on a birdbath. But the pump was still there then, along with the other big stuff, the iron cookstove, the daveno-bed, the matching chair, and the metal bed frames and rusty springs on the bedroom floors. I used to unroll my sleeping bag on the daveno and sleep at the ranch in order to be able to leave for Jones Hole at daylight.

One afternoon I drove out early enough to repair some of the vandalism and also to dispose of a case of dynamite that had been stored for years in a dugout beside the house. I backed the Pig out of the trailer and left her munching at a pile of hay while I went to work. When the repairs to the doors and broken windows were complete, I went into the dugout for the dynamite. It had been sitting there so long that a crystaline exudite had formed all over the bottom of the wooden case. That case would have been useful but the deteriorated state of its contents convinced me to burn the works. I did and was startled by the ferocity of the flames. In minutes the dynamite was reduced to hot, gray ash. Later I mentioned that old dynamite to an Army demolitions expert. "What was that gook that had crystalized over the case?" I asked him.

"My God! That was pure nitroglycerine! If you had bumped it, it probably would have detonated. That's why cases of dynamite have to be turned periodically, to keep the nitro from leaking out of the sticks."

There must have been benign spirits looking over me at the Island Park ranch. Another time I opened a kitchen cupboard there to look for a saucepan and found a rattlesnake instead. He slithered out through the hole he had come in by almost as quickly as I sprang to the far end of the kitchen. Before I lay down on the old daveno bed that night, I beat it soundly with a stick in case any more rattlers had taken lodging there. None appeared, but I never again felt comfortable in the old house. Stumbling on a rattler, as Fat remarked, "sure makes my ol' asshole suck up."

IV / SANTA CLAUS AT THE
FISH FARM

*"This son of a bitch comes up with his hands
cupped together and says, 'See, I got my limit!'"*

—OREGON FLY FISHERMAN

FAT ONCE TOLD ME THAT THERE USED TO BE AN OFFICER IN THE area who couldn't wait for the opening day of trout season. He always rode into Jones Hole a week early to "test the fishin'" and returned carrying a creel filled with proof that the fishing looked good for the coming year. No one seemed to mind this violation; in fact, they seemed to appreciate it.

If I were going to rob a bank in Utah, I would do it on the first Saturday in June. The streets of every hamlet throughout the state are practically deserted. Almost everyone—at one time, over a quarter of the state's population—is out fishing. Utah is an arid state, and its trout rivers would be mere creeks in most other parts of the country. Nevertheless, Utahns must be the most trout-obsessed of all people. I know of no obstacle, including snowdrifts, ice-choked lakes, quagmire roads, and big, mean rattlesnakes, that can discourage a determined Utah fisherman.

I well recall one eager motorist who braked to a gravel-spewing stop beside a lake where I was fishing. He leaped from his car (he had been driving with chest-high waders on) and ran down to the water's edge. When he reached it he kept right on running, as fast as one can run in waist-deep water. All the while he was running, he was casting, and he did it as a Roman charioteer might whip the galloping horses before him. The fellow was way out in the lake, casting furiously, when his rod-wielding wife reached the lake shore. By the time she had waded out near her husband, he was surging out of the water and hurrying back to the car to try another spot.

Before becoming a game warden, I spent several summers working in Utah fish hatcheries and on fisheries research in Montana. My first job was at the Scott Avenue Hatchery, in what was then a residential section of Salt Lake City. The water supply there came from artesian wells at a constant fifty-six degrees. It was sparkling clear, beneficial to trout production, and wonderfully palatable on boiling hot Utah afternoons.

Sometimes, while driving the fish-planting truck, I used to pass the home of a polygamist and at least three highly fruitful wives. An acquaintance who knew the "cohabs" used to snort. "He says they're his 'sisters,' but every one of 'em has a kid each spring."

Bill Jacklin was the Scott Avenue superintendent. He had worked in hatcheries since boyhood, learning from his father, who had been a hatcheryman before him. Bill could raise handsome thick-bodied trout without seeming to half try. Helping him was the late Ras Peterson. Ras was a deeply browned and severely weathered little man from the Uintah Basin. He seemed never to tire, and when the work was at its wet, miserable worst was fond of saying, "What're you crying about? I hired on here five years ago to drive truck."

Some state jobs become soft sinecures, and those who hold them become self-righteous sloths. I've known tobacco-chewing wardens too lazy to roll down their truck windows when they spat. But fish hatchery work, at least in my time, was hard, evil-smelling labor that often had to be done while standing deep in icy water. Dry socks were a luxury, and my water-softened hands were always acquiring new cuts that were slow to heal.

Visiting a trout hatchery can be fascinating and because we were near Salt Lake's large population, we had lots of visitors. One persistent guest was a Negro. The man came day after day to stand around in garrulous fascination. Each day he became more of a nuisance, standing in our way, giving suggestions that became orders, and finally following us to the privy in order to continue his unending conversations.

"Jesus," Ras complained, "haven't you got someone else to bother?"

"Oh, now, I ain't botherin' you all—'sides, this yere is public works. Why ain't you sorted them fish in the gravel ponds yet?"

Bill would come out to "Goddamn" and "Fer Chrissakes!", but the man continued to make his long, unwelcome visits. One day he followed Ras into the meat house to supervise the mixing of the trout food; a grain-based mash was blended with the meat, and sacks of it were stored in an unused meat locker. This day, the man followed Ras into the locker, and when he tarried there, Ras closed the heavy door on him. Then he switched off the light in the locker room and began mixing the trout food. He intended to release the Negro when he'd finished, but some emergency arose that kept us running all day and it was early evening before Ras remembered the man.

"My Gawd! I hope he didn't croak in there," he said, hurrying to open the locker door. Fortunately, the man hadn't died. When Ras threw open the door, the man bolted through it and never stopped running until he'd cleared the hatchery gate. He never came back.

Another employee had a harelip. He was a competent and industrious worker, although he would come into Bill's tiny office to report, "Mill, nam nodnammed nish omner nere needa ne norted" ("Bill, them goddamned fish over there need to be sorted.")

Some trout grow much faster than others, and they must be sorted to prevent excessive cannibalism. To do this, we seined a pond, then dipped the splashing fish into a sorting box. These boxes came in various sizes and had dowels running the length of their bottoms to form a sort of grate. The dowels were spaced so that fish under a certain width slipped through them and fell back into the water. The retained trout were either placed in a screened live box for transfer to another pond or loaded into a tank truck for stocking.

Most hatcheries specialize in rainbow trout. These natives of the Pacific slope have proven easiest to raise to catchable size. They are good fighters and in their original state were more difficult to catch than cutthroat or brook, but easier to hook than the wary brown trout. They are good, stolid, middle-class fish for middle-class fishermen. Their spawning cycle has been manipulated until some fish spawn in the fall, rather than spring. This allows the hatcheries to stay in full-scale fish production the year around.

Unfortunately, the rainbow's propensity for domestication has resulted in a race of stupid fish that any child can catch, one after the other.

It had been so long since any appreciable number of wild trout spawned in Utah's lakes or her dammed and dredged streams that most citizens believed in fish planting as wholeheartedly as they do in their Mormon religion. As a result, the state that ranked about forty-sixth in water supply is near the top in hatchery trout production. Before the season, the department's public-relations men organize popular hatchery tours so the citizens can see their fish milling in anticipation of the planting trucks. And although the local sportsmen's club was not especially active in other conservation work, it always produced ample volunteer help on fish-planting days.

We planted fish on an irregular schedule. But every morning, no matter what the day's schedule was, there were from one to three cars waiting outside the hatchery gates. When a truckload of fish emerged, the cars' occupants started their engines, and the race began. These truck-followers had all the tenacity of wolves on the blood spoor of a gut-shot caribou. We sent our fish trucks careening across dubious-looking bridges, slewing on two wheels, and we hid in the bushes to protect our cargo from the rapacious anglers. Despite our efforts, these grinning road-racers often pulled up beside the truck the moment we began unloading. As a fish planter I understood how Santa Claus and the Easter Rabbit must feel when in season.

The trout's size and the trip's length governed the number of fish we could carry. Our pickup-mounted tanks usually held three hundred trout averaging eight inches in length. Mounted on the tank was a water pump driven by a gasoline engine; this pump circulated water in the tank and kept it filled with oxygen. If the engine stopped, which it loved to do, there were no more than five minutes to restart it or to dump the load. This is why trout occasionally began leaping in turbid irrigation ditches.

One day a driver had his pump stop as he was passing the home of friends. He quickly checked the engine and found its gas tank empty. Even worse, he found he'd left his reserve can of gas back at the fish hatchery. So he sprinted to his friends' door, yelling for a hose with which to siphon gas from the truck's tank. The lady appeared, looked momentarily bemused, then turned back to reappear seconds later waving her douche bag. The driver grabbed the contraption and dashed for his truck with the lady at his heels. Just as he was about to run the hose into the gas tank, the lady stopped him for a moment, "I'd better not let you have this," she said, removing the spray nozzle.

On hot days we put chunks of ice into the fish tank before starting on long trips. Without ice the water would warm and lose its capacity to hold oxygen, and the trout would begin to die. Unfortunately, we didn't then use the technique of circulating through the tankload of fish water taken from the stream or lake to be stocked. This tempers the water and reduces the shock trout suffer if summarily dumped into water of markedly different temperature.

I planted a load of good-sized trout in Big Cottonwood Creek one afternoon, and many were partially stunned. They struggled to the shallow pool bottoms and lay panting there in total vulnerability. Because the fishing season was open, planting policy required that I scatter my fish along the creek, a dipnetful to a spot. When I had finished and was driving back downstream, I noticed a smartly dressed Abercrombie-and-Fitch-type angler squatting in a pool. He had put aside his rod and was attempting to catch the sluggish trout with his landing net. He was so intent upon his work that he didn't hear my truck as I drove it up behind him. I blasted the horn. The beautiful creature stared at me, then tried to run, jump, and turn around simultaneously. He failed and made a terrific splash as he fell, full-length, into the creek.

People who considered themselves wags often said our trout whinnied when pulled from the water. They also claimed that a rod and line weren't necessary to catch them. "Just clank two horseshoes together over the water and the fish'll jump out on the bank."

Our trout were fed horsemeat, but they also received the offal of every slaughterhouse in the area. There simply weren't enough decrepit horses around to feed Utah's millions of trout. One packing house sent us great, brown, squishy things called "beef melts." There were enormous bull livers of such poor quality that only fish (and, as I later learned, Navy men)ate them. Gallons of sheep lungs arrived in filth-incrusted oil drums with about eight million flies flying fighter-cover above them. These flies mated eagerly with those crawling happily over the mounds of semi-cooked trash fish that were piled in a corner of the meat house.

Unbelievably, there was no refrigeration and our only means of sanitation was to wash down often with cold water and sprinkle rock salt on the concrete floor. In July and August the meat house exuded a stink that would knock a fly off a gut wagon. After a day of working with this stuff, I would get indignant looks from people in cars stopped next to mine at traffic lights. And at home Mother insisted that I undress in the backyard.

This mass of meat had to be ground into varying consistencies for the various sizes of fish. After the tiny fry, who were kept indoors, absorbed the natural food in their attached egg sacs, they received a watery puree of straight meat. The larger trout were fed a blend of meat and mash, which was rather tricky to mix. It had to be of a texture similar to that of damp peat moss, and we achieved this blend using a cement mixer and slowly adding ingredients from five-gallon buckets. If the stuff was either too wet or too dry, it killed the fish. Apparently, trout can eat anything just so long as it is properly moistened.

Occasionally, however, they began dying for no good reason—at least, not one that we could understand. So we gave the fish a shot of brewers' yeast and hoped that a good cleaning-out was all they needed. Usually it was, and the physic soon returned the fish to normal, gluttonous health. But once a malady attacked the fish in the midst of their meal. Dead trout began piling up at the pond outlets and many others surfaced, writhing in unmistakable signs of anguish.

Bill hurtled into the meat house where I was working innocently. "Jeezus Key-rist! What're you doin'?" He rapidly checked the day's menu—sheep lungs—then stirred thoughtfully with a stick through the buckets of pale-pink goop. "It's them goddamned hard parts," he concluded. "Throw this shit out. Then cut the hard parts outa' all these lungs before you grind 'em." I did as ordered, carefully cutting the windpipes and their fibrous extremities out of hundreds of pairs of sheep lungs. Bill's diagnosis was correct, as was his treatment; the fish were fine again within a few hours.

Some trout ignored the food we offered them and dined on their fellows. They often worked by night and hid from us during the day in crumbled-out holes in the concrete ponds' sides and bottoms. Bill could look at a pond teeming with fish and know if cannibals were working on them. If they were, we plugged in a primitive but potent electro-fishing contraption and probed its leads through the cannibals' hideouts.

When the current struck them, the great, fat gluttons came spiraling up to float, stunned, on the water's surface. Before they could recover, we netted and killed them. (These were the only hatchery trout any of us would eat.) Our rubber waders protected us from the electric current, but one day Ras got between the two poles. "Woowoo! *Tee*-ake it *out!* Woowoo! *Jeezus!*" I lifted my loop from the water, breaking the electrical field, and asked Ras what had happened. "I gotta leak in the crotch of my waders," he explained.

Working in the hatchery made me a celebrity to some anglers. For despite all their protestations about planted fish, many fishermen eagerly seek tips about planting sites. I was glad to tell them where the week's production had been planted. For one thing, it kept them out of my favorite spot. On my days off I fished some lovely alpine lakes at the head of the Weber River. There were three lakes, tiered above one another, on a fold in the mountainside. The first lake was called Lily, the second, Frying Pan, and the third, which was above the timberline, was known simply as the Upper Lake.

It was six miles from where I left my car to Frying Pan. The trail led uphill most of the way, and the first time I fished there with a casting rod and large spoons, I didn't catch any trout. A huge brook trout, indescribably beautiful, did follow my spoon to the lake shore. When he saw me he whirled and flashed back into the lake's blue-green depths. But I had seen him, and the next week I was back, armed with what was probably one of the first spinning outfits ever used in the Uinta Mountains. Today I couldn't be less proud of that than if I had been the one to introduce gonorrhea into the student body at Vassar.

But on that day I sat on the lakeshore and re-read the directions that had come with the strange-looking reel. Finished, I stood and made a prodigious cast that carried the tiny lure up and out and then down the lakeshore, where it landed in a pine tree. An article in *Field & Stream* had convinced me that anyone could cast with the new tackle. But at the lake my conviction weakened. I couldn't cast the thing. The fact that the outfit had cost nearly a week's pay kept me from wadding up the tangled line and pitching the works into the lake. Finally, I somehow managed to send the little silver and brass lure sailing far out toward the lake's center.

It landed there with a satisfied plop, and I began reeling. *Thump!* I had a fish. It struggled futilely against the reel's unrelenting brake, and then came thrashing into shore. It was a grayling. The slender fish had sides of radiant blue marked with minute dark spots. The long, purple-blue dorsal fin was flecked with delicate pink. And, as millions of crass spinning-rod wielders have done since, I horsed that lovely fish from the water and broke its neck.

I caught eight more in quick succession and killed them all. They were big grayling, and while the law specified twelve in the limit, I stopped fishing for fear I might exceed the weight limit. I cleaned the fish, then slipped their open mouths over one prong of a forked carrying stick. Despite my haste to get them home, the beautiful grayling turned a sickly gray long before I left the lake.

The grayling used to attempt to spawn in a small spring that tumbled down a rocky hillside into Frying Pan Lake. Dozens of them would crowd frantically into the tiny flow of rushing water. It was a scene of such frenzied, but often frustrated, power that watching it made me uneasy.

Virtually no one ever fished those lakes but me. I used to leave at four A.M. and arrive at the trailhead by six. With weekly practice, I was soon able to hike up the steep trail and never stop for breath in the six miles. Going down again with a light pack on my back, cased rod in one hand and flour sack of fish in the other, I would try to see how many deer I could count watching me from the timber. One day toward the end of the summer I counted twenty-five head. I wish someone had told me, "Savor this day. Days like these will not come again in your lifetime."

In the late 1950s the Utah Game Department began surveying the fisheries potential of the high Unita Mountain lakes. The crews mapped the lakes, sounded their depths, and netted samples of fish. Before leaving they also took a water sample, which was forwarded to a lab for analysis. Going in to receive the results of a water test one day, a biologist was met by a very indignant chemist. "Think you're pretty damn smart, don't you? Well, we haven't got time for fun and games with distilled water."

The chemist had difficulty believing that water so pure could exist, even in the relatively unpolluted Uintas. There are hundreds of lakes in the Uintas, ranging in size from about fifty acres down to ponds of less than city-lot dimensions. Originally, very few of these lakes contained trout. At first, sheepherders stocked some by the simple expedient of carrying cutthroat they'd caught from a creek in a nearby lake in lard pails. During the 'twenties the state began stocking the lakes. Iced ten-gallon milk cans containing fry were laboriously packed into the high country by men and horses.

Until recently the western states were invited to send egg-stripping crews to Yellowstone Park. When the Yellowstone cutthroat began running to their spawning areas, they were caught in traps and their eggs taken. Later a proportionate share was shipped to each participating state. In Utah the resultant fry often ended up in the Uintas. There were times, however, when the trap watchers had nothing to do. And as stags will, even educated ones, they often indulged in low humor. One season the men catalogued the flatuses that echoed through their bunkhouse. Like Krupp cannon, each type had a name, from "pipsqueak" to the monumental "commode cracker". One afternoon a bored Ph.D. came leaping into the barracks dayroom and, at the height of a joyous, heel-kicking bound, fired off a commode cracker. But no one laughed, which caused the doctor to look more closely at his audience. To his dismay, he saw that a colleague's wife had dropped in for a surprise visit.

The Yellowtsone eggs were fertilized by the simple expedient of holding a ripe male over a basin of eggs and giving him an appropriate squeeze. The milt was gently stirred through the eggs, which shortly became "eyed" or fertilized eggs. When the supply warranted, the eggs were packed in trays and stacked in big wooden cases. These were ice-packed and insulated with moss before shipment. On arrival at the hatchery the cases would be carefully opened and the trays of eggs removed to troughs filled with running water in the hatchery building. I remember Bill and Ras working far into the night to care for these eggs.

Every day the hatcherymen uncovered the troughs of eggs, which had to be protected from the light, and with large rubber syringes they sucked up each whitened egg. These were dead eggs, whose presence among the pinkish-orange live ones was inimical to the latter's development. The syringe nozzles were pointed at the trays of eggs with the bulbs squeezed tightly. An experienced worker could release a tiny amount of this pressure over each dead egg so skillfully and yet so quickly that he gave the impression of being an animated, super-precise vacuum cleaner. I am afraid that when I "sucked eggs" some viable little embryos went up the tube with the dead ones.

The hatchery visitors' interest in trout increased with the size of the fish. Not many lingered over the fry or the translucent eggs, where the embryos could be seen developing. To see these things was to see a synopsis of our origins, and perhaps it made people uneasy. Anyway, they were soon outside and looking for the pond with the largest trout.

Illegal fishing was common at the hatcheries. I have actually seen youngsters joyously arrive at the hatchery with rods in hand. More covert anglers would sneak a set line into the pond waters, then return later to haul out a fish. Hatchery personnel quickly thwarted most of these forays, but a pleasant old man fooled the employees at one plant for weeks. His bib-overalled figure could be seen on any summer afternoon standing benignly beside a pond of huge spawner rainbows (which cost about twenty dollars each to raise). After a while the superintendent noticed that his spawners were fewer. He gave orders and surveillance was increased, but the prize fish continued to disappear. Suspicion centered on the old man, but he never seemed to be doing anything but placidly watching the fish.

Finally, someone saw a great trout come zipping out of the water and disappear up one of the old man's floppy trouser legs. Day after day he had been standing beside the pond, dangling a handline down through his clothing and into the pond. When a fish bit, he'd jerk it up into his pants, then amble out of the gate.

So great is the trout's allure that many people cannot bear to release them once they're caught. People have been arrested coming out of the Uinta lakes with dozens and even hundreds of trout over their limits. One gang reported the fishing had been so good that they had felt compelled to bury their catch in order to be able to go fishing. I have watched a man force his small, shivering son to stand with him in a lake while the father, having caught his own limit, proceeded to catch his son's. As I recall, Utah law was actually changed in order to prevent adults from exploiting their youngsters' fishing privileges.

One day a warden caught a fellow with an illegal concoction

of rotten hamburger and chopped nightcrawlers. The angler denied using this repulsive substance as bait. "What're you doin' with it, then?" asked the warden.

"I'm eating it for lunch," said the man, swallowing a gob and simultaneously securing his release.

People sometimes came to the hatchery for samples of the mixture we fed the trout. They were dismayed to find that its use for bait was illegal. Nowadays, I suppose, they gather spilled pellets of the modern trout rations, then sneak them home and try to figure how to bait their hooks with the stuff.

I don't know how the new pelleted food works as bait, but with its antibiotic ingredients, it certainly raises trout faster and with fewer losses. When the fish are of proper size they are bombed into alpine lakes from airplanes; more accessible waters are stocked by specially built planting boats and tank trucks. Some of these trucks are as modern and almost as many-levered as jet planes. They have many times the range of the old pickup mounted tank and can disgorge five thousand trout at a load.

They do it at night now, because all the old truck-chasers are still around and seem to have used the off-seasons for breeding purposes.

In the hatcheries biologists are experimenting with trout raised in jars. Outside, merry-go-round type aerators rotate over circular ponds, increasing the water's oxygen content and the pond's normal carrying capacity. There are now aquatic vacuum cleaners for ponds that formerly were scoured by hand or horse-drawn wooden scrapers. My friend Max North has even invented a machine that crawls along the troughs, feeding the small fish automatically. Geneticists are investigating ways to put some life and wariness back into the hatchery trout, while other scientists work out new defenses against fish diseases.

But despite the many technological improvements, the public's demand for fish and fishing increases its lead on scientific progress every year. This is true because only a percentage, often a tiny one, of stocked trout live long enough in natural habitat to be caught. Fewer still ever live to spawning age, and then only a fraction of these can find suitable spawning areas. We have built a tottering empire of fish hatcheries and called that conservation. It is a misnomer. For what it's worth, however, we've had a hell of a lot of fun doing it!

It is easy to adopt the hatchery mentality when you are fishing but not catching much. Fat had come back from Jones Hole convinced that the stream needed restocking. I disagreed, not from the standpoint of numbers of fish but from the desire to keep meat fishermen away. On previous trips I had seen and caught some nice brown trout. They are notoriously hard fish for the average angler to decimate; still, they are a great game fish and capable of restocking a stream such as Jones Creek naturally.

Just horsebacking in there from Island Park was an adventure. The range had been badly overgrazed by cattle, deer, and sheep. But the livestock had been removed and the trail, no longer ridden by stockmen, had become a faint trace marked here and there by deeply rusted tobacco cans. In places the eroded gullies were deep enough to bury the Pig with me sitting on her back. Occasionally, a small sign tacked to a juniper announced PARK BOUNDARY. A lot of Jones Hole was in Dinosaur National Monument, although the state was responsible for the fishery there.

On a typical trip, my capacious cavalry saddlebags were tightly packed with food, some utensils, a pint of whiskey, and a book of game laws, along with a pad of citation blanks. I generally carried a .45 revolver in a belt holster around my waist until I reached the creek and could cache my groceries in the little cabin there. After that, I carried the gun in my saddlebags.

My light, down-filled sleeping bag was tightly rolled in a plastic groundsheet, which in turn was rolled inside a big, waterproof nylon tarp. The tarp could be used as a groundsheet, lean-to, or pup tent as the need arose. Before rolling the bag, I slipped a paperback book into the bundle. Then I tied the roll behind my saddle. I carried a coiled lead rope and cotton halter on the saddle strap cowboys use to carry lariats. Over this I hung my rifle scabbard, which on these trips held a cased fishing rod and a small tackle box secured by a rolled poncho.

With all these western trappings, I felt constrained to stuff a pouch of Velvet into my hip pocket and put an orange packet of *Riz La* cigarette papers into my shirt pocket. It was practical as well as picturesque, because you can carry a lot more makings than you can packages of tailor-mades.

I planned to catch a couple of trout to supplement my simple grub list. There was a tiny stove in the cabin, and I cooked on that, or over a campfire outside if it was too hot to fire up the stove.

The trail in, as I've said, was very steep once it started down into Jones Hole. Carl Staley, who owned property in the area, had a pack horse fall off the trail and into the rocky abyss beside it. The horse was killed and most of its load destroyed. I took that as a warning and led the Pig down the more precipitous sections of the trail.

Beyond the switchbacks the trail curved beside sheer stone cliffs. In their stark, unyielding way, they were lovely in colors of straw, buff, and reds that graded to brown. Sometimes I glimpsed buck deer with big, velveted antlers, which would be even larger by September. In cool nooks I often saw inquisitive, big-eared does and occasionally a spotted fawn. As the mare took me down and down, her large round rump switched rhythmically from side to side. It is reassuring to know that a horse is almost as fearful of falling as you are. Then, suddenly, the switching gait stops, the mare strides ahead more easily and faster, swirls gracefully around the last blind curve, and we are enveloped by the soft greenness of Jones Hole.

The mountain men categorized anything they went down to as a hole. There is Brown's Hole, a huge basin where rustlers once held their cattle. There is Pete's Hole, a canyon on the Green River. Little Hole is a basin counter sunk in the Green River Canyon, and Jones Hole is a deep, slowly undulating gorge.

The Park Service built the mid-canyon cabin I used and another much larger one at the Creek mouth. At one time the service employed a teacher and his wife as fire guards, and I used to visit them. They were fine amateur naturalists, and they seemed to enjoy their isolation. The Park Service supplied them by boat (although some supplies were also brought in by pack train), and I enjoyed several home-cooked meals in the wilderness with this couple.

They had a radio transmitter and sent daily fire-condition reports to Monument Headquarters near Jensen. When that was done, they did some trail maintainence and cleaned up after the float trippers who stopped at the mouth of the creek for everything from a quick beer to a laid-on barbecue.

The boaters came downstream in huge black rubber rafts. Bus Hatch of Vernal guided many of these parties, but others were outfitted by people from all over the intermountain west. One of them had circulated a brochure that promised superb trout fishing and subsequent dinners as a feature of his tour. Unfortunately, most of the float trips began in Colorado, and would-be anglers weren't able to get the required Utah fishing licenses. Some guides pooh-poohed this and opened the season by all the authority vested in them. Fat had once nearly gotten into a battle with a young Salt Lake City guide over this illicit fishing. Taking a nonresident out of the remote canyon to a Vernal court was well-nigh impossible, so I tried to prevent violations, rather than springing out of the bushes crying "Aha!"

Most of the time there was no one to surprise. The most solitary fourth of July I ever spent was within the silent walls of Jones Hole. But one afternoon I did ride around some streamside bushes to find an elderly man trying to cast a fly into a small pool. His rapt attention, together with the creek's music, had permitted the Pig and me to come very close before he noticed us.

"Hel—*lo* . . ." His face fell when he connected my badge with the Utah Fish and Game patch on my sleeve. He looked something like Anthony Eden, and his expression must have matched Eden's when the first reports of the Suez debacle arrived.

[70

"How's fishing?"

"I'm not doing very well, really. I haven't fished in years, but this is such a lovely stream, I just had to try it. The guide loaned me this rod." Under his new patina of river tan, the man was pale, and he had a sick look that transcended being caught in a misdemeanor.

"Where you from?" I asked.

"San Francisco. I'm a stockbroker." He named a number of somebodies comprising a firm on Mountgomery Street. "But," he said, "I had a nervous breakdown a while ago. I haven't been working. My doctor took a float trip last summer and recommended it. This is our third day, and I'm certainly enjoying it."

If he was trying to talk me out of asking to see his license, he was succeeding. He continued talking, telling me how he used to enjoy secluded streams like this one in California, and how they were all gone. "I didn't think there were places anywhere like this one."

"This is about the last one," I said. "Say, when I left the river, your gang seemed to be about ready to eat."

The elderly man smiled, then looked at the stream and back at me. There seemed to be a kind, genuine humility in his expression. Then he stroked the Pig's nose gently and was gone.

I rode on upstream to the cabin. The sun was below the canyon wall, and shadows cast by the cliffs had fallen in broad, purpling planes. There was a flat-surfaced pool in front of the cabin, and I saw the soft splashes of two feeding trout at its head. After I had unsaddled I jointed my rod and crawled to a spot just above the feeding fish. I cast and hooked one. He tried to dive, and when I stopped him he jumped, a silver shadow vibrating the water. Then he surged across the pool, but I turned him and led him back across the pool and slid him out onto the bank. He was a brown trout, and was actually golden under his dark spots. When I cooked him he curled in the pan, and his translucent bones popped from the orangey flesh as the heat enveloped them.

Later, I sat on the cabin's stoop, enjoying the gloom with a cup of coffee. The Pig was a few rods off, baling the lush grass swiftly, methodically. I could make her out by her blaze and her single white stocking. Eventually the rhythmic "chumping" sound of her feeding stopped, and she ambled over to where I sat. She seemed to enjoy examining things I held, and the coffee cup was no exception. Delicately she sniffed the cup, never quite touching it or the hand and knee that held and balanced it. Finally there was a satisfied exhalation of breath. I got up and replaced her bridle with the halter and tied her under a nearby tree for the night.

Then I went back into the cabin and refilled my coffee cup. I sat down on the stoop again and lit a cigarette. Hell, I knew that old guy didn't have a license. He knew that I knew. But I think he needed the canyon and its stream. We didn't have a license for that kind of need—possibly because there are so few places left where a man can go to satisfy it.

V / PRINCELINGS ON THE PLAIN

"There's about two acres of public land for each of us. I want a deer or antelope on mine."

—FAT GARDINER

ONCE THE THOUSANDS OF HATCHERY TROUT HAD BEEN HIDDEN away in the streams and reservoirs, our next task was to make an aerial census of the antelope on the Bonanza Desert. Before taking off, the department pilot called from his home in Price for a weather report.

If the sky looked clear Fat or I would be waiting an hour or so later, in the day's first gray light, for the little Cub to come winking in over the blackness of the distant Book Cliffs. For one accustomed to scheduled airlines, flying in the Super Cub could be a leveling experience. No stewardess took your coat or offered coffee, tea, or milk. You just piled in behind the sleepy-eyed pilot, clapped him on the shoulder, and sprang into the slowly lighting sky.

The names on the land we flew over would have delighted Stephen Vincent Benét. No sooner were we airborne than Naples was beneath our wings. It is a Mormon ward, similar to a parish, although the inhabitants never call themselves Neapolitans. To the south, on the edge of the brick-brown Bonanza Desert, stands a lonely little mountain that some people call Gobbler's Knob. To the west of it, along the wooded bottoms of the Green River, is Horseshoe Bend, and west of that is the stand of cottonwoods known as Chepeta Grove. Beyond, out in the Ute Indian share of the Book Cliffs, is BP Springs, the full name of which is Bull Prick Springs. As if to make up for that vulgarity, the Indians also had a place with the name of Moonwater. Looking back toward Vernal, you might just make out the canyon called the Little Vee. It is north of Doc's Beach (where there is no shoreline and very little water). In the haze to the north and east, close under the rounded crest of the Uinta Mountains, is intermittent Pot Creek. I understand it was so named because gunman Matt Warner once held up a peddler there and, finding he had no money, scattered his goods along the stream.

Pot Creek is a tributary of the Green River, whose course we flew along. The river looks placid out here, but there are some fearful rapids farther on. One is called "Sling-a-Ring Rapids"—the polite

[74

name. This exploding rush of white water is known to boatmen as "Shit-a-Ring Rapids," and well-named, too, because a trip through the boiling froth is said to induce a violent laxative response, capable of circumnavigating the moon.

Boone McKnight and Green River veteran Bus Hatch floated hundreds of passengers safely through that spot. If Utahans have given their landmarks interesting names, they have done even better by their offspring. I knew a couple of men who had grown up to be salty six-footers despite the first name of June. When other mothers were naming their sons El Ray, at least one called her boy Ray El. Names of earlier currency, such as Nymphas and Mahonri, aren't as popular as Odell, Udell, or Golden. Given names like DelMar, De-Loyd, DeLayne, and Denzil are as common in Mormon country as LaVere, LaVon, LaVar, and Lael. While many Saints don't accept Negroes as spiritual equals, some have named their baby boys Othello. I have known Ebs, Almas, Voyles, and a couple of guys named Shirley. The game department employed a lady by the name of RuDell Sudweeks. Twila, LaPrielle, and Utahna are fairly common girls' names. My wife has a pair of aunts called Zoa and Zola, and two friends, twin sisters, named Wyoma and Neoma. She doesn't think these are particularly unusual names, because hers is Rodello.

Fat Gardiner was not the only man in town with that nickname. The proprietor of one of Vernal's nicest restaurants was called Fat Belcher. But whether the name was on the land or a person, I think my favorite was Chepeta Wells.

Named for the previously mentioned Ute princess, Chepeta Wells had been a freighter's way station in the desert between Bonanza and Ouray. According to Fat, water wagons periodically went out to replenish the reservoirs there, because there is no live water at Chepeta Wells. But when I saw them, the freight wagons no longer rumbled across the desert, and Chepeta Wells was only greasewood, shadscale, and yellow-brown earth smeared here and there with alkali.

If you follow the dirt road past the abandoned tanks, you come upon the White River, a muddy stream coming from Colorado to merge with the muddy Green near Ouray. If you drive slowly and watch carefully, you might see a white stone marker almost hidden by greasewood and weeds. It solemnly announces that a man and his two wives drowned here while trying to ford the flooded river.

The stone is easily missed. The road is now lined with distracting windrows of glittering beer bottles and cans. Conspicuous among these and the low ledges are tiny, white-bottomed antelope ground squirrels. Their flight is a combination scamper and headlong dash, and the last thing you see of them as they disappear is that big, white behind.

They are the namesakes of the pronghorn antelope, whose white rump patches can be equally revealing. From the air, however, the color-camouflaged animals aren't easy to see. Often we looked for a band of horses, because for some unknown reason antelope often were nearby.

The airplane offered the only practicable means for counting the elusive animals. We took off at daybreak because the game was easier to find then, and the air had not yet built up turbulence from midday heat. From the air the western brush lands often appeared to me to be covered with frieze. The color was brown or green according to the season. But as we roared down the long dry valleys to zoom up over the rocky buttes at the last instant, I could see small pebbles on the butte tops. Up close, the hard land certainly was not upholstered.

Once, just as Hank West was descending to land at the Vernal airport, the plane's engine stopped. I thought he had cut the switch somewhat early, but didn't think more of it until the Cub glided down and bounced on the runway.

"That's the first time that ever happened," Hank said.

"What?" I asked.

"The engine quit on me." I was thankful it hadn't stopped just a few minutes earlier as we were scratching over that last butte top.

When we spotted antelope, the pilot would buzz them, flying

alongside the running animals while his passenger counted and classified them. Antelope are fascinating at any time, but to see them surging along just below your plane is a special thrill.

Part of the thrill is the promise in the numbers of fawns running easily at their mothers' sides. It was a promise that nature reneges upon before fall comes, but in June it is there and alive. We were almost sure that finally the herd was about to really grow. We knew that many of the bucks were not with the herds, the older males spend solitary summers on the desert and can seldom be seen from the air. When the rut begins in September they move in on the does and are likely to drive off the young bucks that have followed the females with such devoted anticipation all summer.

Unlike the mule deer, which often thrive on unstable, evolving range, antelope seem to prefer a stable range. Their favorites are often those ranges where plant succession has reached the climax stage. Until the west was settled, antelope lived harmoniously with buffalo, one species complementing the other's existence. But when the buffalo were virtually exterminated, the grasses they had grazed flourished—to the detriment of the leafy plants and shrubs the antelope depend upon. Next, disease, overshooting, and overgrazing by the recently introduced cattle and sheep sent antelope into a swift decline that stopped just short of extinction. From a population estimated at forty million, the antelope in North America dwindled to a few thousand.

But with protection and, in some areas, more favorable range conditions, antelope have increased, even flourished. In Utah, however, pronghorn births barely exceed the deaths, primarily because the ranges are so badly overgrazed. Still, beginning about 1945, carefully regulated hunting has been allowed.

Antelope are polygamous, and biologists feel that a cautious removal of some bucks does no harm. It may even be beneficial, because hunting chases the animals into areas they might otherwise not occupy. Also, some legal hunting thwarts poachers by keeping the animals alert and discouraging them from bunching together in overly large numbers. Finally, the antelope evolved as a prey species. They were an important source of food for the Indians, who were not always successful in getting buffalo. If the pronghorn had not been pursued, it would never have developed its remarkable eyesight, swiftness, or the handsome, protective coloration. Even the giveaway rump patch serves to keep the fleeing animals lined up on one another and, perhaps, to offer a pursuing predator a false target.

I have always resented the appellation "goat" being given to antelope. The early Spanish explorers referred to the pronghorn as *la cabre*. The pronghorn antelope is not even remotely a goat. Nor is any mutual genealogy shared by African antelope and the North American variety. Nevertheless, there is probably a similarity between hunting antelope in Wyoming and hunting them in Kenya.

Like many others before me, I became really fond of antelope only after I had hunted them. Our family friend Rex Hanson convinced my father and me to take our first trip after antelope. We bought Wyoming hunting licenses, because they were much easier to get than the Utah permits, and made plans to hunt in an area north of Casper.

After leaving Salt Lake City we drove across the Union Pacific's vast domain, Evanston, Green River, Rock Springs, and on toward Rawlins. There was little to see between the grimy Wyoming towns but desolate distance, and I began wondering what Rex had found to enjoy about antelope hunting. Then Rex said, "There's some." I looked but saw nothing. Mile turned upon tiring mile, and every so often Rex would say, "There's some more." Finally, in the waning sunlight, I saw several buff-colored smudges hovering in heat waves above the buff-colored land.

Casper was even less impressive than the antelope had been. At night it was all neon-ugly and obviously booming on a tide of black oil. In the cafe where we sat down to eat, the Kemtoned walls resounded with the oil talk of drillers and tool pushers. Even the air smelled of oil, to such a degree that it seemed to have permeated the food. We hopeful antelope hunters ignored the cafe's other patrons and concentrated on our rubbery steaks.

George Davis, a business associate of my father's who lived in Casper, came in. He waved and then walked over to our booth. George shook hands all around, then said he had arranged for us to hunt next day on a ranch about fifty miles north of town. He talked a little business and a little antelope, then left us with our dishes of oily ice cream and an early-morning appointment.

The next morning George met us in his jeep. With him were his teen-aged son and another man. They were extremely friendly, although I got the distinct impression that George's friend had come along as a back-up gun. It was a little embarrasing to be considered a bum shot without a trial.

After a long drive we arrived at a tiny knot of ranch buildings. Set in that rolling, treeless landscape, they looked as temporary as military Quonset huts. As we drove up before the ranch house, the rancher and his wife came out and made us welcome. They had a pet antelope in their yard, and as we talked it ambled up for a sniff and a tenuous pat on the forehead. "Don't shoot our pet!" the rancher called as we drove out of his yard.

The jeep was hardly away from the ranch when George stopped it. A young buck antelope was standing a couple of hundred yards off and looking at us curiously. Rex nudged me. "Your shot."

I looked at him and then at the motionless buck. I whispered that Rex should shoot, but he insisted, "Go ahead, you've never hunted these things before."

I climbed slowly out of the jeep, loaded my rifle, rested it on a convenient fence post, and pulled the trigger. My bullet made a tiny puff of dust at the antelope's hooves. He hopped, mildly surprised, then ambled off a few yards to stop and resume watching us. I looked at Rex sitting in the jeep, shrugged, and nodded for him to take a shot.

Rex was an above-average rifle shot. He brought his .270 over to the fence, rested it, aimed, and dropped the buck. Then it jumped up and shuffled off, trailing its entrails. Rex ducked through the fence after it; when the animal paused and let Rex approach, he shot at it a couple of times with his .22 pistol. The buck shied away, although the dragging intestines hampered his movements. Rex followed and when the animal stopped again, he shot at him some more with the pistol. The buck lumbered away again, dragging and grotesque, across the golden, rolling hills. When he stopped the next time, Rex unslung his rifle and killed him.

I walked over to where he was cleaning it, with a big knot growing in my stomach. There was a buzzing sensation along the top of my skull and I was intermittently blinded by flashes of light. Between them I saw the antelope's dead gray paunch; the greenish dirt covered rolls of intestines. I had to turn and walk away. I walked to the top of a knoll, where I sat down, feeling faint and chilled. I was sick and embarrassed to be sick. I put my head down and willed the nausea to go away, I also wished I had not come antelope hunting. When I was sure I wouldn't vomit, I walked back and helped Rex and George load the little buck into the jeep; I doubt if it weighed ninety pounds. No one said much to me but I saw George's son working to suppress a grin.

We motored over some more hills and a young doe trotted in front of us. George suggested I shoot her—she was bouncing along easily, only sixty yards away. "I'd rather try for a buck," I said. George shrugged and said something about not getting another chance.

There is a code, or used to be, that you do not quit in the middle of a hunting trip. It may be a barbaric or juvenile expression of the stiff-upper-lip philosophy to go on when you do not want to, but it is the only thing you can do. I have been with men who quit when the going became unpleasant, and I learned that it is the only thing worse than going on. It is an old and respected western tradition to "get your time," but it is never done at noon. Some members of the present generation, which I call "the give-up generation," may disagree. That is their right.

George seemed to have been correct about not getting another chance at an antelope. They were everywhere, but we could not get near enough for a shot. Herds of fifty streamed over the low hills, to disappear into draws that suddenly spewed fifty more of the fleet animals, all running wildly far beyond rifle range. After lunch (which I ate only out of courtesy to George), a middle-aged man come out from the ranch in a pickup. They called him Herb. He asked with quiet interest about the hunting and barely grunted when someone joshed me for being sick. He looked at me with a gentle friendliness before we all piled back into the jeep again. Maybe he said, "We'll get you a buck," and maybe he didn't, but somehow I knew he would get one.

Herb sat in the back seat and guided George's son, who was driving, with shoulder taps and finger-pointing. Herb obviously knew every hill and swale and "let down" in the miles of sheep-tight fence. He also seemed to know the hold of every band of antelope, and he could estimate to the inch which route they would take to escape us. When a band started he would tap the boy on the shoulder and point. We bucked and roared to the spot Herb indicated, and the antelope would suddenly come flashing out of the draw, right in front of us. The man was like an old bird dog, doing a job of work he loved and did in the easiest possible way. The gently rolling grasslands and patches of low sage offered no obstacle to the growling jeep. It was an inexhaustible predator, roaring and springing ahead, then quartering across country to intercept the fleeing game.

At one intercept point, two dozen animals came careering across our front. The jeep slammed to a stop, and George's friend and I jumped out. There were several bucks in the herd, and they spurted forward, nearly merging with the leading does. We fired. The buck I had picked slowed to a lazy, burlesque walk, and I shot him again. Herb walked up to where he lay. "Nice ivory tips on his horns," he said. He took out his pocket knife and while he was saying "I've dressed some of these," he did it.

My dad got his antelope under Herb's guidance that same afternoon. We took them to a shed, where they were hung, then skinned and sacked. The rancher stood by and watched us as we worked, pleased that we were so pleased. As we skinned, he told us about a doctor who sometimes hunted on his ranch. The physician had insisted upon using a cased set of surgical knives and wearing rubber gloves when he dressed his antelope.

It was dark long before we returned to Casper. Before saying good-by, George invited us to come again. We said, "You bet!" In the cafe we ordered steaks, and while we waited for them Rex said that he never wanted to shoot an antelope that way again. My father praised Herb, and I praised my rifle and opined that once you learned the lead, antelope shooting isn't as hard as it looks. We all felt very good.

When I learned to know antelope better, I was much less pleased with myself than I had been that night in Casper.

Ernest Thompson Seton wrote that the antelope's worst enemies were "repeating rifles, next, sheep which destroy their winter range, and finally, deep snow." I learned about the first of these enemies shortly after I arrived in Vernal. A prowler east of town had killed every member of a tiny band of five that we had watched over hopefully. The killer left them where they dropped, to bloat among the greasewood. The gobs of protoplasm (and there are too many) who do this are rarely caught. It doesn't seem to me that they are worth a scintilla of what an antelope is worth. But then, I have an admittedly odd way of totting up values.

Seton's lethal list has been added to in the forty years since he published it. The fences that cross and recross the western plains are far more dangerous to antelope than deep snow. Antelope can move ahead of a storm, but virtually none of them can slip through the viciously tight fences—many of which are built by, or at least with the approval of, federal "range conservationists." Apparently the skeletons of antelope lying along one of these execrable erections move certain people to cut the wire. They do it expertly by cutting the entire panel from between two posts. Then they roll the wire and dump it far away where nothing will later become entangled in it. Others who have scruples about cutting a fence, kick a few staples out of the posts. The wire sags in time and allows the antelope to crawl through it.

[82

The latest enemy of antelope is the jeep. This machine and its many counterparts are very like DDT. When they first appeared, most of us considered them a panacea. But, indiscriminately placed in the hands of fools and self-servers, they have done incalculable harm. Hunting by jeep is not easy, due to sand and wet sinks on the Bonanza, where even the trucks that had brought the antelope down from Wyoming originally had not dared to venture off the established roads. Fat Gardiner had driven some of the carefully blacked-out van loads. The vans had to be completely dark or the frightened, high-strung animals would have rushed toward the light and broken their legs or necks.

Under the transplanting agreement, the antelope were not legally hunted for five years. When the time was up, our aerial counts showed an increase, and we recommended a limited hunt for bucks. For some reason, perhaps better range and water, many of the pronghorns were on the Ute Indian Reservation, not far from the village of Ouray.

"The Utes are an interesting people" it says in the travel brochures. If the Utes were to publish a travel guide, I doubt that they'd say white people are interesting. I became friends with one Ute and came to know many others. They do not think as whites do, and so their philosophy is as different from ours as their values are.

Whites have been cheating and abusing the Utes for a couple of centuries. So any agreement they make with us now is understandably of a tenuous nature. But we did believe we had worked out a suitable antelope-hunting arrangement with the Tribal Council, (at which one old buck wearied and said, "Huh, all white man want to do is sit at desk and shuffle paper."). We agreed to issue twenty-five hunting permits. Fifteen would be distributed in a game department drawing, and ten given to the Tribe, to be issued as they saw fit. Hunters who got the permits would then be allowed to hunt anywhere in the district, either on or off the reservation.

The Indians seemed satisfied, even pleased, with the arrangement, so on the morning preceding the hunt, I was shocked to hear the following announcement on the bilingual Ute radio program: "The Tribal Fish and Game Department will issue fifteen buck antelope at Chepeta Grove tomorrow morning."

There followed some hurried council, in which the Indians didn't seem too interested, and, bang, the season was open. As it developed, Indian hunters shot three or four antelope, while the whites killed ten or so bucks and one illegal doe.

Recently I saw a picture of a nattily dressed, horn-rimmed college professor holding a tape recorder's microphone to the smiling lips of an elderly Ute lady. The photo's caption explained that the professor was collecting authentic Indian lore. But from the expression on that old gal's face, the professor just thought he was collecting lore. A Ute will tell you what he believes you want to hear. The best illustration of this was told to me by a friend who had been visiting an old Ute man in his cabin almost every day. My friend was collecting Indian lore, too, and after many visits, he felt he was finally getting somewhere with the taciturn old Indian. But when the fellow arrived at the Indian's cabin for an appointment one day, he found it locked and the windows boarded up. He was very disappointed, and asked a neighbor if the old man had been called away suddenly.

"No. He fix trip for long time now."

"But he was supposed to meet me here today," my friend said.

"He tell me. But he know it make you sad if he go away, so he not tell you."

The mute Bonanza was a macerated testimonial to Seton's indictment of the sheep. Fat used to say that "even the rocks have teeth marks on 'em." The doe antelope would regularly bring forth twin fawns in early June, but by mid-July the overgrazed range would take them away. The poorly nourished doe simply couldn't feed their tiny fawns. They would die, perhaps as one I found had died, on a black, sun-baked plaza of flint. The delicate skeleton's hooves were no larger than a man's thumb. Its mouth was open.

[84

Soon afterward, I met two sheepmen on that range and asked them if they'd seen any antelope.

"Nope, and we don't want to see none, either." They probably won't.

I drew a hunting permit on the Bonanza that year, and near the close of the late August season killed a buck beside the Green River. Fat and I cleaned him and then took the carcass to a nearby grove of cottonwoods. We hung it from a tree and quickly skinned it. Despite the quick kill and the equally fast care of the carcass, I had doubts about the quality of the venison. Beef or mutton fed on such a range would have been "starvation poor," but the antelope venison was sweet and succulent. None of the many other pronghorns I've killed on much better range has tasted better than that Utah buck.

The antelope is a most unpredictable animal. They will stand well off a road, then, as your car approaches, begin to run—not away from, but parallel to, your car. When you accelerate, the pronghorns will drop into overdrive, and when your speedometer is nudging fifty, the antelope will turn and zip across the road in front of you. Afterward, they may run back to the area where the race began.

Antelope love to race. I have watched them suddenly quit their placid grazing, race pell-mell for several miles, then suddenly stop and begin feeding again. At other times, you may see a buck running free across the prairie apparently just for the joy of it.

At some hours the antelope will act quite tame; then, for no apparent reason, they will become as unapproachable as the stars. On one game range, the manager kept a pet buck, which was everyone's pal. Then a professor of wildlife management came out for a visit, and the buck put him up a tree.

During some antelope-hunting seasons, I have seen tiny puffs of dust spring up several miles away. If you look at the base of the dust spire, you will see a speck so small that only its speed tells you it is antelope. It may be frustrating to hunters, but it is also marvelous to know that such eyesight as the pronghorn's exists.

85]

Antelope seem to prefer running to thinking. I only once remember seeing a particularly sagacious act performed by one of them. I was hunting in Wyoming's Big Sandy country. It's sagebrush range, broken by abruptly rising buttes and long, deep valleys. Sadly, it is also sheep range. On the bare ridges you can see numerous cairns of piled slate—sheepherder monuments, built to mark the dragging passage of time. I had been watching a buck on top of a ridge bearing one of these monuments. He was oblivious of me, intent instead upon the bug-sized pickup that was steadily approaching in the distance. As the truck reached the section of road below the buck, he stepped behind the monument. As the truck moved, the buck did, too, carefully circling the cairn, and keeping it between himself and his enemies.

There are a lot of cheesy ways to kill antelope. Hunting from cars is the worst, but by far the most popular. A few hunters wait for them in blinds near waterholes. Some others try the ancient dodge of flagging the curious creatures into rifle range by waving bandannas tied to sticks. I have attracted does by flagging them, but have never been able to fool a buck.

There is only one real way to hunt antelope: stalking. A car should be used only to get into the general area. When the game is sighted or suspected, it should be stalked on foot, then on hands and knees, and finally on your belly, if necessary. More often than not, the stalk will fail. When he thinks about it later, the hunter will understand why the failures are even more important than the successes.

VI / AND WE HAD TO
KILL THE DEER

*"I don't care about getting some meat;
I'm not shooting any doe."*

—MY FATHER

ALTHOUGH IT LACKED ANTELOPE, FOR WELL OVER A DECADE UTAH was the mule deer capital of the world. When the first green wisps of grass appear on the foothills in late March and early April, the deer congregate there in almost undreamed-of numbers. I have driven along a highway in April and counted over five hundred animals in less than thirty minutes. Except for its western desert wastes and some of the slick-rock country in the southeast part of the state, all of Utah is good deer country. A motorist driving up Emigration Canyon east of Salt Lake City early on a summer morning has to proceed cautiously or risk hitting one of the deer that habitually sleep on the warm pavement.

But the magnitude of the deer population impressed me most when I saw the truckloads of deer hides being loaded and hauled away from the hide buyers. At one lot the hides were packed in bales nearly as large as cotton bales and then loaded into huge tractor-trailer rigs that hauled tons at a load. When fully laden, one such truck pulled out onto the highway and its burden didn't seem to have made a dent in the piles of hides awaiting shipment. At that time, Utah hunters were killing over a hundred thousand deer each fall. In addition, they wounded fifteen to twenty-five thousand animals that died and were lost.

The deer bonanza of the mid-twentieth century could never have been dreamed of in the early 1920s when Utah closed its hunting seasons for lack of deer. Some ecologists equate the mule deer with the annual weeds that spring up on disturbed land. The pioneers had not found their Zion particularly blessed with deer, and they quickly slaughtered most of Utah's original big game. When they were done with that, they slaughtered the grassy ranges by overgrazing and injudicious logging. Shrubs began to flourish on the raped land. Bitterbrush, cliffrose, mountain mahogany and serviceberry filled the grasses' empty niche. Where sagebrush had always done well, it now did even better.

[88

To protect their livestock while it overgrazed the land, the old-timers exterminated the grizzly bears and wolves, and mounted an ever-more-successful war of attrition on the coyotes and mountain lions. Then, with pious mien and the best of intentions, they controlled the range fires that had for eons prevented the growth of brush on the grass ranges. When they realized that their big game was almost extinct, they made game preserves of many of the abused foothills. Inadvertently, the pioneers and their offspring created superb deer ranges throughout the state.

The well-fed does took advantage of the rhapsodic conditions and reliably produced two healthy fawns each June. Given a year to mature, the healthy fawns also began to reproduce, and Utah's deer increased geometrically until there were probably a half million of them. When over one hundred thousand starved during the bitter winter of 1949–1950, the loss went virtually unnoticed by hunters the next fall. There was another sizable loss the following winter, but it too was easily absorbed. Many deer fanciers, including some older wardens who could remember the deer dearth of twenty-five years earlier, refused to admit that there were too many deer. Fat told me that one old warden had hurried out to the scene of a severe deer die-off and hauled the carcasses away when he heard that biologists were coming out from Salt Lake City to assess the situation.

Actually, many hunters had already grown weary of the abundant deer. They were badgering the game department to provide them with more elk. They could not understand that this was an ecological impossibility, as the grassy ranges upon which elk thrive best had been long overgrown with brush. Elk often do best on a climax range, where the forage is not in a stage of succession. Of course, both deer and elk dwindle when a climax forest of conifers begins shading out the aspen, grasses, weedy plants, and brush.

Included in the various vegetative changes to the range were the dark, green phalanxes of juniper trees. Probably because of fire control and overgrazing, juniper and piñon pine began advancing

down the ridges to choke the swales and valleys with their seed-
lings. Deer will browse certain individuals among the common
species of juniper, but they leave most of the trees untouched.
What makes one tree more palatable than another of the same
species is unclear, although botanists think it is due to the amounts
of essential oil in the foliage. When the juniper or piñon trees invade an area, practically all the other plant life disappears. A
range that supported twenty deer per square mile might support
only five after a juniper take-over. This condition was occurring
on our ranges, and west of Vernal stood what some misguided Jay-
cees bragged was the "Largest Cedar Forest in the World." Cedar
was the local name for juniper.

The thoughtful game biologist could go nuts worrying about
his deer, for the ranges were declining in productivity while the
number of hunters was increasing by the tens of thousands. Stockmen hounded us to get rid of the game, which competed for food
with their animals, and the Federal land managers wanted a reduction in deer and elk, both to get the politically powerful stockmen off their necks and to preserve the land. Conversely, sportsmen
demanded more game and put DON'T KILL DOES signs in their car
windows and hung placards reading THIS IS A DOE-FREE CAMP outside their hunting tents. Fat remarked that it seemed foolish to
"bust our ass runnin' down deer poachers in August, then turn
around an' coax hunters to kill more deer in October."

Really, each deer has a double image: one is a biological power-
house eating up its range and destroying the soil; the other is a
beautiful creature whose very presence is a tonic to the soul. And
I suppose it was these latter deer that we looked out for in August.

Once we had made our recommendations for the forthcoming
hunting season, we could give our time to the frustration of the
poachers. One evening Dick Bennett, one of the two wardens in
remote Daggett County, across the Uinta Mountains to the north,
was sitting in his living room when he heard a shot. He rushed outside to his truck and drove toward some alfalfa fields, where the

shot seemed to have originated. Just as he reached a gate in the fence surrounding one of the fields, he met a sedan coming through. Dick flashed his red spotlight on the car and it stopped. He walked up to it. "Been doing any shooting down here?"

"No." The driver was positive.

But Dick let his flashlight beam play over the car anyway. The light illuminated the back seat. "If you haven't been shooting, why is that deer standing in your back seat?" The deer had been only stunned, and had taken that supremely opportune moment to regain consciousness.

One summer night I went out with the Colorado warden to patrol our mutually shared border. About eleven P.M. we stopped a jeep on a remote back road. The two occupants each held a fully loaded deer rifle. "What're you hunting?" I asked.

The driver looked at us blandly and said, "Rabbits."

One warm evening I took a lady friend on a moonlight drive. We parked on a back road beside an alfalfa field and proceeded to become better acquainted. After our acquaintance developed into warm friendship, I suggested that we could carry it on more agreeably in the back seat. We were just getting comfortably established there when a shot rang out.

"Spotlighters!" I dived into the front seat and drove toward the source of the shot with a very surprised female in the back seat. I found that the hunters had missed their deer, and I will not enlarge upon my own success that night.

I can say that such goings-on never occurred in the department's accounting office, where Armond Carr ran things with punctilious perfection. Mr. Carr flawlessly handled millions of dollars and often was aghast at the wardens' casual business practices. All state monies had to be handled according to strict regulations. For instance, all the money that was received for special deer permits by an agent in Vernal had to be sent in full to Mr. Carr's office in Salt Lake. On receipt of the cash and a correct accounting, Mr. Carr sent the agent a voucher for his sales commission. It was slow but correct. One year the agent pressed Fat for his commission, and Fat finally paid it to him out of the license receipts. Fat then sent in the rest of the money, along with an explanation about paying the commission. Immediately, Mr. Carr was on the long-distance line. He heard Fat's explanation.

"But Mr. Gardiner, you cannot do that." Fat tried to explain his side of it, but all he heard was, "But you cannot do that." Fat finally said, "Well, by gawd, I done her," and hung up.

Mr. Carr suffered many such experiences. One time some wardens spent several hundred dollars on liquor while entertaining politicians at a state fishing cabin. Although the technique worked to the department's advantage, it was reprehensible in pious Utah, so the wardens turned in their whiskey bills as purchases of cabbage. Mr. Carr was on the phone again, "How am I to explain eight tons of cabbages to the state examiner?"

After he had given me time to get settled, Fat asked me to choose the half of Uintah County that I wanted for my district. I took the eastern half, which included about half the town of Vernal, all of Jensen, Jones Hole, a small duck marsh, and two thousand square miles that included the big-titted blonde at the Gateway Café. Ah, that pneumatic girl! She never knew that on stormy days when even the seconds dragged, we bought her atrocious coffee and drank it simply to restore our confidence in the development potential of the human mammary glands. An envious female once said of such endowments, "Hmph! She can't even wash her knees when she's sitting down in the bathtub."

I had apparently gotten a reputation for jumping across car seats and consequently, the ladies I found interesting often were not interested in me. So, like most of the other game wardens, I spent my days off on the job. It became an admission of guilt as well as a sign of shirking if an old-timer mentioned some remote spot in the area that I had not recently visited.

Once summer was secure in the Basin, the townspeople invariably asked about conditions "on the mountain." This included

[92

every sort of intelligence from "How cold is it at night?" through
"Are the ticks bad?" and "How do the deer look?" Some people
remarked that if Fat met them coming off the mountain with a
gun in their car, "He always wants to look in our trunk." Perhaps
the most flattery we got all summer was from the fellow who said,
"You guys are just like horseshit—all over".

I enjoyed getting around the country, for most of it was beautiful. Diamond Mountain was partially separated from Taylor
Mountain by Brush Creek Gorge and the equally spectacular abyss
called the Little Vee. The mountain had a sort of elephant's-back
for a top. At its crest were conifers that gave way to aspen, which
in turn yielded to grassy expanses of sage that extended down to the
mountain's precipitous edge. Some mountains are described as
glowering, towering, or majestic. To me, Diamond Mountain was
peaceful.

But, like the old gentleman dozing in his club chair with hands
folded on his paunch, Diamond had known some livelier days.
The mining hoax mentioned earlier happened here, some said
right in Diamond Gulch, which, when I knew it, was a grassy draw
that nearly always held some sage grouse. Anyway, in the early
1870s two prospectors salted low-grade diamonds on the mountain.
Somehow they were able to fool mining engineers and a Tiffany's
diamond expert, who recommended the spurious mine to their
financier employers. The two prospectors sold out to the con-
sortium for thousands of dollars and in the best tradition of a Peter
B. Kyne story, vanished.

Diamond Mountain's eastern edge, however, was all business,
for it ended abruptly on the rugged, unforgiving rocks of the Ladore
and Jones Hole Canyons. The Green River came surging out of
Ladore to burst from the mountain at a place aptly named Split
Mountain Gorge. This point was also the headquarters of the Dinosaur National Monument, a wildly rectangular preserve partially
in Utah, partially in Colorado, which kept most of the Green River
Canyon Country safe from the Bureau of Reclamation and also

protected the petrified remains of ancient reptiles from unofficial disinterment.

Across the Green River from Diamond Mountain was the butte-shaped, brooding hulk of Blue Mountain. Blue Mountain was divided by the Utah-Colorado boundary, and the park service owned its middle. It seemed to be that no one had decided quite what to do with it. The Colorado and Utah roads leading to the Monument were rutted, high-centered horrors, although the park service had provided their section with a serpentine road of coral-colored gravel, very neatly tended. This road led to some breath-taking overlooks discreetly marked with interpretive signs (THIS IS A CANYON) that a tourist with decent bifocals could read without ever having to leave his car and actually peer over the brink.

Fat half-seriously accused the Colorado warden of moving the state-line boundary signs back and forth to suit his current notions about deer hunting and management. But as soon as the season's first shots were fired, many of the deer piled over the mountain's abrupt edge to the sure safety of its rugged flanks. Other deer fled behind the Monument boundaries, where they instantly changed from prey into pets.

Out on the Utah portion of the lonely, uninhabited mountain top stood a grove of magnificent conifers. Fat took me out there on the chance we might see one of the rare blue grouse that lived near the huge trees. Under those great trees, with their orangey-brown trunks lined with black, one felt as if he were in the presence of kings.

The blue grouse didn't cooperate, so Fat took me around to several "gallinaceous guzzlers" that had been laboriously constructed on the mountain. One of the reasons Blue Mountain was so blissfully barren of humanity was its paucity of water. The concrete guzzlers were adaptations of a water-catchment design used in California. Rain and the melt water from snow collected on the catchment's wide concrete apron. It then ran down the apron into a large tank that was earth-covered to reduce evaporation. The

[94

devices were so built that thirsty sage grouse could walk down the apron to the slowly receding water's edge. We could see from the droppings that the big birds were sharing the tanks with cottontails and the occasional deer.

Blue Mountain had once sheltered a huge deer population but, as had happened throughout Utah, the excessive numbers simply couldn't be kept on the depleted ranges. At the same time, the number of hunters doubled, and in the twenty-five years after World War II the number of deer was cut almost in half. There were too many deer, and some hunters, taking advantage of all the special seasons and hunting permits, could legally kill thirteen deer in one year. But that is over now and a good thing, too. Mule deer deserve a better fate than to be slaughtered wholesale.

Deer management nowadays has two aims. One is to keep the herds in check, and the other is to provide as many animals as possible for the hunting masses. The biologists do this by establishing hunting regulations that assure a heavy deer kill each fall. This harvest, as the biologists like to call the annual bloodletting, keeps the herd young and often below the carrying capacity of the range. Such a young herd is a kind of biological bomb, reproducing itself frantically and filling up the range. The typical, leggy buck with four points on each of his antlers probably isn't four years old; he's more likely twenty-seven months old.

One way that a biologist can determine a deer's age is to tag it as a fawn and then collect the lower jaw when a hunter later brings the animal through a check station. A fawn has baby teeth, which are replaced by permanent ones on a regular schedule. Thus, a collection of jawbones from tagged deer provides the basis for determining the age of any deer. The hitch has come in getting the deer to tag in the beginning.

Deer can be trapped in winter if their hunger overcomes their fear of the baited traps. During the fawning time in early June, fawns up to a week old can be caught by men searching for them on foot. But for the rest of the year there was no way to get a deer without harming it. I say "was" because the biologist now has a tranquilizing gun that, if everything goes well, can temporarily immobilize deer.

Jess Low of Utah State College and the U.S. Fish and Wildlife Service came out to the game farm that summer. He brought with him a student and an ebullient salesman who was trying to sell everyone in sight one of the first tranquilizing guns. They came because we had a doe and two big fawns in a large paddock which we had offered up as guinea pigs. The student hoped to tranquilize some deer in the course of a range study and wanted to experiment on our deer first. The salesman was long on cheer but woefully short on knowledge of deer, their physiology and how to shoot them.

The air-powered gun fired an ingenious development of the familiar hypodermic syringe. The syringe had a wooly ball at one end which sealed the bore while the projectile raced down it and also was supposed to serve as a stabilizer in flight. The needle end of the syringe was barbed so that when it struck flesh it stuck and, through a release mechanism, simultaneously injected its load of tranquilizer. The tranquilizer was a nicotine derivative, which supposedly could be counteracted by a follow-up injection of antidote.

The gun came furnished with some dummy projectiles for target practice. We set up a piece of beaverboard about fourteen inches square. But even from a steady rest, we couldn't often hit the big target from a distance of thirty-five yards. The gun was terribly inaccurate. While we were standing around ridiculing it, Ruth Jensen's pet cat went trotting past the target. "Fat," I said, "let's see you hit that."

Fat aimed quickly and nearly knocked the cat through an adjacent garage door. "God! I hope Ruth didn't see me do that!" The cat quickly recovered everything but its smug look, and we decided to try shooting the deer.

In the paddock the salesman saw the deer and beamed. "Oh,

these are fine . . . mule deer?" He didn't seem too sure, but went on. "Now you boys are going to see something."

The animal we selected eyed us warily and kept itself just beyond accurate shooting range. Finally, the student crept close enough for a shot. The syringe went zipping over the deer's back. He continued missing, and each time the syringe had to be retrieved, refilled with tranquilizer, and then reloaded. Finally Fat took the gun and shot the deer in the butt.

"That's the way!" declared the salesman, who had started to blush. "Now watch him go down!"

We watched and watched, but the deer just trotted testily around with the big syringe flopping on his hip. "How do we get the needle back?" I asked.

"This never happened before," said the salesman.

"Hittin' the deer, or havin' it stuck in his ass?" asked Fat, who was inclined to be blunt.

The five of us began following the deer around so that when the syringe finally came out we could recover and reload it. Around and around the paddock we went. "This is bullshit," I said. The salesman looked hurt—he had bought me a steak dinner the night before. Jess grinned and shrugged, and the student kept his mouth shut. You are not allowed to say "bullshit" in front of your professor until after graduation.

Finally the syringe fell out of the deer and we recovered it. As the student began reloading, the salesman said, "Guess you'd better add a bit more juice, heh, heh, heh." The student measured some more of the tranquilizer into the syringe. This time Jess took the gun and shot another deer in the shoulder. It fell, quivered, and died. "Hmm, guess we got too much," said the salesman. He looked like Willy Loman after two bad weeks on the road.

Another batch of the drug was loaded, and after several misses all around we managed to plant the syringe in the doe's rump. She took a few steps and then spread her legs wide like a drunk bracing himself. Next she began to sway and then lay down as the drug took greater effect. While we watched her she began to breathe with gasping violence and the student quickly gave her a hypo to counteract the tranquilizer's effect. "Poor bastard's havin' a fit," said Fat. The doe began a series of spasms and twitches that resembled a grand mal seizure. The salesman was wiping his face with his handkerchief and saying, "This never happened before."

"I gave her a lot less than the one that died," said the student.

"What about the first dose that didn't take?" asked Jess.

"That was heavier than this one," said the student.

"There has been some variation noted in individuals," said the salesman.

"Why don't you let me shoot you in the ass?" Fat asked the gun peddler.

"Heh, heh, heh." The salesman's smile was ghastly.

Since then both the guns and the tranquilizer have been improved, although the drugs used now are not foolproof. They have, however, been used to immobilize Utah buffalo so that the animals can be tested and treated for brucellosis.

All people who work with game live with the remote but nevertheless real fear of a disease breaking out among their wild charges. Years ago a disease identified as hemorrhagic septicemia caused many deer to be destroyed in western Utah. Deer also can become infected with hoof and mouth disease and become a deadly threat to livestock. One summer some deer and at least one elk died unusual deaths across the divide from us in Daggett County. When jumped by a passer-by the affected animals would run a few feet, then collapse and die. Some of us suspected a parasitic infestation, and one dead deer was flown to the veterinary lab for examination. This produced no positive results but the game stopped dying after that, so everyone relaxed.

The cost of the examinations and much, much more was paid primarily by the sale of deer-hunting licenses. For deer were one of Utah's biggest cash crops; they even paid for the damage they did. Farmers and ranchers who were able to prove damage to their property from big game could collect cash payments. Settlement of these claims was often acrimonious, because some landowners seemed to think having a few deer on their property was tantamount to damage. Bob Jensen told me that he knew farmers who prefaced their claims for damage payments with, "Well, Bob, it's about tax time."

Some wardens authorized damage payments, not because there was damage, but because they felt the landowner "had something coming." It was an easy way to stay popular in the community, although it could make life miserable for the next warden who got the district. We had one fellow who claimed recurring damage from deer, although neither Fat nor I could find evidence of it. We refused to pay any damages, but did stake out the man's farm on several evenings, hoping to ambush the elusive deer. We never saw one, but the farmer continued to complain. At last we gave him a box of cartridges and told him to shoot the deer himself. His only obligation was to notify us of any deer he succeeded in killing so that we could salvage the carcass.

Nothing happened for several weeks. Then, in late summer, I got a call to go out and pick up a deer at our friend's farm. I went there and got a doe, although the farmer refused to let me dress it on his property. As I was loading the doe, the farmer said that now we had proof of deer damage. The doe did have a stomach full of his alfalfa—perhaps ten cents' worth—but as I left I refused his claim.

No more was heard from the fellow and we all hoped we were through with him, but in the early fall he called Bob Jensen. "I got another deer."

"Okay," said Bob, "where is it?"

"It's in the northeast quarter of section sixteen," said the farmer, giving the location's legal description.

"Oh, hell!" Bob said. "It's after midnight. How do you expect me to find and dress that deer before it spoils?"

But the farmer was adamant, and the deer spoiled. However,

its death seemed to end the nebulous depredations and the ensuing damage claims.

In cases where a landowner claimed damage that we disputed, we had learned to suspect him of an ulterior motive. One orchardist complained that deer were ruining his fruit trees and even taking bites out of his apples as they hung from the tree limbs. "I seen where their front teeth come together," claimed the farmer, describing how he had seen marks in his apples where the deer's upper and lower incisors had met. His "proof" vanished once someone reminded him that deer have no upper incisors. Domestic sheep had been in his orchard.

In another case, a rancher rode roughshod over the local warden, claiming deer damage the officer couldn't find. Finally one of the perplexed officers sought an answer from a prominent churchman who was acquainted with the case. The churchman said that years earlier the rancher had gone to his bishop, the equivalent of a pastor, and asked for a "Temple Recommend," a permit to enter a temple, which Mormons believe contains a preview of their Celestial Kingdom. The bishop asked the farmer if he had paid his tithing, and received affirmation. Then he asked if the farmer had broken any laws. The farmer admitted poaching a deer some years before. "Well," said the bishop, "you'll have to surrender yourself and make this right with the law before I can issue your recommend. But I know the judge and I'll put in a word for you."

The bishop saw the judge, who listened to the circumstances and then intimated that the farmer's redemption would cost him around ten dollars. The farmer heard the news, went to the judge, and willingly pleaded guilty to poaching a deer. The judge nodded and assessed a fine of a hundred and fifty dollars. The rancher was dumbstruck but paid the fine. After he had been to the temple, he must have decided that his preview of paradise wasn't worth that much, and he'd been trying ever since to get even by collecting deer damage.

That same summer another rancher came to us with recognizable deer damage. The animals trailed through his ripening grain, shattering some of the heads, and when they jumped the surrounding fences they often kicked the wires loose. This man's grain was adjacent to some rough, juniper-clad breaks, where deer could hide unmolested all day long. And, although we could see no reason for it, he prohibited hunting on his property. So, in addition to repairing his fences and authorizing the maximum damage payment, I killed about twenty-five deer on his property. In addition to the deer I shot, several others were killed by men who accompanied me on the shooting trips. Finally, in the hope of mollifying the rancher, I held an impromptu auction for him and his son and "auctioned" off a prime buck to the boy for three dollars.

But the only thing that really satisfied this man was to see me kill deer. One evening as we left his ranch house, I saw two lovely fawns, one on each side of the road ahead. I stopped the truck and looked at the face of the man beside me. It was impassive. There was nothing left for me to do but kill the little animals as painlessly as possible. I did, and the heavy rifle smashed their spotted bodies into bloody obscenities. When I returned with a tiny corpse in each hand I said, as sarcastically as possible, "Sorry they're only fawns."

"That's all right," the rancher said, "it'll help take care of next year's crop."

VII / AND NOW, THE

BEAR STORIES

*"We treed the bear 'n' Curly shot him nine times
with his bow and arrows before he come down."*

—Ute game warden

ONE PLEASANT SUNDAY MORNING, I FOUND A MIDDLE-AGED SEDAN abandoned in the middle of a country road. The keys were in the ignition, but there were no signs of breakdown or foul play. I reported the car to the police dispatcher, who radioed back.

"That's Dempsey Brush's car," he said. "I heard he was in town last night. He probably just wandered off and left it. If the car's not a hazard, leave it there. Dempsey'll be back for it."

Dempsey made a living, such as it was, for himself and his family by tending some ranch property for a nonresident owner.

One day he was hoeing the family's garden spot when he happened to look up into a large tree beside the plot. Hanging there, sort of hugging the trunk with his forelegs while balancing his rump on a lower limb, was a small bear. Dempsey walked over to the tree and looked up at the bear. The bear looked at Dempsey. Suddenly, in the midst of this mutual examination period, Dempsey reached up and grabbed the bear by a hind foot. Then, with a prodigious heave, the mighty Dempsey jerked the bear out of the tree and down onto the ground. The bear roared and began a furious, three-legged race to pull out of Dempsey's grip. But Dempsey held tight and the bear decided he'd have to whip the man before he could run away. When the animal turned on him, Dempsey began bawling for help. "Git the gun, gawddammit. Git the gun out here: Halp!"

Dempsey's wife, inside the cabin, heard and got the .30-30 down from the wall. She stepped outside and levered a cartridge into the rifle's chamber. Then she paused, for the bear and Dempsey were wheeling round and round in a dizzying circle, the bear trying to get the man and the man afraid to let go his hold.

"Shoot the son of a bitch! I can't hold it much longer!"

With the steadfastness inherited from her pioneering forebears, Mrs. Brush raised the rifle and steadied it against her cheek. When the bear loomed alone in her sights, she killed it. Later a friend re-

[104

ported to me that he had told Mrs. Brush, "You mean you had the gun in your hands—and you killed the bear?"

Originally, there were grizzly as well as black bears in Utah. The grizzlies were exterminated by the time World War I broke out, but the black bears have held out to the present day. About the time I was working in the trout hatchery, there were several black bears in Lamb's Canyon, just east of Salt Lake City. A federal trapper killed them before any had apparently thought of harassing the sheep herds that used to fester filthily around the city's water supply. I have seen claw marks on the aspen trees along the trail to Lily and Frying Pan Lakes. But the bears were offered no protection by the state, and by the time I became a warden their numbers were minuscule.

Most of those that remained were in the Uinta Mountains or the Book Cliffs, where they were harried incessantly by sport and professional hunters. I tried to pooh-pooh the sort of fun to be had in shooting a treed bear off a limb, but officially I was powerless to help the beleaguered bears. Typical bear-slayers would swell up like poisoned pups while their pictures were taken for the sports pages of *The Deseret News*. There would follow a great deal of what amounted to dancing in the moonlight and peeing on "scent stations." When the hunter had sufficiently inflated his glands, I assume he went home and took a jump at momma.

I met one of the west's most proficient bear hunters when I was still a kid. Every summer for a number of years I was sent out to help Clay Paulhamus watch his stump ranch in the dripping rain forests of western Washington. It was there that I saw the waterproof old brush-rat named Bill. He was a professional bear-hunter, and certainly the equal of the legendary Ben Lilly. Besides killing hundreds of black bears, Bill hung up many a dead cougar in front of Vean Gregg's saloon.

Bill used to come to Clay's ranch to look for his hounds. They would get lost on a hunt and board with us until Bill came for them. Clay taught me to judge a hound's worth by the number of rips in his ears.

Clay had been briefly married to an aunt of mine. I think I
was the main beneficiary of that marriage. Clay was a skilled out-
doorsman and a thorough, patient teacher. His place was a paradise
of deer, elk, ducks, and trout, and salmon used to leap the beaver
dam in the creek below the kitchen window. At one time there
must have been a black bear for every seventy acres in the six-
hundred-forty-acre section that Clay still owns. In comparison,
Utah had about one bear for ninety square miles.

It was common to start a bear as we rattled out the timber-lined
road to the mail box. I have also met them while walking or riding
horseback along that same road. The bear would *"woof,"* dive for
cover, and after the initial crash I would never hear him again. In
the summer I saw their tracks and scats, which looked like berry
jam, along every muddy log road and trapper's trail. Sometimes
we'd get a bear ahead of Clay's old Dodge pickup and run him
down the road so fast that he didn't have time to dodge into the
brush.

When World War II broke out, troops were rushed into the
area to repulse the feared Japanese invasion. Some of them surreptitiously established a garbage dump on Clay's property. This
delighted the bears, who had never had it so easy, but it frightened
Clay's first wife. She liked the bears but not so many, so close.
When Clay protested, the Army closed the dump and the bears
went back to making a living on their own. This was the only trouble Clay ever had with black bears during thirty years of raising
cattle on his ranch.

When the war ended Clay got himself a new Nash car and
roared off, leaving me to superintend his wilderness. I had charge of
his chickens, a cow and calf, and approximately twelve Labrador
Retrievers. There were two older dogs, Ginger and King, plus a pen
that was constantly alive and awash with fat black puppies. I fed
the chickens, milked two of the cow's quarters for the pups and myself, let the calf suck the others, and spent the rest of my time doing
as I pleased.

And Now, the Bear Stories

I often took a lantern and the two dogs down to the Cougar
Hole on the Humptulips River and fished till midnight for blue-
back salmon. Other times I would walk up on top of the logged-
over hill behind the house and watch for bear in the salmonberry
pitches below. There was one spot where you could climb up on a
tall stump and see a whole berry-filled ravine. It nearly always held
a bear or two. King and Ginger knew this, too. They would lift their
ears and hackles and whine at me with impatience once we were up
there.

"Get 'em out! Go get 'em! Get 'em out!" Before I was half
through my exhortation, the dogs had dived into the brushy ravine
and were generally driving a frightened bear from it and into the
great hemlocks bordering the slash. Then the bear could be heard
splashing across the creek and I would "Hi!" in the dogs and walk
home, feeling very pleased with myself.

Across the yard from Clay's house was a weathered building
called "Joe's Shack." Joe was an Indian who had lived there when
Clay needed help in clearing the trees and brush from what is now
a verdant pasture in front of his house. After the Indian left, his
shack became a catchall and, when I knew it, housed great reeking
tubs of pickled bear meet. It was my job to go there each day,
grapple out a chunk of meat, and put it to soak in a bucket of fresh
water. Larger pieces to be de-pickled were hung on baling wire and
lowered into the creek.

The buoyant puppies thrived on the meat but Clay would suffer
none of it on his table. "There's a lot of poor sonsabitches that has
to eat this stuff. We don't." Recalling now all the wood we cut and
split by hand, the eggs we gathered and the hay pitched, the kerosene lamps, the stale-smelling ice box, which rarely held ice, and the
hand-cranked churn—all that makes me think we weren't exactly
rich sonsabitches ourselves. Yet, somehow, we were very rich; I just
didn't realize it then.

I call it rich when you can take the dogs to a hilltop behind your
house, then sic them on a bear. One evening when I was alone I

took the two older dogs up on the hill and they immediately sensed a bear in the bushes below. They began to whine and raise their hackles, and I sent them hurtling down after it. They had no sooner crashed into the enveloping brush when a small, black cub went scuttling up a lone tree off to my right.

Immediately there was a cacophony of roars and snarls and the sound of smashing twigs and berry canes from the ravine. I saw none of the battle, but I could sometimes follow its progress from the violent rippling of salmonberry leaves. At one point there was a colossal splash and I imagined a valuable dog being belted into a bog hole by a furious she-bear.

"Hee—ow!" I called but the dogs didn't come. The invisible battle continued to rage over an ever-widening field below me. The cub clung silently to his perch near the top of the tree. It began to get dark.

My excitement from the battle quickly faded before the fear and anxiety I felt for the dogs. I called once more, then went back to the house. I got the gas lantern from the porch and lit it out on the planked sidewalk. Then I went into Clay's room and took the heavy Remington .30-'06 from his closet. I opened its bolt and found the magazine full. There were some more cartridges on the dresser, and I stuffed them into my pocket. Finally, I got the flashlight off the kitchen table and went outside. The lantern was burning brilliantly on the walk; with it in one hand and the rifle in the other, I started back to the hill. I knew Clay would skin me alive or, worse, send me home if I let anything happen to those dogs.

On the dark hilltop, I called again for the dogs. But the ravine was still. The night had enveloped the cub's tree so completely that I couldn't tell if he was still there. I set the lantern on top of the tallest stump around and clambered half-way down into the ravine. I balanced the rifle's forearm on top of the flashlight in my hand. If necessary, I thought, I could flick on the light and be able to see to shoot.

But first I decided to shoot anyway. Sometimes, when the dogs strayed, Clay got them back by going out on the porch, firing into the air, and then bellowing, "*Hee—air!*" I looked back at the lantern on the stump; for all its brilliance, it seemed an awfully weak safety beacon. I worked the rifle's bolt and pressed the trigger. In that black pit the blast and flash were as frightening as the thought of an angry bear lurking in the brush. I halloed the dogs; nothing. I called again. From very far away, I heard a rustling. I scrambled back up to the lantern and jumped up on a stump. "Here King! Here Ginger! Come *on!*"

The rustling came nearer, and I aimed the rifle at it. Then, into the circle of light burst two wet but joyous dogs. I jumped down from the stump and hugged them. They licked my face, delighted at the fervor of my welcome. When we were through greeting each other, I carefully examined each dog in the lamplight. Neither of them had a scratch.

The next morning the cub was gone from the tree. All that was left was the question, What had really happened in that brush-choked ravine?

Most of Clay's stump ranch was indistinguishable from the green wilderness that spread out for miles around it. The higher ground was covered with vast stands of hemlock, which had been considered virtually worthless until the war. The bottoms were filled with great gray-barked alders, gigantic spruce, and cottonwood trees that were often six feet through at the butt. Sword ferns grew waist-high and, in the wetter spots, vine maple and the murderous devil club formed impenetrable thickets.

I have stood in these dank jungles never glimpsing the elk I smelled and heard all around me. Bears roamed these wilds, too. But we never gave them a nervous thought when we jumped off into that wet, enveloping forest armed only with an ax or fishing rod.

When the summer ended and the fall rains began to drift in cold and gray over the tree tops, Clay gave me my summer's pay: fifty dollars. I went home reluctantly, even tearfully, but nevertheless rich.

I got my Father to order a Springfield .30-'06 through the N.R.A.

The rifle cost thirty dollars and when it was delivered I found that it was brand new. After some fumbling attempts that winter, I rasped and sanded the military stock into what I considered a sporting rifle's lines.

The following summer I took this rifle back to Clay's. He was kindly and suitably impressed with my work, and took me out to a spot a hundred yards from a scarred, dead hemlock. He handed me some cartridges from his vast supply of World War I ammunition. "Let's see you hit that place on the tree where the bark's knocked off." I did, proudly thumping shot after shot into my silvery target.

Walking back to the house, Clay said, "If you shoot a bear, come and get me right away. Don't go up to it." He repeated his warning in the house while I pumped hot, soapy water through my rifle's barrel to remove the primer salts left by the old ammunition.

On our next trip to town I bought a county hunting license, which would have allowed me to shoot every bear in Grays Harbor County that I could find. At that time the *Aberdeen World* was printing pictures of bleeding hemlocks barked by bears who occasionally crave the cambium. Standing beside the injured tree would be a woebegone forester who looked like an ad for the Foster Parent's Plan. Timber was the area's mainstay, and all but the loggers were exhorted to spare trees. These pictures alternated with those of Bill the Bear Hunter posing with yet another bruin. (As I recall, his toll of black bears ran well over one thousand.) The paper also printed the harrowing stories of berry pickers who had been startled by a bear, or some siwash down on the Queets would report that a bear had killed his pig.

All the anti-bear publicity made my hunting plans that summer seem almost holy. Clay had already shot four before I arrived.

One of Clay's kills was a huge boar; the first shot had only knocked it down. "King ran in and tried to grab him but the bear got hold of King with his paws. I shot the bear in the head just before he bit the dog." The hams of that bear weighed ninety-six pounds, which would make its live weight almost four hundred pounds. He was exceptional, however: most of the black bears I saw weighed between one hundred fifty and two hundred pounds.

The boar that raided Ernie Childs's beehives was one of the larger ones. He had come in the night to rip open the hives Ernie had placed on the front porch of an abandoned house. Ernie was from the old school; no wild animal could interfere with him and live. So Ernie set a trap with a log toggle chained to it and sat back to wait. Some time during the second night of waiting, the bear stepped into the trap. As Ernie told it, the bear dragged the trap and toggle off to a patch of vine maple, where he became entangled. "That ol' bear cleared a lot of ground a'tryin' to git loose. An' when I come up, he took for me." Ernie told us how he had knocked the enraged bear down twice with his Marlin .30-30 before it stayed down.

I think Ernie ate that particular bear. His old school was also strong on "waste not, want not." The only trophy I saw of that kill was the bear's baculum. Ernie had carefully removed it to send to a friend in Chicago. The Childs were good people. They lived simple lives under the watchful eye of Jesus, whose idealized portrait hung in their living room. (I saw so many of those as a boy that I naturally assumed that Jesus had looked exactly like the late Errol Flynn with a beard.)

I got my first bear near where I had almost lost the dogs the summer before. He came wandering out of the logging slash to climb a downed log that was lying aslant the knoll across from me. I aimed carefully, though a bit breathlessly, at his shoulder and squeezed the trigger. The bear slid silently off the log and disappeared into the brush below it. I ran for the house and Clay. But he was already coming up the road, suppressing a grin. "You get one?"

"I'm pretty sure. He fell off the log when I shot. I watched but I didn't see him move—I didn't go near him."

We went on up the hill, then clambered over the logs and logging refuse to where the bear had fallen. "You got one, all right,"

Clay said, "now put a shell in your barrel and walk up behind him. Poke him in the back with your gun muzzle. If he even wiggles, plug 'im."

The lump of black fur did not move, so we wrestled it up on a log. I gingerly inspected its strong white teeth and the small bleary-looking eyes. It was a young bear, and the coat was coarse and lusterless.

We dragged the carcass to the road, then fetched it home in the pickup. Clay stopped in front of the barn and had me hook a gambrel to the haying tackle hanging from the barn's peak. We hoisted the bear and under Clay's guidance, I gutted it, letting the entrails drop into an old wash tub. Then Clay helped me skin the carcass. "Bastards look just like a man," he complained. If you overlook the massive musculature, they do.

We pickled the meat for the dogs. Later, as we drove out to the mail box, we stopped along the road and wired the tubful of offal to an old spar tree. "We'll watch when we come by here," Clay said. "You're likely to get another one." A bear did clean up his relative's insides, but I didn't see him do it.

In the next few days I proudly received the rustic laurels that are bestowed in rural communities when one kills a bear, catches a big fish, or sires a man-child.

And I played on my moment in the sun by reserving a bear roast from the pickling solution. Hot from the oven, it looked, smelled, and was delicious. But before I took the first bite, Clay warned me to take only half of what I thought I could swallow because "it'll swell and ball up in your mouth to twice its size, might choke you." My first bites were dainty, and I paused between them to see if the meat would swell in my mouth. Mine didn't, but Clay said his did.

The pickling tubs were filled to capacity, and Clay clearly would suffer no more bear in his kitchen, so I asked, "What'll we do with the next one?"

Clay overlooked the bloodlusting enthusiasm common to those who have just killed one of something. He said, "There's some niggers in Aberdeen. People say they eat bear meat."

In the days that followed I saw two more bears. One offered no more than a glimpse, and the other dodged a hail of long-range shots to skedaddle safely into the timber. The bears were learning to pick their berries after dark.

Then, one afternoon I spotted a patch of black through the dark-green leaves below me on the bear hill. Crackling sounds drifted up to my seat on a stump. I waited and the sounds continued. Still the bear revealed no more of himself. I sat nervously above his noisy feasting for half an hour. Nothing. I picked up a heavy piece of hemlock limb and lobbed it into the bear's vicinity.

It crashed down, and the bear crashed out. I stood on top of the stump to see it better. The bear was running parallel to my stand, crossing the welter of downed logs with amazing speed and ease. I began to shoot. Each time I flipped the bolt and fired, the bear's speed seemed to increase. I got off my last cartridge just as he dove into a patch of berry bushes. I stood still, refilling the rifle's magazine and watching for the bear. It didn't reappear, and I began feeling optimistic about the way it had vanished.

Clay was in the house, sitting in his big, old-fashioned rocker. He raised a questioning eyebrow and I began my story. When I got to the part about the bear getting into the brush Clay went, "Hmmm." Then he got up, put on his cap, and got his rifle.

When we started up the hill, he made the dogs go back to the house. From the hilltop I pointed out the berry patch where the bear had disappeared. "Toss a few of these limbs down in there," Clay said.

I flung them down and they crashed loudly all around the bear's exit point. Nothing stirred, and Clay said, "Well, let's go down and see what you've done. Your gun loaded?"

We crawled slowly down toward the bushes. Part-way, Clay stopped. "Here's some blood, you hit him." Then he said, "You better let me go first." He poked his head into the bushes, then retreated, looking relieved. "He's here, deader than hell."

We hung this bear where we had hung my first one. I dressed it but left its glossy, blue-black pelt in place. The next morning we drove into Aberdeen. After Clay got the directions, he drove to an older section of town and stopped in front of a one-story, gray bungalow. The paint was peeling on the house but the profusion of roses that grew over the front gate and up lattices on the house added charm that the stark Scandanavian homes beside it did not have. The blinds in the house were drawn, and it looked as if no one were home. But at Clay's knock the front door opened slightly and I saw Clay tip his cap. He talked for a moment. Then I saw him smile broadly and swing away from the house. "Just the Missus was home. She wanted the meat, but said she'd have to wait for the old man to come home. He must be the boss."

The next morning, about eight, the dogs began barking, and soon a big, black buick sedan appeared on the hill above the house. It stopped there, and I peeked out of the window. "I think it's them."

Clay went out, calling in the dogs, and two portly Negro men got out of the Buick. The bear was still hanging from the barn's peak, but neither man looked pointedly at it. Instead, one stepped forward, removing his felt hat. "Mister Paulhamus," he said through teeth that flashed ivory and gold, "we received your message and have come to see about the bear."

Clay shook hands with the speaker, who introduced himself as Mr. McCoy, and then his companion, George. They were both middle-aged and, as Robert Ruark wrote, "plum black." Mr. McCoy, who did the talking, wore a comfortable-looking brown suit with a gold watch chain draped across his well-filled vest. George wore an old fedora and a shabby suit jacket over his freshly laundered shirt and blue bib overalls. His black, high-top shoes glistened.

Clay waved me forward, introduced me as the bear's slayer, and we shook hands all around. Then Clay introduced the bear. The two men turned to meet him with drawing-room civility. "That appears to be an unusually fine young bear," said Mr. McCoy. The other Negro grinned and nodded in agreement.

Clay explained the nature of the bear's wounds and the care we

[114

had thus far given it. "We figured, if you wanted the bear you might want the hide, too, so we left it on."

Mr. McCoy in the brown suit stepped over to the bear and examined it briefly but thoroughly. "One shot," he said flashing his big, expensive smile. I grinned back. He then asked for the loan of a knife. I ducked into the barn for the skinning knife and steel that were hanging there. George stepped forward and took them. Then he whipped the knife expertly up and down on the steel. When he had achieved the desired edge, he confronted the bear.

Mr. McCoy stood back and gave orders for each cut. "That's far enough on that side, George, now go to the other side and work the hide off evenly. That's the way."

As the hide came away the spokesman turned to us for a moment and smiled. "Fat," he said. Then he re-anchored his thumbs in his vest pockets and continued supervising George.

George was not a fast skinner, but he went at the task with methodical precision. He soon had the hide off, and Clay handed him a saw to remove the head and feet. That done, the man quickly quartered the carcass.

The quarters were laid on clean sheeting the men had placed in the car's trunk and on the back seat. When the meat was loaded, they covered it with more sheeting and finally a light quilt. They worked so carefully that not one drop of blood fell on the Buick's glowing finish or on its well-brushed upholstery.

When the car was closed again, the men came down to the house to wash. They exclaimed over the house, although it wasn't a speck nicer than the home we had visited in Aberdeen. After they washed the men drank a cup of "swamp coffee" with us. They couldn't have been more courtly if they had been sipping champagne with Queen Marie.

Then we walked them to their car, but before getting in, Mr. McCoy turned to me. "When I was a boy in Kansas a man gave me one hundred dollars for the first buffalo and bear I killed." I'm sure my eyes widened in surprised anticipation. "So," he continued, "I'm going to give you five."

My heart sank a little, but I hadn't really expected anything, and Clay nodded for me to accept. The Negro took a worn but neatly folded five-dollar bill from a plump coin purse. I accepted it happily. Five dollars was lots of money; it would buy a box of shells with plenty left over for fishing tackle.

We shook hands all around again, and I promised to sure let them know if I got another bear. Then, with two more broad and flashing smiles, the Negroes waved and drove away.

I didn't shoot any more bears that summer. An afternoon wind began springing up regularly from the ocean and carried my scent, warning the bears every time I approached the hill. Then the salmonberries were gone, and the bears with them. I have never shot another one.

But Bill, the super hunter, did, hounding them relentlessly, sleeping in the rain beside downed logs and then rising to resume the chase at first light. We saw fewer and fewer bears and finally none at all. But the timber barons kept whooping for their blood. The last time I visited Clay, there were big signs on the road. They advised that bear snares were set throughout the area and to watch your dog.

Anyone who visits Grays Harbor today and sees the countless miles of razed and ruined timber land, the rotting stumps, the worthless ferns, the decaying towns and collapsing saw mills, might think, "Perhaps the snares were set for the wrong predators." A few cambium-seeking bears are no match for a screeching phalanx of gluttonous chain saws.

VIII / MRS. GARDINER

COOKS A GOOSE

*"Ducks fly on windy days because if they
sat on the rough water they'd get seasick."*

—Utah game commissioner

I T IS ALMOST TWENTY-FIVE YEARS SINCE I FIRST VISITED CLAY Paulhamus's isolated stump ranch. He became my friend and mentor then, and he has remained so throughout the years. Although he is well past seventy, Clay still lives alone, fishing for steelhead all winter (or at least until the dark "come-backers" begin appearing) and observing the ebb and flow of wildlife on his land. He recently wrote to say that he has landed eight fish so far this season but has seen only one flock of geese.

City people seldom realize how significant the comings and goings of geese are to people in rural areas. Canada geese beat robins as harbingers of spring as well as fall, and so long as a flock or two lingers in the Wyoming valley where I now live, I don't honestly believe in winter.

My father was a goose hunter. He used to arrange his work so that he could be in places like Klamath Falls and Coos Bay during the waterfowl seasons. And from such places immense shipments of geese used to arrive at our home. Dead game has little charm, and to my notion dead geese have none at all, especially if they haven't been cleaned and picked. Mother and I used to muster unhappily in our garage and flail away at shipment after shipment that frequently numbered a dozen geese. I grimly chopped off scores of heads, wings, and black reptilian feet, while mother unreeled dark miles of goose gut. Picking so many birds was impossible, so we skinned them, and then, in a blaze mixed of gratitude and relief, we gave them all away.

Sometimes these birds were the big, familiar Canadas, but often they were the highly prized "Specks" and "Cacklers" (White-fronted and Cackling Canada geese). My father was disappointed to learn that mother and I weren't as delighted to receive his birds as he was to send them. To prove how wrong we were, he selected a young White-front especially for our Thanksgiving dinner. Mother gave it her best attentions, and when it was cooked she placed it

[118

prominently among the trimmings on our holiday table. When the bird was served, I looked at the slices of dark meat on my plate. Then I began to bawl. Mother joined me, and from that sad day to this happier one not another goose has ever crossed any of my thresholds.

I was surprised to move to Utah and find blatant goose worship flourishing nearly as well as Mormonism. Every duck hunter carried a couple of shells loaded with Number 2 shot in the usually vacant hope a goose would pass over him. These hunters were as delighted with an unpalatable, lesser snow goose as they were with a fine big honker. Unfortunately, would-be goose hunters often mistook the big, whistling swans for snow geese and illegally killed hundreds of these stately birds each fall.

Early one morning, I happened upon a swan shortly after it had been crippled by hunters. The bird was standing unsteadily on an open flat many yards from cover. My dog ran up to it and the swan raised its wings with a vengeful defiance that cowed the dog. When the dog retreated, the swan scuttled piteously toward the distant cover. No defeated champion ever slumped from a prize ring with a greater aura of angry, uncomprehending humiliation than that swan had. I had thought to put the bird away with my shotgun, but as I watched it I hadn't the heart. Maybe it got well after all.

Whistling swans aren't particularly rare. They have been protected as much for the sake of the rare trumpeter swans as for their own. Even experts have difficulty telling the species apart. The only sure way is to have one of each on a table before you, and to do this the birds must be dead, so the identification loses a lot in the transition. Lately, a limited whistling-swan hunting season has been held in Utah with no apparent damage to the look-alike trumpeters, who rarely if ever venture into Utah.

For years, however, the fine for illegally killing a swan ran about two hundred and fifty dollars, and no sensible hunter got near a dead swan. There was one hunter, though, who tried to talk a swan through headquarters at Bear River Refuge by claiming that it was an Ogden goose. Another hunter was so proud of the bag of "white geese" he'd made that he had himself photographed with them. After the picture appeared in the newspapers, he was kidded so unmercifully that he welcomed the inevitable arrival of a game warden.

I had a case once that was nearly as simple. I came on a young man hunting ducks long after hours and found that he had an overlimit of birds. I cited him into court for the overlimit but told him I would give him a break on the following infractions: shooting after hours, using an unplugged shotgun, failure to validate his duck stamp, and failure to display his hunting license. Then the fellow didn't show up in court, and I cited him for that, too. But he was an elusive lad, and I didn't locate him until he came into town for a funeral. I shadowed him all during the day of the services, and picked him up as soon as they were over. My solicitude wasn't appreciated by an indignant prisoner, and as we drove toward the jail he told me what an S.O.B. I was because he "just didn't feel guilty."

In the Uintah Basin, as elsewhere, recognition of species didn't go much beyond "this is a duck" and "that is a goose." Any large bird was usually fair game if it had the bad luck to fly over the average duck hunter. I even had eager gunners come running up to my stool of decoys with their guns ready.

Some years ago an old-timer called Zelph stocked his Diamond Mountain ranch with two dozen domestic geese. In no time hunters reduced the flock to six birds. Then a past president of the rod and gun club saw them and bagged the lot. On his way home he stopped at Fat Gardiner's to do a little bragging.

"My God, Av, those are Zelph's tame geese!" Fat said when he saw the birds. The hunter was thunderstruck, but he recovered to realize, "Zelph will want a fortune for these birds when he finds out I've killed them."

The hunter, however, had time to think as he drove to Zelph's,

[120

and when the two met he asked, "What'll you take for those geese you've got up on Diamond?"

Zelph frowned. "I really had hopes for an increase in those birds. But the hunters have killed all but six; I guess you can have 'em for two dollars apiece." The hunter agreed and handed over the money. "When do you want to get them?" Zelph asked.

"I already have," said the hunter, making for the gate.

The only marsh of any size near Vernal is the state-owned section south of Jensen called Stewart Lake Refuge. When Fat first took me there I was immediately impressed by the large, rustic sign at the entrance on which was artfully emblazoned the figure of a flaring pintail. But the marsh itself looked like hell. Rank legions of tamarisks were everywhere. Much of what should have been marsh was a thick mat of cattails, and the grassy glades were choking with cockleburrs.

"We've had trouble with people letting the water out," Fat explained. In one of the weedy glades stood an impudent-looking black horse. His mane was plastered with burrs, and his tail was so clotted with them that it resembled a club. When we approached him, the plug trotted insolently away, and Fat said the cattle and horses had a peculiar way of appearing on the refuge at the first rise in winter hay prices.

The marsh lay along one slowly curving bank of the Green River. In its center was an irregularly shaped lake that was bordered in places by fine stands of hard-stem bulrush. On one side the marsh was limited by low bench land that farmers planted to alfalfa and small grains. I could imagine dozens of cock pheasants deserting the bench for the safety of the marsh once the hunting season opened. Across the marsh from the bench, a long dike had been built to maintain the water level and prevent the silt-laden Green River from washing out the refuge during its spring rampages. The main water source was a sloughy creek whose waters reached the marsh via a diversion canal. When I first saw this, it was filled with debris and the working of beaver. Additional water came from small springs near the bench and these, I think, had been keeping the marsh alive.

A huge, primitive wooden headgate in the dike provided means for regulating the water level in the marsh. At the end of the duck season the gate was opened wide to lower the water substantially and prevent the impending ice cover from damaging the dike. We fought a limited war with local ice skaters over this procedure. Every time I opened the gate, the skaters would come along and close it in order to buoy up their sagging rink. Finally, I took several timbers out of the headgate and hauled them away to the game farm. That ended the skating. (In the spring, spear fishermen frequently reopened the gate to get at their prey more easily. Such activities often caused Fat to say at the close of a day's futility, "Well, we didn't do much today, but we'll give her hell tomorrow.")

There were cottonwoods all along the river bank. They grew rapidly, only to go crashing into the river when its abrasive-laden waters finally undercut them. The Green accumulates tons of silt once it leaves Wyoming's mountains and high meadows. At that time there were no Fontenelle or Flaming Gorge dams to restrain the gook. It all gurgled through Utah, plenishing and replenishing itself, until it reached its oozy rest in Lake Mead.

The Green River provides a secondary route through Utah for migrating waterfowl. Their big arterial highway is farther west, across the Great Salt Lake marshes. Still, it was fine to go down to the refuge on a spring morning and find the deep-water areas dotted with resting scaup. These handsome divers didn't stop long before resuming the journeys that might take them another thousand miles north. I never saw the scaup during the fall hunting season. In their place came blue-wing teal, which I rarely saw in spring, and they, too, had vanished by late September.

In a way I envied these migrants: they had a definite goal and flew there. A game warden is often frustrated by the lack of any definite end point in his work. I never felt that getting a conviction against some poacher is much of an accomplishment; most of them are miserable human beings living lives of unenviable smallness. But at Stewart Lake I found work that could have tangible results. I needed no excuse to be there, because it was deep in my district. So, before the runoff began that spring, I made some plans.

The first item was repairing the diversion dam that turned water into the canal. That done, I cleaned the canal and dynamited the small beaver dam abuilding there. Then I dug lateral ditches out from the channels in order to flood areas of burrs, cattails, and tamarisks. When the stray stock was rounded up and ejected, I repaired the fences. The first high water of spring appeared in the creek, and I closed the headgate in anticipation of the surge of run-off water that I hoped would transform my squishy weed patch into a vibrant marsh.

As the water rose, I shot exploring muskrats with my revolver. No one trapped them, and their burrowing menaced the dike while their voracious appetites threatened marsh vegetation. The famed muskrat-mink relationship seldom exists on Utah marshes. Unless the rodents are trapped or otherwise controlled, their numbers fluctuate wildly. A naturalist friend recently told me he had witnessed a Utah muskrat migration similar to the famous exodus of lemmings. Muskrats and people exhibit comparable signs of stress and disintegration of personality when too many are crowded too closely together.

Most of the muskrats soon learned to stay out in the marsh and away from the dike. Out there they seasonally cut cattails and piled them on their cone-shaped houses. Surprisingly, cattails aren't particularly welcome on a waterfowl marsh, for they provide little food and are poor nesting material. The plants survive fluctuating water levels well and spread into open water areas, which they eventually clog with worthless vegetation. The more desirable hard-stem and three-square bulrushes disappear before them. As my ecology professor used to say, "the cattail is a good 'compeetor.'" Cattails tend to dry up a marsh, and as this happens the exotic tamarisks (pronounced "tamarack") come invading. They quickly grow to heights of six feet, and while their soft green, lacy foliage is attractive, it offers poor cover and worse food for wildlife. And, like the cattail, tamarisks use large amounts of water.

One way to eliminate or impede the growth of both plants is to keep them flooded. I did this until water began creeping outside our refuge fences. Then I pulled a board from the headgate and sat back to watch the customers.

Among the first were Canada geese, who moved in when the marsh was still the color of cold oatmeal. The goose built her nest on top of a muskrat house, and while she lay and then incubated her eggs, the gander maintained an incorruptible vigil. Toward June the eggs hatched, and through my binoculars I could see the golden-brown goslings dutifully swimming after their parents. When danger threatens, the goslings often hop on the adult's back for a faster get-away.

It isn't unusual to see paired Canadas after the nesting season that have no broods. These are often young adults who have courted and "married" but will not nest until the following spring. "Canada geese," someone said, "are nice people."

As spring's green began brightening the marsh, the cattle came back. What tender new shoots their mouths missed their hooves hit, trampling them into muck. Many stockmen act as if they are terrified by the color green, and at the first sight of any of it they sic their animals on it. As fast as I ran the cattle out, someone else ran them back in again. At last I got the Pig and used her to herd the cattle out of the gate and down the county road, where, I suppose, they scattered and were a problem to gather. But at least they never returned to the marsh; one light blow had been successfully struck against the utopian notion of multiple use.

As water and June's warmth spread across the marsh, the last brown stalks of winter disappeared in a sweep of brilliant green that reflected darkly on the water's surface. Suddenly, shy mallards peeked out at me from a nest among the rushes. Other ducks made busy sweeps across the lake, the twinkling whistle of their wings drowned by the reedy calls of a hundred blackbirds. A hen pheasant carefully led her ten carefree chicks across the dike. And at the end of the dike, where it dropped into the brushy river bottom, I found a doe and her two wondering fawns. For the first time, Stewart Lake Refuge really was a refuge.

At the first hint of warm weather, fishermen begin coming to the refuge to try for the Green's small catfish. But unless they have some of Grady Russell's super bait, they catch bonytails and carp more often than the edible cats. Carp are nearly as successful breeders as humans. They used to school below the headgate and dart out of the quiet water in futile attempts to breach the gate. As they fell back to rest, I shot them with my revolver. Shooting fish is not as easy as it's supposed to be, although shooting carp is immensely satisfying.

Europe's carp may have come into Utah in casks fastened to the pioneers' wagons. Others are said to have been brought in by Chinese laborers building the Central Pacific railroad. Still more came under the benevolence of the Federal government's fisheries experts. It was a fair trade for the syphilis that some say the New World sent to Europe.

The bottom-feeding carp muddy marsh waters, and the turbidity filters out sunlight, which is vital to aquatic plants. Among these aquatics is pond weed, *potomageton*, probably the most important of the duck foods. Game-fish populations usually decline when carp invade their water, but little could be done about it until fish toxicants were developed.

In Utah, carp and other trash fish were seined in an often-futile attempt to keep them under control. At the Strawberry Reservoir this work was done by a crew of convicts. The men enjoyed being outdoors, and a warden friend who supervised them said they were good workers. One day he took his wife to watch the operations and she soon struck up a conversation with one of the men. As often happens, the lady couldn't understand how such a seemly chap had landed in the penitentiary.

She asked, "What were you convicted of?"

"Oh," he shrugged, "murder."

We partially controlled the carp that inevitably got into Stewart Lake by draining it in winter. Fat Gardiner had seemed relieved to turn this and the other refuge routines over to me. He was an infrequent duck hunter who favored late-season, jump shoots along the creeks. And I think he resorted to those only because the Canada geese had gone south. Fat watched the first flights of geese to see what fields they used; unless they are disturbed, the big birds will use the same fields two or three days in succession, so it's fairly easy to set up for them. After one successful shot, Fat invited me to a goose dinner at his parents' home. I had avoided goose dinners since that long-ago Thanksgiving, but this invitation couldn't be politely declined, and besides, a bachelor learns never to turn down a home-cooked meal.

So on the appointed evening I presented myself at the Gardiners's. Their farm home stood across a field from Fat's house. It was an old place with rough, unpainted siding and aging trees in the yard. The rustic finish made the house look more like a cabin than a bungalow. I parked in the moonlit yard, and as I got out of my truck I could see a glimmer of light down in the barn where Fat's father was milking. Fat met me at the door and took me into the kitchen. It was warm and brightly lighted but, aside from running water in the sink, the kitchen was old-fashioned. It had been built in a time when dishwashers were female and deep freezes were nails pounded into the north outside wall.

There was a long table in the center of the room. Places were neatly set on the embroidered tablecloth. The service at each place was different, just as each chair was different; they ranged from old, straight-backed oak to Sear's chrome and plastic. A million steps had worn distinct trails in the faded linoleum—they ran from stove to sink to table, then back to the stove again.

Fat's mother was gray and slightly bent. Life had not been gentle with Mrs. Gardiner, but I could see in her face that it had not been unkind, either. She was wearing a house dress under her big, old-fashioned "apern." Mrs. Gardiner welcomed me with shy grace. "We're just common people, not fancy. Now you set down and make yourself to home." Then she turned to the black coal stove that filled one corner of her kitchen, and adjusted the location of a pot. The old range seemed a bit bent, too, but from its oven drifted an aroma that was almost thick enough to cut and certainly good enough to eat.

Fat's younger sister was there, along with his younger brother, a tall and fair youngster who had won an athletic scholarship at the state agricultural college. Two of Fat's little boys were there, too, slick and scrubbed for their first goose dinner at gramma's.

When Mr. Gardiner came in from his milking we shook hands while he, too, bid me welcome. He was elderly but still solid, with the broad face so typical of many Saints. Mr. Gardiner had clear blue eyes that always seemed framed in wrinkled amusement. He washed in the sink and took his place at the head of the table. Everyone ducked his head as Mr. Gardiner intoned the old Mormon blessing, "Heavenly Father, we thank Thee for this food prepared for our use, and pray that it may nourish and strengthen our bodies . . ." When the blessing ended and had been "amenned" all around, Mrs. Gardiner took a big enameled roaster from her oven. She lifted its lid and deftly removed the goose. It glowed a rich brown from the basting and the slow, even coal heat. It was magnificent—a Dickensian goose, truly a ghost from Christmas past that was miraculously back and whole again. When it was set upon the table the painted water glasses turned to crystal and the flatware became silver. The magic lasted until we dazedly pushed back our chairs while the youngsters cleared the table.

My tribute was wholehearted: "Mrs. Gardiner, that was the best goose dinner anyone ever ate."

There is a knack to cooking waterfowl that few women possess. Mrs. Gardiner had it, and so do some of the good sisters around Brigham City. The average duck dinner usually tastes like duck guts smell, or else it is so fancied up with herbs and spices that you think you're eating one of Julia Child's old hand towels. Because of a light pocketbook, one fall I fed rather heavily on ducks and I did learn to cook and enjoy them. You must have a duck that is good; you can't make a bad one good, so start with a mallard, pintail, or canvasback. Jump-shot birds are generally best, because they are killed while going away and have no shot in their breasts. Clean the birds quickly and hang them on the inside of your blind or on a bush to drain and cool. Carry them on a strap slung over your shoulder, not stuffed into a rubberized pocket of a hunting coat. I let the birds age at refrigerator temperatures up to a week before picking them, although some hunters prefer to pick them while the birds are still warm. (I never shoot ducks until November because they are too full of pin feathers before then.) Finally, cut off the tail before freezing or cooking. When you prepare it, boil the duck for at least a half hour. The latter is almost sure-fire preamble to any of the standard roasting procedures. Incidentally, cold duck and goose combined with mayonnaise make excellent sandwiches. If these instructions seem too complicated, you might do what a friend did; he got a retriever that ate any duck he was sent after.

I think far more hunters enjoy shooting ducks than enjoy eating them. It is indescribably thrilling to watch the birds turn, then turn a little more, then circle before they finally drop into the decoys. The nearer the birds come, the higher your tension, and you breathe a teaspoonful of air at a time. Then, with a great *whoosh!*, the ducks are over you, hanging in the air like drooping petals of huge flowers. These seconds are the ones most hunters savor, for they are exciting and beautiful. Next, there are a couple of milliseconds, when the gun kicks and the bird first falters, that are charged with exultant satisfaction. But when the bird crumples and comes crashing to earth as a grayish, blurred blob, my exultation falls down around my ankles like a pair of old shorts. I always wish I could put the dead bird back into the sky and restore its marvelous symmetry.

I don't think this is a unique reaction. Ducks have a special effect on hunters; I have known men who once hunted for the market and who still enjoy going out after today's small limits. Of course, it isn't just the limit they're after, any more than it's just the trout the fly caster wants. Many old market-hunters have since given far more to wildlife resources than they ever took with their guns.

One former market-hunter became a foreman on some of Utah's first marsh-restoration projects. They used horse-drawn fresnos and picks and shovels in those days, and human sweat was cheap. The foreman thought it was free, according to the men who worked for him. One of them told me how he was put to working swinging a heavy sledge hammer.

"I bounced on that damn hammer until I was give out, an' I asked George if I could take a few puffs. 'Why, sure,' he said, 'but while you're restin', carry some a' them timbers over so's the boys can set 'em.' "

Marsh improvement and restoration is by far the brightest gem in Utah's not-always-sparkling conservation crown. There are nine hundred thousand acres of wet lands and permanent water in the state, and about two hundred thousand of them are devoted to waterfowl. Over a dozen species of ducks use these marshes, and the hunting is as good or better than any you'll find in the other forty-nine states. Veterans of the huge Bear River Refuge, west of Brigham City, could name a species of duck and then go out on the marsh and bag a limit of them, seemingly without half trying.

Bear River and the numerous other public marshes are not slaughterhouses. Utah duck hunters take a disproportionately small share of the Pacific Flyway bag. But how long these marshes can exist is problematical. Utah politicians enjoy running on water platforms, and they often inveigh against "phreatophytes," meaning marsh vegetation, and ask rhetorical questions about "ducks or people?" Reclamation is so overdone in Utah and throughout the west that authorities estimate enough water storage exists now to last until the year two thousand, but unfortunately there is more money in dams than in ducks. Some of the marshes now suffer from lack of water, and it isn't too difficult to imagine them dried and dusty. When the politicians have talked us into committing this crime, I suppose the next step will be to have them measure their bladders. Then the public can still elect the man who'll give them the most water.

The public marshes are watered much the way the farmer irrigates. A vast system of dikes has been built to keep the water in bounds, and walking out one of them is an excellent way to see what ecologists mean by plant succession. At Ogden Bay Refuge you encounter first the cattails, bulrushes, and even some shrubs, but as you go west toward the Great Salt Lake you find alkali bulrush giving way to saltgrass and finally glasswort.

I loved to hunt on that refuge, too; the shooting was good even on bluebird days. One day I took an acquaintance out there and stationed him on a muskrat house. He hadn't done much duck hunting, so I outlined the process, telling him to announce any ducks he saw approaching. He soon hollered. "Single from the north!"

I ducked, hiding my face in the musty fragrance of my 'rathouse. After a time I asked, "Still see him?"

"Yes, keep down, he's coming!" I waited and waited for what was the world's slowest duck, although my partner continually assured me it was coming. Finally, I yelled, "For Chrissakes, I've been down for fifteen minutes—how far can you see a duck?"

"He's right there, see," said my wounded partner, pointing. I looked where he indicated.

"Jesus, Keith, that's a butterfly!"

Unless you can hunt ducks with a kindred spirit, I think you are better off going alone. There's just you, the dog, the sky, and, hopefully, the ducks. Unless you fuss overmuch with your call or fiddle with your decoys, it is impossible to imagine a more uncomplicated way to spend a day. And yet, when you have finished that day, you feel a remarkable sense of accomplishment.

MRS. GARDINER COOKS A GOOSE

Recently, I've been sitting beside a small spring that meanders through snow-covered meadows behind my Wyoming home. I use clumps of willows for blinds, and unless I sit very still with my face hidden, the mallards spot me every time. I put out five decoys, four ducks and one drake. They seem to be more attractive if they're placed at a bend in the spring's channel. Sometimes I can pull a willing drake in with my duck call, but I rely mainly on the decoys. I let hen mallards and the teal come in and land in the decoys—if they can be fooled right down to the water's surface. My old dog looks at me on these occasions with disdainful impatience, for she fails to realize that we are hunting ducks, not necessarily shooting them.

One snowy day, a fox came and sat down across from my blind. We three studied one another for twenty minutes before the fox lost interest and trotted off through the snow, dodged under a fence, and disappeared. The foxes in this valley are a mixture of wild animals and the escapees from a once-flourishing fox farm, and are quite unusual-looking.

Another time, near the spot where the fox appeared, two mallards dropped into the spring without my seeing them. They punted majestically about in the small spring channel, sometimes stopping to sip at the water's surface or to pump their heads up and down in remarkable unison. (I can't understand why this "dance" looks so good on ducks and so awful on teen-agers. A mallard drake is a grand creature, impeccable in dress and, in late fall, as charming as an urbane old uncle. There is real character in that black eye, and also an intelligence that is too rare in most of the eyes we see. The hens just miss being dowdy. They're like the plain but alert lady who plops down beside you on the bus and talks and adjusts her packages for the next six blocks.) Presently, a muskrat swam up in the pair's wake. The ducks ignored him, but he remained in their wake much as I imagine a bookmaker might follow a lady and gentleman at the opening of Ascot.

When the ducks at last recognized me and sprang frantically into the air, the muskrat went back to his *tick-tick-tick* nibbling from under a willow that overhangs the spring. Then an ermine came by, moving in slow-seeming undulating bounds that belied the sinister purpose of his travels. Later he returned carrying a dead mouse. I never see an ermine without remembering one I saw in 1963. I had just heard the first fragmentary radio bulletin announcing the shooting of President Kennedy, and for some reason glanced out the window. An ermine was passing with a mouse in its mouth.

Just before closing time the mallards began coming over, and I killed two drakes with three shots. As I came with them across the snowy fields that were blue in the waning light, a motorist passed by on the county road. He slowed to examine me and then hurried on. He obviously thought I'd been hunting ducks, but when I reflect on that afternoon, I can judge him only half right.

After I've picked my ducks I clip one wing, slip it into an envelope, and mail it to a fish hatchery in California. There federal biologists examine the wings, noting species, sex, and age of the duck. Hopefully, this information will be helpful in the future management of our ducks. The federal government is the chief steward of waterfowl. Its Fish and Wildlife Service has its odd little ways, but I think the service tries to do a good job and generally succeeds. They have fusty bureaucrats and egregious old bullshitters on the payroll, but they also have many dedicated men of surpassing warmth and ability.

The latter men make the biological jokes seem even funnier. I remember one lad who was getting his doctorate by finding out what baby ducks eat. (Every few years someone finds out what baby ducks eat.) This fellow announced, rather smugly, I thought, that ducklings ate midges when the wind blew them in their direction. However, they did not eat midges when the wind blew them in the opposite direction!

The boy who thought he was doing the really monumental work, however, was the one recording duck blood pressures and respiration rates at various altitudes. He presented himself at the game department offices and explained his quest: to string nets across Utah's mountain passes and therein catch his birds. As you see, the commissioner quoted at the beginning of this chapter is not out there all by himself!

Utah's marshes attract all kinds. At the close of a fall day the hunters can be seen straggling in across the flats; guns angled across their shoulders, they form picturesque silhouettes that are distinctly American. Behind them the sun is slipping below the horizon west of Great Salt Lake. Nowhere do days end so beautifully. The western sky is ablaze with hot reds and flaming oranges that fade to soft pinks and cool lavenders as you turn to watch. Stitched in awesome skeins across the day's last fires are the ducks and geese. In formation they are long armadas moving relentlessly, although the swiftness of their flight is arrested by the majesty of their numbers. If you try to count them you will fail, for at this moment on the marsh you don't count things.

IX / MISS JOSIE AND

OTHER OUTLAWS

"I'd just as soon stay outa' sight while you check
people from around here—lot of 'em's my relatives.'

—DEPUTY GAME WARDEN

Nonth over Diamond Mountain from Vernal lies the old bandit retreat of Brown's Hole. Major Powell renamed it Brown's Park during his descent of the Green River, but many of the old-timers still call it Brown's Hole. Until Flaming Gorge Dam was built across the Green River in the early 1960s, Brown's Hole was among the most remote and forgotten areas in the west. The district embracing the Hole bordered mine, and I often crossed the line to work or visit with Steve Radosevich, my opposite number over there. Steve owned a big ranch in Brown's Hole and was one of the finest men outdoors.

The most direct road to Brown's Hole from my district crossed Diamond Mountain on its eastern side and then bounced down Crouse Canyon to the "swinging bridge" on Green River. This bridge was nothing but loose planking laid on top of some cables that had been suspended across the river. To keep their cattle from straying across, ranchers sometimes picked up a few of the planks near the bridge's center. The result was one of the world's most effective cattle guards.

The road on either side of the bridge is a segment of the old Outlaw Trail, an ill-defined track that extended from Wyoming's Hole-in-the-Wall to, and beyond, Robber's Roost in Utah's rock-bound eastern quarter. Looming at the head of Crouse Canyon is a gigantic bluff of dark red rock called Flynn's Point. It was from an overlook on this point that Tom McCarty earned five hundred dollars for ambushing accused rustler Mike Flynn.

McCarty did the killing in the style, and at the salary commanded by Tom Horn, a rancher-hired murderer who, during a brief stay earlier, had earned a frightening reputation in Brown's Hole. One story about Horn and the panic he inspired concerns a bone-lazy fellow who lived with his wife and young family on the margins of Brown's Hole. One winter day shortly after the turn of the century, the man was handed a note in the Hole's tiny store.

[136

Since he was illiterate, the fellow asked the storekeeper to read the note to him. It didn't take him long; all it said was, "You have 36 hours to clear out of Brown's Hole," and it was signed "Tom Horn."

According to the story, the man blanched, lurched from the store, and dashed home as fast as his horse could take him. When he arrived, he threw his family and their few possessions on horses and began frantically driving them over the wintry mountain toward the Uintah Basin. Somehow they made it, and the ranch that was begun where the berserk trek ended still exists. I have visited there many times. Brown's Hole was never the same after its visitation from Tom Horn.

Another occasional resident of Brown's Hole was Butch Cassidy. He is said to have had a winter cabin near Crouse Canyon and another at Little Hole farther up river. Every boy who grew up in the intermountain west during the first third of this century knew about Cassidy and his band of outlaws called the Wild Bunch. (A recent motion picture about Butch and Harry Longabaugh has revived that interest.) Their banditry and wonderfully prodigious horseback escapes across the west inspired countless pulp magazine thrillers. Writers of Sunday supplements never failed to praise Butch for never killing a man until the blazing finale of his career. (Actually Butch hadn't needed to kill at all; some of his loosely-knit Bunch were homicidal psychopaths.)

During one deer season, I stayed for a few days with Dick Bennett at his Sheep Creek ranch, to the west of Brown's Hole. One evening, over drinks, Dick told me that Cassidy and members of his bunch had often stayed in that very cabin. "They kept fresh horses here and changed when they were making their long rides," Dick said. How staying in that cabin would have thrilled me back in the days when I watched for Indians while my Uncle Ransom gathered firewood!

Still, there was an air of unreality about the old outlaws; to me they were blurred faces from pulp fiction and Saturday matinees.

I said as much to a Ranger friend at Dinosaur Monument one day. "Did you ever meet old Jos?" my friend Paul asked.

No, but of course I had heard of her, an old woman living alone at the foot of Blue Mountain. So Paul checked out a park service four-wheel-drive truck, and we started for Josie Morse's (some said "Morris"). When the gravel road ended, Paul steered on up what was partly trail and partly cattle track. We forded a small stream and bounced along a brushy route until, suddenly, we were in front of a strange-looking little house.

Behind its veil of unkempt shrubbery, the place appeared to sag under a variety of building materials. If a tired old gnome had decided to build a house, this is what he would have built. The tarpaper roof was what I remember best—it was quilted! The roofing material reached the roof's low ridge by going over uneven puffs and depressions that created the quilted look. I finally realized that Josie had put her roofing paper on over a dirt or sod roof. "Josie built this house all by herself," Paul explained.

In addition to her shrubs, Josie had planted fruit trees along the tiny stream that wandered happily through her grove-like yard. Across from the house was a small shed with the stretched hide of an animal tacked on its wall. And almost hidden in the burgeoning shrubbery by the house gate stood a tiny, gray-haired woman. She was very old but still quite erect, like a solid old juniper post, silvered with years.

Her eyes were quick and bright, and when they rested on me, I saw that they were wondering. She welcomed Paul, and after he had introduced me she asked us in for coffee. "I made it this morning, so it might be pretty strong by now." We followed Josie onto her enclosed porch, where there was the usual clutter of rural apparel, implements, and utensils. There were some cartons of canned goods.

Off the small kitchen, to the right, was a grayish parlor and it seemed to me that the walls were stuccoed. It was an unusual room with a few odds and ends of old furniture and little glass ornaments from a Woolworth's store of long ago.

[138

Josie's coffee was strong all right, and not really very good. While we held our mugs, she sat down across from us and visited. I had been warned that "she won't say much until she gets to know you." Josie did not trust strangers wearing badges. I kept quiet and let Paul do the visiting. Josie said that she hadn't been feeling well and had just returned from a daughter's in Vernal, where she had "wintered." Josie said a young relative had been staying with her, but he had wearied of the isolation and pestered her until she gave him the money to buy a car. Once he got that he had left. As she talked, she sat primly in her chair, back straight and feet close together as young ladies of the 'nineties had been taught to do. Like all grandmothers, Josie spent most of our visit talking about her grandchildren.

Only, Josie really wasn't like all grandmas. When she was Josie Bassett of Brown's Hole, they said, she had rustled cattle and could ride and shoot with the best in Cassidy's Wild Bunch. In fact, Butch Cassidy had courted Josie. But his attentions, owing to his "traveling job," weren't steady and she married a man named McKnight. It wasn't a happy marriage and Josie finally told McKnight to clear out and shot him in the leg to prove she meant it. Dick Bennett and Fat both told me how Josie had poisoned another of her husbands (she had had several). It seemed that after Josie and the decedent had rustled some cattle they were subsequently tipped that a posse was coming after them. The husband panicked—this was in the time of Tom Horn—and Josie began to fear that he would blab. Josie had the cattle hidden, and her only problem was the nervous spouse, so she poisoned him.

Dick said a woman acquainted with his family had told of seeing a full package of rat poison in Josie's pantry a day or so before the fellow died. When she saw it again, soon afterward, it was empty. One version of the story says that Josie stored the corpse in a cool room until the posse arrived. The other states that she rolled the body into a buck board and then drove out to meet the posse. Then she received the condolences due a bereaved young widow. The rustled cattle stayed rustled.

As I sat there drinking Josie's coffee, it didn't occur to me that she was an accused poisoner. She appeared to be a lady possessed of good grammar and her strongest oath was "Oh my!" She must have been over eighty but she seemed much younger; her mind was quick and sharp, and she lived in the present, not the past. Perhaps that had helped to preserve her, but I would have been delighted if she had done some reminiscing.

Josie had known Tom Horn. He had once given her brother a warning to clear out, and vigilantes had hung a renegade from her dad's gate. Her sister, "Queen Ann" Basset, was said to be the riding, shooting darling of the Wild Bunch. Ann was tried, unsuccessfully, as a rustler, and she in turn claimed that Tom Horn tried to kill her. Harry Tracy, that incubus of a million turn-of-the-century nightmares, barely escaped being hung from the Bassett gatepost himself. But Tracy got away and killed twenty men before he killed himself in a grainfield. And little Josie, sitting across from me so sweetly, had known them all! If ever there had been a Wild West, she had helped to make it so.

By the time I came along, Josie had been given an unwritten license to kill a deer whenever she needed one. She was a kind of living memorial to the vanished frontier and a time that perhaps never really was. "Why, they'd lynch us back in Vernal if we ever gave old Josie a ticket," I said to Fat and he agreed. The old lady really didn't kill any more game than the average hunter—she just preferred getting hers out of season. As she told Fat one day, "Oh my, I never go out when all those hunters with their big guns are around. I wait until after the season, then plug mine down in the orchard."

Josie never shot or killed things, she always "plugged" them. Once she told Fat and me that a beaver had been girdling her young fruit trees. We both jumped at the chance to do her a favor by removing the beaver, but she said our help was unnecessary. "I waited for him one morning and plugged him. I didn't skin him, though." Apparently she felt that pelting the illegally killed animal would make her liable to arrest. Technically, she was right but we were not disposed to haggle with Josie.

As we were leaving, Fat chuckled. "She said she didn't skin that beaver but I saw a beaver hide tacked up in her shed. Reckon she'll git someone with a trapper's license to sell it for her."

Though I never saw the evidence of it, I was told that Josie's pleasant manner could give way to icy hate—especially when she saw a certain neighbor. One day she met him far out on Blue Mountain. Josie was about to cross his range toward home, but he turned her back onto a circuitous route that forced her to ride many extra hours. Josie said scarcely a word at the time but one day she again met him on the mountain. This time, however, he was headed home across Josie's range, and she turned her horse in front of his, a .30-30 aimed leisurely at him from across her lap. If the man hadn't turned back, I'm reasonably sure that Josie would have "plugged" him.

When I knew her, Josie and her funny little house were squatting illegally on public-domain land. Fortunately, the government never found it necessary to tell Josie that it wasn't her land. The range men, like the cowboys, rangers, and game wardens, overlooked Josie's misdemeanors and, very surreptitiously, we all looked after her. Because, Josie Bassett McKnight Morse Morris, you were the sweetest old husband-poisoner any of us ever knew.

The last time I saw her, she was standing partially hidden in her shrubbery, and she was smiling delightedly. A bunch of us had just come clattering into her yard on horseback.

"Oh my!" Josie said, "it's so good to hear men coming in on horses again!" We were no substitute for the long-departed Wild Bunch, but to see her standing there happy and excited had us sweeping off our big hats and bowing from our saddles.

Perhaps we had dwelled too long on stories about criminals losing themselves in the unquestioning west. The "Bull Moose" was the only name I ever heard applied to a wild-looking fellow who worked on a ranch near Vernal. He always kept a horse saddled and waiting—always. And no one could start down the steep, dirt road leading into the ranch without being watched by the Bull Moose.

One evening, as I was passing along a road overlooking the ranch, I saw a huge fire raging below. I inched my pickup down toward the flames, and as I approached them I saw a figure swirling eerily in and out of the flames. Coming closer, I saw that it was the Bull Moose burning immense piles of tumbleweed. But I had to drive to the bottom of the steep road to turn around, and because I felt that I should explain my visit, I parked and walked over to where the man was working. Behind him, waiting in the shadows, was the ubiquitous saddle horse.

The Bull Moose had a weedy beard and shoulder-length hair. And just meeting him in the daylight was unnerving enough, partly because of his badly cocked eye. On the rare occasions when he came to town, he flew wraith-like down the sidewalk, angrily avoiding all the curious eyes that fell upon him. My heart was beating with unusual speed when I approached this rough-looking apparition and asked, "Is the fire all right? Do you need help?"

The Bull Moose lowered his pitchfork, rested on its handle, and said in one of the most cultivated voices I've ever heard, "No. This fire is under control, thank you. Good evening."

"Uh, well, goodnight. I'll just go out the way I came in." When I had reached my pickup and driven it up out of that inferno, I relaxed. I felt like the kid who had taken a dare, raced up on the porch of the neighborhood's haunted house and knocked, then raced away again, unscathed.

The next time I talked to the Bull Moose was in the early fall, when I delivered a load of slabs to the ranch. The game department supplied them to ranchers for use in fencing their haystacks against marauding deer. He didn't have much to say on that occasion, although his manner was pleasant enough. I had just gotten a Labrador puppy, and she was in the pickup's cab with me. "I hope you don't mind riding with the dog. She's too small to put in the back."

[142

The Bull Moose said he didn't mind the pup, and even ran a gloved hand over her little round head. Just before we reached the stackyard he said, "There is only one thing worse than a car-riding dog."

"What's that?" I asked.

"Two of them." There was a brief twinkle in the Bull Moose's wild eye. I couldn't begrudge him his mane and untended beard, they enhanced his aura of mystery. But I do resent the unwashed, scraggly bearded squirts of today. Whenever I see one, I'm reminded of a rhetorical question: Why cultivate on your face what grows wild on your ass?

That summer Fat had been temporarily assigned to Fish Lake. It is a beautiful lake, and assignment there was something of a plum. In fact, some of the older wardens had turned the area into a personal fief, which was one reason wardens from "outside" were sent there. But the old-timers were a good sort, and Fat had enough tact to get along with them. One was a bouncy little fellow with sparkling eyes and more energy than many men have at half his age; he was sixty-five. One night before dinner, Fat asked him if he'd like a drink.

"No thanks," chirped the little warden, "I quit drinkin' years ago." Fat asked why. "Oh, I uster drink my share, but one time I got awful sick and went and passed out back of the saloon. I made such a mess a' myself that when I came to, the flies had blowed me!"

Fat came home in time to lead me and Clif Greenhalgh on a "turkey survey." Clif was head of the state's upland bird program, and I doubt that there was ever a man more loved by the department's rank and file. We knew that Clif's survey was an excuse to go fishing, and we had a seldom-seen lake full of brook trout waiting for him.

Clif was a skinny, middle-aged bachelor with a hairless pate who always sang "Dill Pickles," an atonal song with a two-word lyric, at parties. He had the priceless gift of taking his work seriously, but not himself. No other man in the department had given more help to embryonic game managers struggling through college. Clif had kept me in part-time jobs during two years of graduate school, and later he helped me to get permanent employment with the game department. Clif was a very friendly fellow, but he was not a politician; if there was a biologically "right" answer to a problem, Clif never considered the sociological or political alternatives.

The bane of his existence was a self-assertive, elderly man with an interrupting voice, a political following, and a yen to run the upland bird program himself. He was known as "The Bellerin' Bull of Benjamin." And with a few choice remarks, the Bellerin' Bull annually reduced Clif's carefully thought-out pheasant program to a shambles.

He was Clif's undeserved cross. Clif Greenhalgh had devoted his life to birds and the game department. He was always looking for foreign game birds that might fill some niche in Utah's inhospitable ecology. He was instrumental in establishing chukar partridges throughout Utah, and his introduction of wild turkeys was also successful in suitable areas. He had a vast and vivid interest in Utah's native birds, and lectured before Audubon clubs and other interested groups. He also composed articles for the department magazine; he submitted them printed in pencil.

Clif's yard, surrounding his suburban home, was a mass of shrubs and trees that produced fruit, or color, or were useful to birds. He had cages for game birds he was studying in his backyard, and he had turned one bedroom of his house into a huge aviary in which he studied the behavior of exotic passerine birds. On almost every wall hung original watercolors of birds, each one was painted with exquisite accuracy. But Clif's garage was the highpoint of his avian world. He had converted it into an ornithological library of huge proportions and excellence. Any student was welcome there, and if he showed particular interest in a volume, Clif was known to find another copy and present it to him.

I must confess a growing feeling of nervousness if I'm left over-
long in the company of birdy folk. But I never felt that way with
Clif, for he was not a pedant. One day several of us were questioning him about the method for telling male chukars from female
chukars. They are superficially similar, and Clif nodded at our question, a very serious expression on his face.

"You tell by the feces. The droppings of males have an alkaline
taste, while those of the females are acid." I'm sure our eyes
widened, but our heads all bobbed in feigned understanding. "So
you see," Clif went on, "the mark of a good chukar sexer depends
on how much shit he can eat."

Clif commonly prevented some youthful biological folly with
a single four-letter word. Yet he was not a vulgar man. He had been
born into a rock-poor family that ranched near Kanab, Utah. He
told me that the only toys he had ever owned were a steer's patella
and a cow's urinary bladder, which had been blown up, filled with
gravel, and dried. His Saturday-afternoon treat was to get permission to walk three miles through the hard but colorful wastes
of southern Utah to a little wet meadow. There he would sit con-
cealed in the shade of bushes, watching the birds and listening to
them sing.

Clif was a medical corpsman in France during some of the bit-
terest fighting of the Second World War. He never discussed it
with me except once, and then it was with revulsion. But it was the
war, I think, that had helped to make Clif a kind, though not soft,
man. When cancer struck him, he refused the palliatives that
would have prolonged his disease along with his life. His marvelous
library is now at the University of Utah, where a scholarship has
been established in his name.

Some of my first work for Clif was helping him to trap game
birds for transplanting. The trap is simply a waist-high mesh cage
with a V-shaped entryway. Shelled corn is placed inside, baiting the
birds down into the V, but when they turn to leave, the narrowing
mesh at the V's bottom is too small for them to reenter. Unfortu-

nately, trapping is also the most effective way to poach pheasants. The trapper operates with stealth and needn't go near his catch until after dark. However, a warden to the south of us did catch a pheasant-trapping farmer that summer. It was a coup, but before the warden could paste it on his stick, the farmer collared him.

"Joe, your damn pheasants is eatin' up my grain 'n' I kin prove it. Here's a claim for game damage." The farmer was paid, too, and he ended that year with a profit—at least as far as pheasants and game wardens were concerned.

The mobile pheasant-shooter is far more abundant. A car crawling down a country lane or parked back in the bushes is always suspect. However, a car parked in an out-of-the-way spot is more likely to contain lovers than poachers, so we approached them gingerly; or at least I did. One government man came on such a car near Vernal one day. He peeped inside and saw a couple in flagrante delicto. The peeper, apparently feeling cute, tapped on the car window and, when the man looked up, asked, "Hey, buddy, do you need any help?" Whereupon, a half-clad giant exploded from the car, yelling, "You smart son of a bitch, I'll show you how much help I need!" He chased the voyeur far into the boondocks.

This springing out of the brush and its many variations has been customary for wardens since the days of the king's deer. A friend once sprang out of the brush to capture an early-morning fish dynamiter and found, instead, a lady relieving herself. "Boy," said the ungallant chap, "the piss sure flew!"

This same warden had another leveling experience with another friend of mine, who had purchased a new set of tires for his Model A in Salt Lake City and was driving toward his home in the Uintah Basin. His trip over the gravel roads had been frequently punctuated with flat tires and blowouts. When he had still another flat in the Strawberry Valley, he sat down on a nearby stream bank to think evil thoughts. All the creeks of this valley were closed to fishing and carefully patrolled to protect the huge cutthroat that spawned in them. As my friend ruminated, the warden burst out of the willows, crying, "I gotcha!"

"Jeezus Keerist!" said my irate friend. "If you ain't got nothin' better to do 'n' sneak in the bushes, you kin fix that tire for me." And the warden fixed it.

But, like the semi-chivalrous Wild Bunch, the crafty, imaginative poacher had almost vanished by the time I reached Vernal. Mobile stealth had displaced wit. However, one group of deer poachers used to get a confederate at a ranch from which they operated to take his telephone off the hook. This tied up the party line, and prevented irate neighbors from calling me until the shooting was over and the poachers were away.

Rhy Hyatt, the warden supervisor, used to come over from Price to see, in his gentle but efficient way, if we were staying on the ball. Rhy had been with the department for many years. For a long time he had been superintendent of the Price bird farm, and Clif Greenhalgh's right hand there, but he handled his new job well and found it less confining than the bird farm. One day Rhy told me about some beaver poachers he'd contended with when he was a young warden.

The almost-extirpated beaver were being carefully guarded in these days but, unfortunately, their fur was in great demand. Rhy suspected a halfbreed Indian and his chums of trapping beaver along the Green River, but he could never catch them with any pelts. The wardens tried every trick. They met and searched the suspects at the end of their float trips. When that failed, the wardens followed them downriver and dropped in on their camp. Nothing worked; the suspects never had a pelt, although plews of doubtful origin continued to appear in the fur trade.

Finally, the defeated wardens fell to occasionally harassing the halfbreed and glumly accepting the fact that he was outsmarting them. Their break didn't come until the price of beaver furs dropped and the halfbreed gave up the river for a cattle ranch. Rhy met the suspected trapper some years later and got him to reveal how he'd taken so many beaver through the warden's blockades.

"You know all those cottonwood logs along the river?" the man began. "Well, whenever we'd get a beaver, we'd skin him quick, then peel bark off one of them logs. Then we'd tack the hide to the log and replace the bark. Unless you looked close, you couldn't see where the bark had been removed. Then, after you wardens searched us, one of us snuck back, got all the hides off'n the logs, an' sold 'em. You'd a' caught us if you'd checked us twice, but you never did."

Occasionally, Fat and I were told that old Orson Hall, who herded cows for the cattle association, sneaked a few deer-poaching jobs over to us. It was said that Ors was behind the mysterious elk poaching that occurred almost every summer during the rodeo. But Fat and I were in and out of Orson's sheep-wagon camp all season long without finding a shred of evidence. Many times I found my conscience panging because of the surreptitious examination I was giving Orson's fingernails (anyone who dresses game acquires tell-tale accumulations of dried blood around and under his finger nails which are difficult to remove quickly.)

Orson Hall was another character from a bygone time. I suppose he had poached game—nearly all the old-timers had—but he had also helped restock the area with elk. The pioneers had destroyed almost all of Utah's native elk, and the animals there today are the result of transplants from Yellowstone Park. Orson used to cite this and complain that he had never drawn an elk-hunting permit. "By Gawd, boys, if'n I don't draw a permit this year, I'll hafta' poach me a elk! I'm just gettin' too gawddamn old to wait anymore."

Orson may have finally killed his elk illegally, but he didn't want anyone else to. When someone poached a young bull, Orson firmly fastened the head to an aspen tree. It was his chiding way of warning us to improve our vigilance.

In his turn, Fat would chide Orson about "all them blue-eyed Injuns down by Randlett." I had never seen any, but Ors hee-hawed just the same. As a young cowboy, Orson had reveled and raced horses in the lawless "Strip." This was an area that early surveyors had somehow left off their maps, and for a time it was a sinful reservoir for western dregs.

[148

Orson was a big, round-faced man, with a horsey grin and very little hair. Though he was supposed to be ailing, he ate well and had a medium-sized paunch to prove it. He loved anything that contained alcohol and drank despite the protests of his doctor and his wife. Fat and I often bought him a drink or two in exchange for kitchen privileges in his camp. We thought that anyone who enjoyed a drink as much as Orson did shouldn't have to endure a prohibition placed on him by a couple of townies.

One day I was nursing my pickup over an almost indistinguishable track on Taylor Mountain. When I drove out of the timber and into a tiny clearing, who should be in the center of it but old Orson! He was sitting on the ground with his legs cocked Indian fashion; standing erect between them was a quart of whiskey. "Well, howdy!" Orson bawled, "I was gettin' out some wood and decided to stop here for a drink or two. Here, have one!"

The standard method for taking a drink on the range is to grasp the bottle by its neck, put it to your lips, and tip it up; enough liquor is then swallowed to send at least two huge bubbles convulsing up through the remaining contents. It is something like drenching a horse. The trick is to pour the whiskey straight down your gullet, bypassing the tongue and its taste buds. When you have finished, you can say, "By God! That's pretty good stuff," or "Wah! Cuts like a file!" It is the mark of a dude to be struck dumb after such a prodigious swig.

Orson and I sat there in the pleasant little meadow until all of his whiskey was gone. When it began raining we got into my pickup and sloshed back to Orson's camp. As the rain began falling in earnest, I peeled some potatoes for a late lunch. While I was peeling, Vert McConkie came in lugging a gallon of wine. So we delayed eating a while longer in order to help Vert. When I finally got away from that camp, I could barely "hit my ass with both hands."

It wouldn't have been very wise to take the state highway back to town, especially in a state truck, so I set out at a creep across one of Diamond Mountain's back roads. I thought I might be able to count some sage-grouse broods on the way home. But I'd only gone a mile or two when the truck slewed around and sank to its axles in the muddy road. Perhaps it was Providence's way of protecting me, because as I slithered and struggled with jack, shovel, and tire chains, I began to sober up.

Almost immediately, I was smeared with red-brown mud and soaking in perspiration. The rain had passed on over, and the air was hot and humid; the more I struggled to extricate the pickup, the feebler seemed my results. As I fumbled and stumbled in the muck, a four-wheel-drive truck appeared on the knoll just beyond me. I recognized it as belonging to some men whom I suspected had been poaching deer in the area. The truck churned effortlessly down to where I was.

"Stuck?" called the driver. I nodded, and threw out my mud-caked hands to indicate the size of my predicament. "We'll winch you right out of that," said the driver, while his brother hopped from the passenger's seat and began hooking their winch cable to my pickup.

"Now, when she starts movin'," I was instructed, "hit 'er hard." I followed instructions, and the mired pickup was whisked miraculously from the morass and went fish-tailing up onto firmer ground. "I sure appreciate that," I said, "what do I owe you."

"Nothin'," said the driver with a knowing look, "jes' call us even." When he waved away my thanks, I noticed the peculiar stain around the man's fingernails. I have known wardens who were invited to "chicken" dinners that their palates swore were illegal grouse. Now I knew how they felt.

I didn't count any sage-grouse broods that day, although I probably could have doubled the number of any broods I saw if I hadn't become stuck and dissipated Orson's bottled euphoria. The grouse might have used my help, too. All the species of western grouse have declined, due in some cases to overshooting pioneers, but also because of land use and abuse and the subsequent effects on vegetation. Utah had closed seasons, or strictly controlled, permittee-only grouse hunts, during most of the years that I lived there.

Precedent is old: many years ago, officials closed the sage-grouse season in an area far south of Salt Lake City. Their action upset the grouse hunters of one town, who invited a top game official down to see all the birds they had. The hunters also invited the official to a campout and outdoor banquet on the grouse range.

The official accepted, and as soon as he was in the company of the would-be hunters, he began seeing sage grouse, lots of them. It was embarrassing for him to find such a plentiful supply of birds, but the official refused to admit their plenty even when he saw grouse promenading through the sage around the camp. The season was closed and it was going to stay closed, he said, and that was that.

While supper was being prepared, the undaunted hunters plied the official with choice whiskey. With pointed references to the abundance of sage grouse that year, they totaled up the number of birds seen that day. While all this counting and appreciative clucking of tongues went on the noncommittal game official swigged bourbon from an ever-full cup. His eyes may have widened a bit as the inventory increased, but he kept his own council.

His hosts were a bit surprised, therefore, when, about a half-hour before sundown, the official suddenly rose from his camp chair and weaved unsteadily over to a boulder. He mounted the rock and stood swaying there until all the camp had assembled around him.

"Men," he announced, "With the powers vested in me by the sovereign state of Utah, I now declare the season on sage grouse open, for one half-hour." While the hunters scurried for their guns, the official took out his watch and, amid the popping of shells, timed the season. (Had he consulted his watch a bit longer, he might also have timed the remainder of his period of employment with the game department.)

Unfortunately, stories like that one hung around our necks like ancient, moldering albatrosses. A surprising number of citizens get a weird sort of pleasure when a state employee is detected in some peccadillo. Conservation was little more to them than dumping a load of fish in a stream or closing the doe season. They could not see that slowly but inexorably, their environment was being destroyed. It took a refreshing visit with a Josie Morse or Dale Jensen (who said I was "chickenshit" if I failed to check him any time he "came off the mountain") to break the pall of discouragement that too often hung over a job in conservation. If ever there was a condition of delicious agony, a game warden's job was certainly it.

I remember the fellow who brought the crippled fawn to Bob Jensen at the game farm. The animal was over a year old but only a trifle larger than it had been at birth. Where there should have been slim, graceful legs, there were only hideous appendages so twisted or truncated that the little animal had never been able to stand. The man who had turned in the fawn had hit it with his mowing machine as it lay hidden in his alfalfa patch the season before. The accident was tragic, but keeping the monstrous result alive for a year until, "we got tired of takin' ker of it" was criminal. The fawn had never been able to care for itself. And now it lay trusting and pathetic behind one of our sheds. The periods of affection and care alternating with others of neglect and cruelty had left the little animal a psychological as well as physical cripple.

It bleated at me piteously when I carried it a gallon of water. And it never looked up until it was far into the second gallon of water. I would never have believed a deer so small could be so thirsty; its former custodian must have become very tired of "takin' ker" of it. When the fawn was through drinking, I placed the muzzle of my revolver on top of its head and squeezed the trigger.

Well, as Fat said, most people want to do the right thing, and unless they are totally ignorant or pressed too hard, they generally succeed. Like me—I was a young man, unattached and with all my juices flowing. I tried to be circumspect—but if I failed, I could bank on having Mac Helm corner me in the vacant office of the sheriff the next Sunday morning. While I sat there, Mac would read to me the various penalties for social impropriety from a ponderous volume of the *Utah Annotated Code*.

"See," Mac would say, after reading a particular well-described breach, "see what you could be letting yourself in for?"

"I'll bet those legislators really enjoyed writing that stuff," I would say and Mac would laugh, slam the book shut, and suggest we run out to Artesia and have a cup of coffee. Mac had made his point, though, and I was back to being circumspect.

Mac Helm was in charge of getting the meat for his lodge's annual benefit barbecue. The proceeds went to a crippled children's hospital. It was a good cause, and I usually was able to provide Mac with some fat deer that had made the mistake of marauding the crops of an ungenerous farmer. But needy families took precedence over the barbecue, and they got first chance at the venison.

I remember one family particularly well. They had ridden into Vernal on horseback, the littlest kids sticking to their bony mounts like circus monkeys. All this family owned, or ever would own, were the clothes they wore and the crowbait horses they rode.

The family had squatted somewhere on public-domain land until an inquisitive pilot flew his plane too close and the contentious father took a shot at it. They had been dispossessed after that, and had come trotting into Vernal, probably the last family ever to arrive there on horseback. The county provided them with some groceries and a generous farmer offered them a vacant homesteader's shack on the edge of his pasture. The father was given a ranch job in the Book Cliffs, and his family settled in the shack.

The mother was a wind-worn lump who would have reminded me of a huge animated potato had it not been for her bellicosity. She had a grown son who immediately stationed himself on the shack's front porch with a guitar and stayed there seemingly for the rest of the summer. There were two or three smaller children, who reminded me of half-starved badgers, always ready to either fight or run.

Early one morning I drove into their littered yard. The woman came out, and I asked her, "Can you use a couple of deer? They're dressed but not skinned."

She examined the deer with practiced fingers. "I've peeled these things before." The woman almost smirked. I pretended not to notice and dragged the carcasses into the shack's back room. It was empty except for some old, discarded fruit jars lying around on the dirt floor. "I'll have to get you to sign a receipt for these deer," I said.

The woman nodded and led me into the shack's other room. It had wooden flooring, and it was filthy; the few unbroken windows were yellow with sunbaked grime. Some child's old underpants had been jammed into the hole in one of the panes. There was a crudely made table beside one window. On one side of it was a bench that had been slabbed together with unplaned lumber, while on the other side of the table stood two rickety chairs with soiled clothing hanging from their backs. On the floor were wads of bedding that appeared to have been hastily kicked over to the walls.

The room's only other furnishings seemed to be the little animal-children. They were sitting at the table. There was a quart fruit jar of water and two cracked, dirty cereal bowls on the table between them. The only bright thing in the room was the cornflakes carton standing on the table. There was no sugar or milk on the table, and I had to assume that the children were moistening their cereal with water.

Outside, the clean warmth of the August sun was drying the dew from the grass, and as the sun climbed it reflected brilliantly on the eternal snowdrifts of the far-off Bolly peaks. As I said, a warden's job is one of delicious agony. Sometimes, if I forgot to look up, it was all agony.

X / LAMB WITHOUT MINT JELLY

"When the Army accidentally poisoned all those sheep in
Skull Valley, I took my wife out to dinner to celebrate."

—UTAH NATURALIST

As Utah summer slowly ends in its warmly magnificent way, the sheep begin coming down from the high country. The hazy mountains are often green from equinoctial rains, and some people appreciate the sight of sheep trailing across the freshened ridges.

I do not appreciate sheep; I hate them. They stink. Their stupid and incessant blatting destroys the tranquility of the range, and their nibbling mouths and cloven hooves destroy the range itself. As the sheep come nearer and finally surround you in a filthy, wooly quicksand, you hear a new sound under the blatting. It has the rushing sibilance of wind overlain with a sound like a million cracking knuckles—that is the clatter of the sharp, little hooves. To me the noise is one of bridled but mindless frenzy, the sort of witless energy that is ready to dive into the nearest abyss at the rattle of an empty can.

Paradoxically, I learned to know and to like some of the district's sheepmen and herders. And I was torn in my liking by the knowledge of what their flocks have done to the ranges. A sheep outfit has to work longer and at a lower profit than does, say, a highway contractor, to screw up the country. The owners have had to import Mexican and Basque employees since the supply of American herders began dwindling after World War II. Few Americans want an outdoor job badly enough to accept the sheep outfits' low wages and long, isolated hours.

The foreigners are often good sheepherders, although many are inclined to herd too closely. This concentrates their flocks and increases the damage that they do. Foreigners have also been very hard on the West's once-bountiful supply of sheepherder stories. What they say may be funny but no one other than their countrymen can understand them. But because a lot of sheepherder stories are based in bestiality, the current dearth may be for the best.

A herder whom I knew was once asked by an overly curious

camp guest if "sheepherders really screwed their sheep." The herder threw him an appraising glance and then looked out at the limitless expanse of empty desert. "What the hell do you think we screw!" he answered.

I doubt that anyone would have dared ask Jimmy Nick such a question. He was a spry and sprightly seventy-year-old herder whom Fat and I enjoyed visiting. We would sit in his wagon listening to Jimmy describe his latest romantic adventure in Salt Lake City, while he stirred up a batch of sourdough biscuits. The biscuits were superb, and yet seemed so simply made that I have since wondered why I've never found a cook who could duplicate them.

Perhaps the answer lay in Jimmy's fastidiousness. The typical herder's campsite is memorialized by piles of rusting cans, broken bottles, and, nowadays, fluttering streamers of polyethylene. None of this could be found around a camp of Jimmy Nick's. He even insisted that wash water be carried far away from camp for disposal, not be simply tossed out the wagon door.

Jimmy's wagon, or sheep camp, was like a thousand others on the western ranges. They are approximate crosses between old prairie schooners and modern travel trailers. The wagons are about twelve feet long by six feet wide, with canvas tops almost high enough for a six-foot man to stand erect. The top is a weathered white and the wagon box is customarily a dark green; sometimes the wooden wheels are painted bright red, but more often they have been replaced by auto wheels and rubber tires. At the front of the wagon is a tongue used mostly these days for attaching to a pickup truck, although many wagons are still horse-drawn.

A blackened stove pipe juts up from the wagon's small wood-burning stove to clear the canvas top by a foot or so. You enter the wagon by a fold-up stair and a narrow door on one side of the wagon's front. This is often a sort of dutch door that provides ventilation and also permits the herder to drive his team while sitting inside his mobile camp. In the front part of the wagon, across from the stove, is a table that may be folded up, out of the way, against the wall. When folded, it covers a shallow cupboard that holds culinary equipment and often an array of condiments rivaling that offered by most restaurants. Low cabinets are usually built against the walls, where their tops double as seats. At the rear of the wagon, lying athwart-ships, is the herder's bunk. In some camps these unmade swirls of dirty bedding looked more like nests than beds, although I never saw one that didn't appear to be eminently comfortable. The small sliding windows in the sides of Jimmy Nick's wagon sparkled, although many others admitted light only if they were opened.

The wood stove, from whose small oven came the wonderful biscuits, generally had an ironware coffee pot on its top, and sometimes a blackened steel frying pan, in which you might assay what the herder had been living on for the past few days. In most camps it was fried mutton, fried "taters," canned "carn," and as many cups of coffee as he could hold.

Most herders had a favorite kind of pickle or spiced pepper they served with their meals. I remember a jar of big pickled peppers. They were a sultry yellow color and they burst into flame if you were so foolish as to eat one. A warden friend did. He was tricked into accepting the pepper, and we were all disappointed when he calmly ate it without incinerating himself. When he finished it, and noticed that we were all looking at him expectantly, he observed, "Man eat many a' them an' he'd have to go shit in the river next morning just to keep his butt cooled off."

The herder's dogs (if he had more than one) were long-haired animals with enough shepherd blood to make their ears stand up. They slept under the wagon and ate what the herder wouldn't. Some sheepherders shot jackrabbits for their dogs, or fed them commercial dog food. The dogs were furnished by the flock owner, and they didn't seem to have much life expectancy. A herder might brag on his dog, though I seldom could tell from the way the dogs were treated whether a sheep dog was good or bad. Of course, the really bad ones lay grimacing in death as they dried in the wind, with bullets through their lights.

A good sheepherder doesn't use his dogs too much. If the sheep are dogged, they knot together and churn the range to dust. Jimmy Nick was a good herder. In the desert as well as the mountains, he husbanded his boss's grazing allotments. When he and his sheep left a site, some grass remained, and the shrubs didn't have that cyclone-struck appearance of plants in other allotments.

Such husbandry isn't typical. Nowadays you often see the herder's raw-boned saddle horse tied to the wagon, while the herder lies on his bunk watching the coffee perk. Chances are that both sheep and range would be better off under a more watchful eye. Sheepmen characteristically believe that their range is in good shape if it furnishes them enough lambs and wool to show a profit.

One morning, I was riding with just such a stockman over some of his blasted range. Save for a scattering of high-lined junipers and occasional scraggles of clubbed browse, the thin soil lay exposed and vulnerable to the elements. Near an eroded gully that had once been a grassy swale, we came upon a patch of rabbitbrush. This is a yellowish-green shrub that livestock dislike, and its presence is indicative of overgrazing, poor soil, or both. The rancher waved expansively toward this brush. "My sheep sure like this stuff after a rain," he said. He didn't realize that water was what coaxed his hungry sheep into eating the brush at all.

On ranges like that one, the remaining forage serves mostly as roughage. The sheepmen feed their animals a concentrated commercial ration, such as cottonseed cake, to provide their basic nutrition. The "caking" occurs most often on winter range, but during especially dry periods it's also done on summer range. This subsistence grazing is extremely damaging to the range and disastrous to the wild animals who must depend entirely on the native plants. It helps to explain why antelope, once common in Utah, have virtually disappeared.

One day Wallace Tabee, the Ute Indian game warden, took Fat and me out to a part of the tribal lands called Hill Creek. The huge area forms the western part of the Book Cliffs, and it is the Ute's traditional summer range. White men had used the area for years, but it was eventually returned to the tribe after an adjudication of their rights before World War II.

After we left Ouray and began climbing into the high, canyon-cut plateau country, I noticed that this Hill Creek range was even better than the Book Cliffs's. The deer we saw were huge animals with the blocky bodies of feed-lot steers. The tribe's Black Angus cattle were grass-fat, and seemingly anesthetized by the abundance they found in the canyon bottoms. But what struck me most in that refreshing canyon greenness were the two distinct stands of aspen trees. One group was mature, and some had even died of old age; the other stand was young, with none above fifteen-feet tall. In stands of aspen there are usually trees of all sizes and ages. Then I realized that the young trees dated from the time when the white man's animals had been removed. The difference between the young and old trees proclaimed the start and stop of overgrazing.

During our drive, a ruffed grouse darted across the aspenlined road in front of our pickup. "Do you have many of those?" Fat asked.

Wallace answered, "Quite a few."

"They're sure good eatin'," Fat opined.

"Oh, yes," agreed Wallace. And then we all laughed, for ruffed grouse hadn't been legal game in Utah for decades.

About noon we drove into a dusty little valley and found a sheep wagon there. The herder invited us to dinner and we accepted. Fat and I peeled potatoes while he cut steaks off a leg of mutton. Each time his blade neared the bone, a sickening smell rose from the meat. Fat and I glanced unhappily at each other—the mutton was spoiled.

But we had to eat the meal, for to have walked out was unthinkable. Wallace and I sat side by side, and Fat took a seat by the wagon's open window. As the plate of mutton was passed around, we vied to see who could take the smallest helping but the herder noticed. "Hell, fellers, there's plenty of meat. Here, take some more." With that he forked another piece onto my plate. And while I sat there, manfully swallowing, Fat carried on an unusually animated conversation. He made his points with a mutton-laden fork, and seemed to have forgotten his dinner's dubious origin.

After we had washed the dishes and swept out the wagon, as range custom dictates, we took our leave. In the pickup I asked Fat, "How the hell could you eat that rotten meat?"

Fat grinned. "I didn't. I waved it around on my fork an' when the herder wasn't lookin' I flipped it out the window. His dog was a-settin' out there catchin' every piece."

I should have suspected that, because Fat Gardiner kept his own version of a *Michelin Guide* to sheep-camp dining. At some camps he would not accept even coffee, while at others he always maneuvered himself into the cooking job. Only at a few camps, such as Jimmy Nick's, would be deign to be fed. Like many rural westerners, Fat was extremely particular about the meat he ate.

Once, he told me, he had met a herder on the range and been invited to go to the man's camp and cook a dinner for himself. There was a leg of mutton wrapped in canvas and stuck under the wagon. It was winter and the meat looked good when Fat cut off his steak. But when he placed it in the hot frying pan, little white things began wriggling frantically up out of the meat. After hearing that, Fat was my taster, and I only ate what he did, where he did.

Lacking a sheep camp, Fat and I often stopped on the range and cooked our own dinner. While we ate, Fat would point out landmarks or tell me about some experience he'd had in that place. One noon on Diamond Mountain he noted an open and sparsely grassed ridge. "That's Bullshit Ridge," he said. "All the sheepherders meet up there and see which one can tell the biggest lie."

The herd owners generally haven't time enough to waste any. Many of them are executives, too busy even to see their sheep more than a few times a year. Some of them, I've heard it said, "would skin a flea for the hide and tallow." Together with mining, railroad, and cattle interests, sheepmen wield tremendous, often decisive, influence over the governments of western states. I remember when big bands of sheep were driven through the center of residential Salt Lake City with no apparent concern or redress for the damage the animals did to lawns and shrubbery. Even today, the motorist who hits a wandering animal on a western highway may find himself with a wrecked car and the bill for the animal. A thief who takes a ewe worth twenty-five dollars can go to the penitentiary. On the other hand, a poacher who steals a deer worth a hundred dollars to the state's economy will be charged with only a misdemeanor.

The strongest evidence of the power of the livestock interests, I thought, was in the state law protecting watersheds—it was never enforced. Whole mountainsides have come sliding into Utah cities and towns, carrying with them everything from gigantic boulders to corpses washed down from foothill cemetaries. The federal government has spent vast sums to terrace these ravaged hillsides. Yet no one was ever indicted for overgrazing them and starting the trouble that often ended up on Main Street.

Overgrazing! I used that phrase at a sportsmen's meeting and tied it to the decline in trout fishing. "Well," countered a stockman, "you can't do anything about that . . ." as if western cattle and sheep constituted something as sacred as the zebu of India. Some stockmen actually insist that there is no such thing as overgrazing. And others, who admit it does exist blame it all on big game and suggest they be exterminated. One professor of Utah agriculture went so far as to advocate that all the vegetation be removed from Utah hillsides in order to facilitate runoff into the reservoirs!

Most people don't realize that nearly half the land area of the mainland states is grazing land. This is traditionally the least productive land: it takes about a hundred twenty-five thousand acres of western desert to winter fifteen thousand sheep, and even at that rate the range may be overgrazed. About three-fourths of the state of Utah is under public administration, yet some of these public lands, poor to begin with, are the lands most abused by livestock.

Theoretically, by virtue of the watershed-protection law and public administration of most of the ranges, Utah should have no overgrazing. Nevertheless, the Bureau of Land Management, the federal agency responsible for much of the western range, reported a decrease from 1953 to 1966 of almost one million A.U.M.s (Animal Unit Month, an arbitrary forage measurement based upon the food requirements of one cow or five sheep grazing the range for one month). As more concrete evidence, Utah's annual wool clip is about five eighths of what it was around the turn of the century and the number of lambs saved annually for herd maintenance has been cut almost in half during the same period.

Even from the sheepman's point of view, the ranges are deteriorating. But proving it has been very difficult. Overgrazing can simply mean the almost imperceptible disappearance of palatable and nutritious range plants and their replacement by less desirable species. When halogeton first appeared on western ranges it was hailed as fine sheep forage. Later the government spent thousands of dollars spraying it with 2-4D because halogeton poisoned sheep that had nothing else to eat. There was even a Johnny Appleseed in Utah who used to go around the desert areas sowing halogeton.

In other cases overgrazing is evidenced by a lack of young plants, as had happened with the aspen on Hill Creek. In the always sparsely vegetated desert, more and more space appears between the plants. This opens the soil to increased erosion, as was occurring between Jones Hole and Island Park. Overgrazing is also indicated when certain highly palatable plants begin dwindling on an otherwise healthy-looking range. Poisoning of livestock may also be a sign of a slipping range if the animals' hunger has driven them to eat plants that they ordinarily avoid. Of course, a sheep is so dumb that it may poison itself just because its herd-mates are doing it. Sheep will let magpies sit on their heads and let the greedy robbers pick out their eyes.

A wag advertises his chain of western service-stations by posting humorous signs along desolate sections of highway. PETRIFIED WATER-MELONS, read one in a boulder-strewn waste, TAKE ONE HOME TO YOUR MOTHER-IN-LAW. In sheep country the signs may read

NOTICE, SHEEPHERDERS ENROUTE TO TOWN HAVE THE RIGHT OF WAY. Another proclaimed SAGEBRUSH IS FREE, STUFF SOME IN YOUR TRUNK. This last sign had often been erected in an area of shadscale greasewood, or rabbitbrush. The vast and often desolate-looking west isn't invariably covered with sagebrush. The pioneers learned to homestead areas that were covered with sage because it indicated fertile soil. And the remaining sage has been the wintertime staff of life to deer and livestock for decades since. Sagebrush is also vital to sage grouse.

Big sage, one of the most abundant of the several sage species, has the happy facility for growing the year around. A sage twig that was six inches long in the fall could easily be eight inches long after a winter of deer browsing. Naturally, we opposed the wholesale sage-eradication projects that many range managers and stockmen considered a panacea to forage production. But, for reasons that I have never wholly understood, sagebrush has been a popular whipping boy for generations. Once an eminent professor of range management told a group of us wardens that cattle didn't eat sagebrush. The room became very still and after the lecture a seamy-faced old warden buttonholed the sleek professor.

"Say, Doc, you better come down home an' instruck our cows. They's so damn iggerant that they been eatin' sagebrush all their lives."

One afternoon, as Fat and I were driving across the dry rangeland southeast of Vernal, he began asking me what kind of shrubs we were passing. Not being any shakes as a botanist, I gave him a couple of guesses for the low-growing shrubs he had pointed to. As I did so, Fat checked the names in a crumpled pamphlet he had fished from a shirt pocket.

"What's that?" I asked.

"One of the guys from the office gave it to me. It's a list of range plants. I'm a-tryin' to learn 'em."

Poor Fat! He had carried that pamphlet for months, never mentioning it but hoping to equate plant names he heard mentioned with those on his list. His task was Sisyphean for, to me anyway, plant taxonomy is a tremendously tedious and often frustrating task. There are ten thousand species of flowering plants on the western ranges, and trying to match those you see with a printed list is the stuff of tragedy.

I looked over at Fat concentrating on his list. "This stuff is spiny horsebush," I said. That left him with 9,975 species to go. But at least Fat was trying. Many ranchers have three general names for all the western shrubs; they are chapparal, buck-brush, and sage. This is one of the reasons why it so damned hard to convince many of them they are over-using the ranges. ("Bullshit, sonny, I never seen the chapparal any greener.")

Before World War II the forest service published an opinion that the productivity of the western ranges had been halved since the introduction of livestock less than a hundred years before. It made the livestock interests furious. The ranges were not over-grazed, they said, it was the drought that had set them back. So the opinion was filed and forgotten and nobody mentions that the "drought" has now lasted for a hundred and twenty years. Extremely valuable forage plants such as winterfat have so dwindled on the desert ranges that hardly anyone now alive remembers it as once being common.

Nevertheless, grazing is natural. The ranges developed under the unregulated chewing of millions of wild animals. But there was an ebb and flow in the wildlife population which permitted an over-used area to recover. Also, wandering, high-strung wild animals are seldom the eating machines that phlegmatic domestic animals are. Lately the range managers have been advocating a "rest-rotation" system of grazing. Under this program, parts of a range are periodically left ungrazed for a season. All the bugs aren't out of the method; big-game needs haven't figured strongly enough in the initial management plan. But these needs are beginning to be considered. Actually, rest-rotation was something the wild animals had figured out before we ever got here.

Most public lands in the West are administered by either the Forest Service or the Bureau of Land Management. Generally, though not always, the Forest Service controls the mountainous regions, while the BLM administers the lower, semi-arid shrub- and grasslands. The Forest Rangers were the elite among the echelons of resource managers. In their offices they wore olive uniforms and exuded an air of administrative industry, systematic correctness— and just the faintest trace of condescension when the local game warden walked in.

Across the street and upstairs over the drug store were the BLM's freshly painted offices. Unlike the rangers, the BLM-ers didn't act as if they'd had offices for very long. The whole crew wore cowboy shirts with pearly snap buttons, and held up their Levi's with tooled leather belts wide enough to land a plane on. The atmosphere in their office was relaxed. The men put their booted feet on their new metal desks and tossed cigarette butts into the wastebaskets. They enjoyed making their points by referring to huge, painstakingly colored maps that were displayed on steel wall mounts that could be moved without arising from the desk. The BLM fellows were a good sort and, collectively, the best poker players in the game, forest, and livestock melange.

The BLM I knew was always the fief of the livestock industry. Each office administers the range it controls, with the "advice" of a board of stockmen. In fact, these boards usually tell the BLM staff what time to go to the john, and I have seen board members solemnly vote on matters affecting their own grazing permits. It is sort of like allowing a plaintiff to serve on his own jury. The wildlife member of the board could advise but not vote.

Lately, however, the BLM has begun to consider all the public in some of its land-management policies. And they did consult us when claims were filed on public lands. East of Vernal an oil crew had drilled a well that by chance struck artesian water. The water was clear but hot and reeking with the smell of rotten eggs. But in that sere land any water was a blessing, and the well site had become a tiny green blossom that attracted all sorts of birds and animals. This didn't prevent a promoter from filing on the land surrounding the well. He was going to build a health spa there on the desert. The BLM asked for a game department opinion on the transfer. I went to the well and listed the wildlife I found there. Some mourning doves had fluttered up as I approached, and their flight was followed by that of some stridently calling killdeer. Small, inconspicuously colored desert birds used the well and I saw the simultaneously spraddled and pinched-together tracks of cottontail rabbits close by. I had seen antelope near the well, and guessed deer might use it at certain seasons. To turn this fortunate little oasis into a neon-lighted junk heap dedicated to the marination of hemorrhoids and varicose veins simply wasn't its highest use. The BLM agreed and, at least temporarily, refused the promoter's claim.

Still more was lost than won on the public lands. That summer a sheepman illegally put several hundred sheep on the public range. The BLM notified him of this violation and requested that the sheep be removed. The notification was ignored and after several weeks of futile trying, the BLM finally filed a formal trespass complaint. The sheepman immediately appealed the complaint, which automatically suspended further attempts to remove the sheep. Months later, when the case got to court, the sheep had long been removed and the sheepman offered to settle the case. The Government agreed and accepted twenty-five dollars in damages!

The BLM boys became snappish when we chided them about that case. Yet the fine was only about seven dollars under the Utah average for such cases. Many a stockman has been heard to chortle over the cheapest grazing fee he ever had to pay when he was "trespassed" by the BLM. Considering that the regular fee for a ewe plus her lambs was five cents a month, I often wondered how big a bargain some stockmen expected.

Such machinations are especially cryptic when there is virtually no demand for mutton. A ewe that was healthy but had worn her teeth out by gnawing rocks on the desert used to sell for five dollars. I met a friend in the grocery store one day and noticed that he had purchased some lamb chops. "What's the idea of buying that stuff?" I asked.

"We don't seem to be gaining on them," my friend replied, "so I thought I'd see if I couldn't eat them out of existence.

My own policy is to boycott lamb and mutton, unless I know it to be farm-raised. Not that range lamb and even mutton can't be delicious. An old range trick is to take a shortened rack of ribs and lay them over the coals in the stove's fire box. The baked result is a treat you eat with your fingers.

Another ovine delicacy, but one that I could never enjoy, were lamb's testicles or "Rocky Mountain oysters." Until recently, the docking and castrating of lambs was sometimes done by biting off the tails and the small sex glands. Once extracted, the testicles were spat into a pan or bucket, then fried for supper. An ex-sheepherder once told me it took him a couple of swigs of whiskey and a mouth full of chewing tobacco to get into this work.

Once, at a country dance, a sheepman's son farted loudly while dancing with a friend's girl. He immediately stopped dancing and brazenly asked, "Whats'a matter, honey, am I squeezin' you too tight?"

Naturally, the girl was mortified, but instead of starting a fight, her escort bided his time. Then, when docking began at the ranch, the offended boy took the girl friend of the flatulent youth out to watch him at work. One look at her beau coated with blood, excrement, and tobacco juice ended their romance.

For some reason (sex, I suppose), wild bighorn rams sometimes begin trailing a band of domestic sheep. One afternoon Steve Radosevich called to tell me that he had seen a wild ram with a domestic herd. I drove over the next morning to see it but found the herder moving his sheep and the ram gone. We looked for him for several hours but never found him. Later Steve told me he eventually found the bighorn lying dead on a ridge above the sheep camp.

[168

LAMB WITHOUT MINT JELLY

Wild sheep and domestic ones seldom get along. In the primitive West, bighorn sheep numbered in the hundreds of thousands. But when domestic sheep began flooding into the west after the Civil War, they brought scabies with them. Wild sheep caught it and died by the uncounted thousands. The "mountain maggots" also forced the bighorns out of their ancestral ranges and then were permitted to overgraze them. Then the remnant bands of wild sheep began dying again, this time of pneumonia resulting from infestations of lungworms.

The larvae of this parasite live in tiny snails that are surprisingly common at higher elevations in the West. The bighorns apparently eat these snails in the course of feeding. As the worm larvae develop, some of them are partially coughed up from the lungs, then swallowed and finally eliminated in the droppings. These larval parasites can live for a year in a capsule of dung—ample time for a snail to come along, become the intermediate host, and renew the deadly cycle.

The wild sheep in my district were existing in some of the most inaccessible sections of the Green River Canyon. I liked living on the edge of one of the most isolated and sparsely populated areas left in the west. I could get away from the traffic, the pushy tourists, and the heat simply by patrolling Diamond or Blue Mountain on summer evenings. The deer were getting fat and the spotlighters sometimes prowled the backcountry hoping to pot one. I would park on a darkened vantage point and listen, or drive along the luminescent dirt roads with my headlights turned off until midnight. By that hour the game had bedded down for the night.

If I had been patrolling Diamond Mountain, I often headed for Av Kay's cabin instead of going home. Av's cabin was isolated and he had given Fat and me keys to the door and an invitation to use it, partly to steer away vandals.

One evening about midnight, I was driving toward this cabin when a tawny form flashed across the road in front of my headlights. I stopped and aimed my spotlight in the direction the flash had taken. Almost immediately the beam revealed a big mountain lion. It was sitting down and watching me, a few steps away. It was the first lion I had ever seen outside a cage, so I grabbed my flashlight and walked over toward it. The lion sat there watching me with that detached sort of curiosity you see on the faces of well-fed house cats. I walked to within a dozen steps of the animal and it just sat there watching and occasionally giving its long tail a lanquid twitch. It didn't seem to be in the least afraid. After a couple of minutes it occurred to me that the distance between us was about one and one half lion bounds, and that my revolver was back in the truck. I must confess, too, that I entertained visions of a big lion displayed in Vernal the following morning. But the lion had shown the good sense to leave before I came back with the gun.

Despite the apprehension of a stockman who saw his track, the lion never killed anything that was missed. And I never told anyone that I had seen the lion. The federal predator-trappers were deadly enough without being given clues. Their activities were somewhat restricted on National Forests but I have seen their bait stations and red AVISO signs plastered across BLM lands. The trappers also set tubular "coyote getters" in the ground, loaded with a blank cartridge and a cyanide capsule. When a member of the dog family found the scented wad of wool on top of the getter, he would paw it, roll on it, and eventually bite it. The bite triggered the device, which shot its load of poison into the animal's mouth. Some trappers complained that a coyote who had seen another discharge a getter would never bite one himself. The average dog won't last a half day in an area baited with getters. To protect sheep dogs, the trappers would set poison-less guns, and then let the dogs set off the blank. It usually broke a dog, but made him gun-shy in the process.

These trappers also injected 1080, an insidious, slow-acting poison, into carcasses they found on the range or into carrion they had brought out with them. This poison kills indiscriminately and has long been denounced by those pesky conservationists. Because it kills slowly, even the clever coyotes aren't smart enough to associate their free meals with the slow death that inevitably follows.

[170   •

LAMB WITHOUT MINT JELLY

When the meat eaters were decimated, the prolific jackrabbits and pocket gophers began nibbling the ranges in increasing millions. The howls went up about this, too, so out came the trappers again, only this time they carried sacks of poisoned grain. Of course they didn't get all the rodents but in some areas, including the one where I now live, they succeeded in exterminating all the sage grouse.

The affable boss of the Utah branch of the federal poisoning-and-mutilating society kept telling us, "The last coyote will be around to howl over the last white man's grave." Considering that I never saw and rarely even heard a coyote, I decided that last one had better learn to howl, "Buulll . . . shiiiiit!"

I have known men who followed the trappers around, taking poison out of their getters and urinating or pouring oil on their 1080-laden baits. A word of warning: It is illegal to tamper with these federally sponsored baits, and those who attempt to unload coyote getters without knowing the proper method risk injury.

Until one sees the many deadly devices and techniques that are employed in behalf of the livestock industry, it is difficult to believe any one group could hate its competition with such ferocity. Several years ago a well-known sheepman reportedly furnished rifles and cartridges to his herders along with orders to kill all the deer they saw. From a biological standpoint the herders should have shot, for the deer herds were increasing with malignant fervor. But the average bored sheepherder often enjoys seeing game and wishes it well more often than ill. Not all sheepmen are waffle-bottomed desk punchers, either. The leathery-faced sort whose very being is the synthesis of years on the open range, is most likely a fine man.

I well remember the anguish on some of those weathered faces when I listened to a bureaucrat casually tell them their ranges were about to become a reservoir. In their way, these men loved the blighted, dusty land; it had mothered them all their lives, and they never realized how harsh and stern it was because this was all they had ever known. The land, and their fathers, had taught them that to get a dollar out of the barren soil, they had to beat it out. These men believed in hard work.

171]

My favorite sheepherder story is an old one, so old that it may be apocryphal, yet it certainly typifies the whole sheep business. It seems that a sheepherder got a gallon of moonshine late one afternoon and took it over to a neighboring camp to help that herder decide to drive the pair of them into town in his Ford. The car-owner finally agreed and the two got into the car and started for town. As they rode, the men passed the jug back and forth. Presently they became so numb that they could almost ignore the tooth-rattling road. But they did hit one wash with such violence that the driver remarked that they had been lucky not to break a spring. His partner agreed and they had another drink, and another, and another. As the Ford's engine purred, the men drank and drank until one of them realized that the light on the horizon wasn't from town. It was the rising sun. They had driven all night.

"But this road's so smooth," one of them wondered, "how could we foller it so long an' never git no place?" The strengthening sun-light revealed the answer: the Ford's back bumper had hung up on the edge of the wash they had hit so violently. The two rear wheels had been suspended in the air and there they had spun all through the night.

XI / THE PLURAL OF ELK

IS ELK

"Some Indian people say, 'elk meat sacred, only for warriors.'"

—UTE INDIAN GAME WARDEN

WHILE WALLACE TABEE WAS GUIDING US THROUGH THE WILD canyons and around the flat-topped buttes of Hill Creek, Fat asked him about some Ute beliefs. "Is it true the Ute people won't eat elk meat?"

"Some won't," said Wallace, "they say elk is only for warriors, because it stops bleeding and heals wounds."

For all his hospitality, Wallace was not particularly anxious to discuss his tribe's beliefs. He changed the subject by shyly telling us that there are no dirty words in the Ute language.

Later in September, when the Utes held an elk hunt on their Hill Creek lands, I met some of them coming out with their game. They were in a small caravan of dusty trucks and pickups. Johnny Chepoose, another Ute game warden, was leading the procession in his tall four-wheel-drive truck, which always reminded me of a belligerent bulldog.

I had set out a STOP sign to check white hunters who had elk-hunting permits on Hill Creek, and Johnny stopped beside my truck. Although his brown eyes were bloodshot and tired-looking, they still flashed with hostility. I asked him how they had done. "Everybody's satisfied. We got most of 'em. We're takin' 'em in now." The last sentence was Johnny's blunt way of saying that he had stopped out of courtesy, not out of obedience to Utah law, and that now he and the other Indians wanted to go home. I waved, and the Ute warden nodded and let in his clutch; the caravan lurched away after him. As it passed, I saw some dusty quarters of elk meat roped to the wooden-stake bodies of the larger trucks. In the backs of the pickups were several brownish elk carcasses, hog-dressed but neither skinned nor quartered. It was a hot afternoon, and I thought those elk should have been cut up to prevent them from souring in their own body heat.

A few of the Indians waved or nodded indifferently as they drove by. They looked weary, and it was a weariness that lacked the jubilation the successful white hunter exudes under similar circumstances. The Utes were not jubilant with their elk, merely resigned, and I heard later that the Indian game wardens had done most of the actual killing. The meat was shared with some of the more destitute tribe members.

The white hunters who had drawn permits for the Ute lands drove out of the buff-colored hills alone or in pairs of vehicles. Very often their pickups were fitted with lacquered aluminum campers, which gleamed expensively despite the coatings of dust. Fat had been out on the hunt, and I found that he had already checked most of them. The hunters, many of them pink from two days of unaccustomed sunshine, were all good-natured but universally tired. In their smart red caps and hunting clothes, they were in sharp, though whiskery, contrast to the dour, brown-faced Utes, who rarely wore special clothes for hunting.

No white, pride-flushed with his elk, dreamed that by killing the animal he had chaffed an ancient Ute belief. To kill an elk in white Utah—even to draw a coveted permit—is hailed as a major accomplishment. The rapacious pioneers slaughtered nearly all the indigenous elk in the first bloody decades of colonization. But that all happened so long ago that few remembered that Utah's present elk herds had grown from animals transplanted from Yellowstone Park in the early 1900s. They are handsome game animals, and only a few fussy biologists lamented the extinction of Utah's native elk.

Each year the Board of Big Game Control authorized the sale of about two thousand elk licenses in the knowledge that this issue would result in the killing of about one thousand elk. This annual cropping kept the herds approximately stable and gave Utah one of the nation's highest elk-hunter-success ratios. The hunting permits were distributed after a public drawing; popular areas were often oversubscribed by forty applications for every permit. Overall, there were about five applications for every permit and people drove in from all over Utah to attend the drawings held at the state capitol. Two hardware and sporting goods stores in Vernal each sent representatives to the drawings. They hurriedly copied the names of permittees in northeastern Utah as they were drawn. Then the unofficial recorders rushed home again in order to have the good, or bad, news ready for customers the next morning. People were called out of bed to be told they had drawn an elk tag. And when Fat and I both drew permits that year, it was announced over the usually circumspect radio network of the police.

The distribution of the official lists of permittees was made almost as quickly. When Fat and I received ours, we began checking them. We looked for names of people who were ineligible because they had applied too soon after receiving their last elk permits (permittees were obliged to wait four years before applying again). We also looked for the names of people who had lost their hunting privileges because of gun accidents. If you shot someone to death while hunting in Utah, you couldn't try again for seven years.

"Looka' here!" Fat said, jabbing a finger at a name on his list. "This one had a permit last year, now she's drawed out on the Indians at Hill Creek." I noticed the permittee's address was in Lynn Nickel's district. "I guess we get an easy pinch?"

"No," Fat hesitated, "we better call the office first, this hunter's got some high-powered friends." Fat called the game department offices in Salt Lake, explained the problem, and suggested that they quietly revoke the permit. The boss "Uh-huh'd" but told Fat to let the matter ride for a couple of days. When the instructions came, they were to honor the permit. It had been decided that since this hunt was on Indian land, the department had only acted as the tribe's agent in issuing the permit; somehow, it could not perform in the same capacity while revoking it. So the permittee got an elk, and I got a lesson in pissing backward.

I forgot my sense of outrage when I started setting up our elk camp. A few days before the season opened, I towed our clumsy green house trailer up onto a bare ridge near the Vernal-Manila highway. I established the Pig in a swale where she would be out of the wind and unloaded some bales of hay nearby. I put a pot of coffee on the trailer's stove, and we were open for business.

The interior of the trailer had been built according to game department specifications. Single bunks were double-decked at the rear, on either side of a narrow aisle. Forward of the bunks on one side, a gas stove and sink had been set into a small counter. Above and below them were drawers and cupboards. Across from the stove was a tiny clothes closet, and beside that a very efficient butane furnace. This furnace had been cleverly installed directly under the built-in ice chest. When the furnace was lit, it could reduce a fifty-pound block of ice to the size of a tennis ball in a single night. All our perishables had to be stored in boxes under the trailer.

The trailer's door was next to the ice box, and in front of that, extending across the front of the trailer, was a folding table with wide seats on either side. This could be made up into a fifth bed if someone from the main office dropped in and we didn't want to put up with him for more than one night. Over the table was a gas-fueled lamp. It generated sufficient light to read the pips on a playing card, if not the print in a book. On the walls above each seat someone had pasted colored photographs of glandularly gifted girls.

One of the department's construction crew came into the trailer and, on seeing the busty reproductions, exclaimed, "Gawd! A set a' tits like that sure makes a feller's mouth water!"

This same man, who had twinkling blue eyes and apple-red cheeks, was a wonderful blend of simple goodness and elemental vice. In another camp he had shared some excellent home-canned fruit and vegetables with me when my own larder was down to Vienna sausage and stale soda crackers.

Before joining the game department, this man had owned a farm. One Saturday night, while he was attending a dance at a neighbor's, he was called out by his excited friends to see a fierce orange glow on the dark horizon. "Isn't that your barn burning?" someone asked. It obviously was, and more obviously the flames were already beyond control. My friend flapped his big palms against his rump. "Jesus Christ, fellers," he exclaimed, "ain't that a purty fire!" Then he went back inside and resumed the dance.

Two nights before the elk season opened, I sat alone in the trailer, trying to read in the poor light. A few anticipating hunters had stopped by to ask a question or get directions, but the bulk of them were still in their towns. Nearly all of the human momentum that explodes on the opening morning of a hunting season develops during the single day and night preceding it. The hissing lamp provided all the heat I needed, for it was a warm night after a hot, Indian-summer day. Despite the calendar, it did not feel like hunting season. Nevertheless, I couldn't help being excited because this year I had an elk license. It was restricted to the taking of a bull, but that didn't matter—my hopes all along were for a bull.

I suppose that my desires were similar to those of most other permittees; we wanted to kill an elk primarily because it was a big animal. Elk are usually better eating than deer, and the antlers of mature bulls dwarf those of buck deer, but the down-deep thing about elk is their size.

Bob Jensen once told me how strong this desire can become— at least in one fellow. He had drawn an elk permit and hunted diligently through the season without getting the animal. His failure dogged him all that fall and into the winter. Then, as he was driving along a mountain highway, he saw a herd of elk that winter snows had driven down near the highway. He rushed home, got his rifle, and rushed back to where he had seen the elk. They were still there. And in plain view of several passersby the frustrated hunter finally got his elk. Naturally, he was reported and Bob arrested him and confiscated the elk. That and a stiff fine were only transient inconveniences to the hunter; he had finally killed his elk!

When I was a boy in Oregon, we regarded an elk hunt as just one step short of an African safari. In short, it was glory. Yet the first elk I tasted were illegally killed. My father and Augie Diehl had accidentaly killed a young bull elk while hunting deer. They dressed the carcass and, on the advice of an accomodating rancher, hung it in his barn. When the elk season opened a few days later, the rancher tagged the carcass and brought it into town. In time a thick chunk of the illegal elk's sirloin arrived at our house, where my parents cut it into steaks. Delicious!

The next elk I ate was also illegal meat, killed on Clay Paulhamus's stump ranch by gyppo loggers who had ambushed a herd of Roosevelt elk in a swamp. We dined on the illegal meat all summer, feeling, as I recall, a little smug and as if the venison were our due for "raising it." Since then, the only trouble I have found with the justification of "needing the meat" is that there are more people who profess this need than there are game animals to fill it.

There were a lot of elk on Clay's ranch at that time. One afternoon I stepped out of the brush and into a clearing the loggers had made for their spar tree and a cold-deck of logs. All that was gone and in its place were some fifteen cow elk with their calves. The calves were brownish with white spots. Their mothers were tan, with necks and lower legs of very dark brown, and they were all suddenly staring at me. The calves couldn't seem to understand the sudden tension and looked around with innocent curiosity. The cows made queer little barking sounds and wagged their stub tails nervously. Clay had warned me against interfering with a cow and her calf, so I checked the load in my rifle—bugger might charge, you know. The metallic click frightened the elk, and with a whirling leap they were off on a high-headed lope that the little calves matched as best they could.

On the average, the Roosevelt elk seemed darker in color than the Rocky Mountain variety I had seen in eastern Oregon and Utah. Biologists say the former animals are larger than those from the intermountain west, although the bulls' antlers must be smaller. I never saw a spread from the rain forests that were nearly so awsome as those worn by bull elk in the Rockies. The calves of both varieties are raw-boned little rascals that, while lacking the cuddly appeal of fawn deer, possess an awkward innocence that is uniquely charming.

One day in early fall, I was walking down a mountain ridge when I saw a peculiar round object suddenly appear on the crest of the next ridge. I sat down to watch. The distant, dark ball extended itself until I realized that what I had seen was the top of a cow elk's head. She came on across the brow of the ridge, moving cautiously along a game trail. Following her were her calf and a yearling heifer. The cow led them along the trail until she was within two hundred yeards of me. Then she stopped. She began studying me in that intently curious yet motionless way elk have of looking at things they do not recognize. The cow stared and stared, paying no attention to her calf as it marched around her flanks and took a few exploratory pulls at her udder. He was behaving exactly as a child does when he is bored with his parents' visiting and wants to go home. The heifer elk offered him no comfort. She seemed to be backing the cow's "point," although she had apparently not sensed my presence. The calf walked with obviously growing impatience back and forth between the two females. When neither paid him the slightest attention, he all but shrugged and then flopped down in the trail. He did not get up again until his mother finished her examination and walked on down the trail.

In addition to their coughing barks, bleats, and the stentorian whistles of the bulls in fall, elk have a natural bent for standing on their hind legs. I have often seen two cows rise and paw at each other like inept boxers. And on one occasion a cow that seemed unable to determine what I was walked up very close to me in a meadow. During her approach she hesitated several times and stood on her hind legs as if to see or smell me from another angle. When she at last recognized what I was, she reared on her haunches like a wild Arabian mare and in two great leaps reached the timber.

The older bulls seem to be rather grumpy and take themselves very seriously, although when they are in herds they almost always follow the marching orders of an old cow. At other seasons, the bulls are extremely secretive and spend much time alone or in bachelor parties. A few times I have spotted them spying on me from heavy cover with all the shyness of deer. At other times, however, the bulls with half-grown, velveted antlers have fearlessly disputed a roadway with me—and won.

Another time, in early fall, I saw a big bull walk out on the edge of a bluff almost a mile away. He whistled fiercely. I moved, and the bull must have seen me, for he wheeled and went pacing up the ridge. I was below him in an old burn and sat down to see what would happen. As he went up the ridge the bull whistled repeatedly, and then he turned off the ridge and started down in my direction. The calls and the snapping of twigs and vigorous rustling of bear-berries increased until the bull burst out of some second growth to stand on a knoll above me. He was about thirty yards away. When he whistled again the blast sent a prickle of apprehension along my spine. But he was so magnificently beautiful that I could not be really afraid. He swung his great, reaching antlers, and it was like watching a forest move. The bull was so near that he dominated the deep-blue sky behind him. Sitting there and looking up at that wild stag with his dark mane and sun-splashed antlers, I was not at all sure which of us was the nobler animal. The bull bugled another exultant challenge. Then, after his claim to superiority went unchallenged, he abruptly wheeled and went striding noisily off across the burn, whistling and whistling.

In the green trailer, that evening, the glowing gaslight hissed softly and lured minute flying insects to incineration in its hot allure. Their corpses plummeted down to add specks of annoying punctuation to my book or to float lifelessly on the coffee in my cup. Eventually, the annoying meek inherited that little part of the earth; I shut my book, dumped the coffee into the sink, and turned off the lamp. Before its last vapors burned away, I had undressed and slipped into my sleeping bag. Later I remember hearing the Pig stir outside and I pulled the cover of my sleeping bag up around my neck.

It had gotten cold in the night. The next morning was what Clay Paulhamus used to call "jumping weather." You jumped out of bed, jumped to the stove and lit a fire under the coffee pot, then jumped back into bed again. To the north, out the tiny window by my bunk, I could see that the sky was leaden, and above the camp wind-washed sprays of clouds faded the blue sky. Reluctantly, I made the final jumps of morning, out of bed, into my long under-wear, and then into pants and boots. Once that part is done, putting on a shirt can be an almost languid process.

While the coffee perked, I went out and fed the Pig. The cold that had come in the night had fluffed and softened her thick coat, and there was a frosty rime on the water bucket beside the trailer door.

Fat drove up as I was finishing my breakfast dishes. He swung his bedroll through the door, untied the rope around it, and unrolled the sleeping bag on one of the bunks. Then he tossed his hat on the bunk above, helped himself to a cup of coffee, sat down at the table, and lit a cigarette. He had moved in for the season.

I told Fat that I wanted to ride over the country for a last look around, and he agreed to man the trailer while I was gone. In addition to scouting for elk, I was "showing the flag" to any season jumpers.

Although I was wearing a hip-length down coat and leather chaps, the wind penetrated easily through all my layers of clothing as I rode across open, sagebrush swales between the patches of aspen. There were no signs of game in the open and only a doe deer and two big-eyed fawns moved in all the clumps of aspen that I touched in the first hours of riding. Wind makes big game nervous, and I knew I would have to ride higher, to where the aspen blended into the deep green of the conifers, if I were to see any game.

Yellowed aspen leaves broke off their frantic trembling and came spinning down to lie on the earth like gold pieces. In the next few days countless millions more leaves would blaze yellow and then come whirling away to accumulate in rustling drifts under the trees. If the leaves were wetted by rain or snow, they would blacken and load the air with a musty odor. Today it felt like hunting season.

In the groves the wind rattled dead brances and set one leaning tree sawing eerily against an upright companion. I followed a game trail into a tiny meadow hidden by pines and aspen. The elk were there. They jumped from their beds and went clattering away. When you jump a deer he goes *thump*, but elk clatter; logs bump, twigs pop, and branches snap with the ring of breaking steel pins. It is a little frightening. The Pig had stopped when the commotion began, and as I turned to ride on I noticed her ears were forward, intent. Over them I saw that one elk had not fled; a spike bull was standing between two trees and watching me. I touched the mare, and she moved cautiously toward the elk until we were only feet away. He was a yearling with thin, twig-like antlers that were a travesty on the beams he might someday grow. About his face was a fat fullness that gave him a gentle expression, which was increased by the limpid brown of his eyes. I was so near the elk that I could see his long, soft eyelashes. I found deep satisfaction in seeing that elk's eyelashes; it was as though he had taken me into his confidence and shared a secret that I was too thick to fully understand.

"If you gawk like this tomorrow, you'll be dead." When I spoke, the bull's eyes widened and he plunged away into the timber.

As I rode out of each sheltering copse, the wind beat at me with rising ferocity. Snow began to fall but the driving wind never let it touch the ground. The big flakes plastered themselves wetly against my windward side. Little icicles grew on the mare's fetlocks, and there was mush ice where water had dribbled off my chaps and collected around my stirrups.

The Pig began making little grunting complaints and shook her head angrily if any of my reined directions weren't toward camp. When we came to a line fence, I had to ride down it until I reached a road and gate. After I had opened the gate, led the mare through, then began to remount, the Pig spun impatiently and catapulted me into the saddle. Before I could arrange the reins in my hand, she was trotting toward camp. I slowed her to a more comfortable walk, and turned my face away from the freezing wind and its volleys of snow. The cold dominated my few thoughts, which concerned getting inside that warm trailer, and so I was startled by a pickup truck that loomed suddenly in the road ahead. It was Av

Kay's. He grinned at my frozen appearance and rolled down his window when he stopped beside me. He said he was going over to his cabin to get it ready for some elk-hunting guests.

"How about a drink?" he asked, displaying a bottle of Scotch. Normally I regard scotch whisky as one degree tastier than Absorbine, Jr. But this day it was warm ambrosia running down my last unfrozen pipe. When my toes began feeling warm again, I lowered the bottle and passed it back to the grinning Av. No battlefield transfusion was more efficacious. When Av drove on and I swung into the saddle again, the warmth I exuded must have radiated into the mare, for she steadied into a reaching, comfortable walk that quickly had us back in camp.

I tied the mare in the lee of the horse trailer and unsaddled. After currying her, I cinched on a warm horse blanket and finally, according to the Pig's actions, gave her the only thing in the world that she truly loved, a thick flake of hay.

A sedan was parked beside the trailer, and I supposed that Fat was entertaining hunters. Unless there were too many, we were generally good for a cup of coffee and maybe a cookie or two. People we knew who "worked on the mountain" might even find a stick in their coffee on a cold day like this.

In the trailer I found Fat surrounded by a grinning young woman with a knowing look in her eyes. She was dressed in western-style clothes—fringed leather coat and pants so tight that when she walked it looked "like two pigs fightin' under a blanket." On her earlobes were fastened dangling golden earrings. She also had an elk permit—and a father who watched her antics from behind his coffee cup. Between the two of them, they were trying to get Fat to tell them exactly where to find an elk next morning.

We suggested some places, and as the girl prepared to leave she said, unoriginally, "Well, you boys git one tied up for me an' I'll be up to git it." It seemed to me that every other hunter said this.

Elk hunters were specifically told that we could not offer them guide service. What's more, many of us were not elk-hunting

[184

experts, because we had no better luck drawing permits than anyone else. Of course, Fat could predict as well as anyone else where elk might be found. He could also imitate, and sometimes call in bull elk with his elk whistle. Nevertheless, I certainly admitted to being an amateur and I went at my first elk season as if it were a kind of over-the-weight-deer hunt.

Some time later, after hunting elk for several years in Wyoming, I began to discover some of the nuances involved in hunting the big deer. One of the most important is to be able to get the elk to camp once you've shot it. One fall I killed a very large bull and, after I had dressed and quartered it, went to a professional outfitter's camp to rent a packhorse. The road into camp was a smear of rutted muck and on the grades there was accelerated erosion. No one was in the camp when I arrived, save a big dog chained to the pole at the entrance of the large cooking and dining tent. Dozens of bright cellophane candy wrappers lay all around the dog, and I guessed hunters had been whiling away their camp time by tossing candy to the dog.

Beside the dining tent were three, smaller wall tents. Inside each was a rusty little airtight heating stove and a log that lay on the ground across the width of the tent. This log kept the straw that had been dumped on the ground from being scattered to the front of the tent. On top of the straw were sleeping bags, wadded and twisted like huge green worms. There was no other furniture in the guest tents. The hunters had left the tent flaps untied and the wind had certainly blown dirt into their sleeping bags. Plastic sheeting had been spread over a couple of tents as a hasty stopgap against leaks. Across from this rather dreary scene was the outfitter's camp trailer. He seemed to live more comfortably than his guests. Beyond the trailer, and across a tiny spring that had been churned to lifeless mud by innumerable horses' hooves, was a dirty and sagging old wall tent that probably sheltered the camp's employees.

In front of the tent row, mounted on a small trailer, was a war-surplus electric genertaor. The electric wires leading from it were patched with friction tape and carelessly strung from scarred tree trunks to tent poles, from whence they snaked into the various tents' interiors. Apart from the dining tent and the outfitter's trailer, the whole camp appeared to sag or lean in 360 different directions. Empty beer and pop cans were scattered lavishly under the trees. And there was mud everywhere, thoroughly peppered with bits of litter.

I walked out behind the tents to appraise the horses in the corral. They had been well fed. That was evident both from the condition of the animals and the knee-deep state of the ground inside the corral. Dumped carelessly here and there on the ground were pack and riding saddles. The canvas pack bags were caked with the blood of countless deer and elk. It had apparently never occurred to anyone to scrub them. The outfitter had still not returned when I finished looking at the horses, so I left a note stating my requirements and promising to return early that evening.

When I did return, the outfitter wasn't there but my note was gone and I assumed it had been received. I began waiting. In about a half-hour two red-clad hunters rode in, each leading a saddle horse. The men were unshaven and their once-dashing new hunting clothes looked as though they had been slept in for a week. The two hunters steered their mounts into the vicinity of the corrals, dismounted, and jerked their gun scabbards off the saddles. They left the horses standing there and walked back to the tent row.

While they were fixing themselves a drink, a mud-splattered pickup came howling and slewing up the camp road. When it stopped, four hunters tumbled over its tailgate. I noticed that they had been riding on top of some elk quarters.

The outfitter flung open the pickup's door and swung stiffly out from under the wheel. He was a lean, long-faced westerner, with a big brown Stetson shoved far back on his head. A wide crimson band had been added to the hat's crown. The outfitter wore a tight, western-cut shirt, cowboy boots, and Levis that seemed to suit his slim hips. But he marred his tonsorial effect by

[186

walking bent over, the way Groucho Marx used to do in the movies.

"You look tired," I said, hurrying to catch him before he went into his trailer.

He threw me a baleful look. "I'm always tired."

"I left a note, I want to rent a pack horse."

The outfitter veered away from his trailer and duckwalked into the dining tent. "What do you want it for?"

I explained that I had seen his sign advertising horses for rent and that I wanted one to pack out an elk.

The outfitter didn't answer but went to a cookstove at the rear of the tent. On its top there was a pan of water in which a slab of blackened liver seemed to be soaking. The outfitter took this repulsive object from the water and began rubbing it over his big hands. It undoubtedly was the filthiest washcloth in the state. "That's too damn much work for one horse," he said.

I assumed that this was the point at which I was about to get the business. I began watching the man to see how he would do it. There had been no perceptible change in the cleanliness of his hands, but he dropped the rag back into the pan and trudged over to the dining table. He sat down on it and began half-heartedly digging dirt from under his fingernails. I noticed that some of this material was falling on the table. "Nooo," he decided, "to get that elk out you'd have to take two pack horses and a guide." He gave me a superior look, and then let a long, plopping fart.

If I was not his favorite person, he could rest assured that neither was he mine. But my elk had to be moved, and I agreed to his price for four horses and a guide. (The guide would not hike to where the elk lay, and therefore I would have to hire a saddle horse to keep up with him.) "A'course," said the outfitter, "I don't know if the guides will want to go. And I got a new bunch a' hunters comin' in tomorrow, and they might wanta hunt. I'd need all my horses then. You come back here about nine tomorrow morning and I'll letcha know."

Needless to say, I did not go back. Delos Sanderson, my neighbor and generous friend, lent me a saddle horse and half of his big work team. We fitted them with pack saddles, and my friend Mel Hoopes helped me pack out the elk.

Some game warders are even more helpful than many guides and outfitters. Fat brought an old and ailing farmer to our trailer soon after the elk season opened. The old man resembled Sir C. Aubrey Smith as he would have looked after farming in Utah for fifty years. For many of those years the farmer had applied for an elk permit, and now, on the heels of a major operation, he had finally drawn one. Despite his condition, the old boy was bound to go, so his wife packed special meals for him and swathed him in the warmest of under- and outerwear. He couldn't walk a hundred yards, so each morning Fat loaded him into the jeep and drove him to places where a lot of men couldn't have walked. Each night the jeep returned with some appurtenance either bashed in or ripped off. First to go, just as Fat had predicted, was the flimsy spare-tire mount. Then the side-view mirror disappeared, followed quickly by both running boards and the tow-bar latch. All that came to replace these things were a myriad of paint scratches and a rip in the canvas top. I began to wonder if the jeep could outlast the old man, who actually seemed to be thriving. He had thrown over his diet for fried camp fare, and he had begun sleeping at night. When he got up in the morning he dutifully drank his milk, and then tied into a plateful of greasy eggs and spicy ham. One night, after a long day of jeep jouncing, he came lumbering into the trailer's gaslit interior wearing a grin that outshone the lamp. Fat and I hung his elk that night, and the next morning packed it and him into a pickup and bundled him off home. He died a few weeks later—which just goes to show you what home can do for a fellow.

The elk season was open for sixteen days, but after the first week most of the hunters had either bagged their elk or wearied of the effort and gone. Fat came in one morning with a good-sized bull that he had killed, dressed, and somehow loaded into his pickup by himself. After he ate breakfast and happily described how he'd

[188

bagged the animal with one shot from his new .243, I helped him hang, skin, and quarter the carcass. But I couldn't help feeling a little jealous, for I had been out every day and had yet to even see a bull.

Then, one morning before sunrise, I spotted a big bull on a hillside. In the poor light, it seemed far off, and I began an elaborate stalk, which ended with the bull's disappearance just when I thought he should be looming in my gunsights.

My mother and father were coming to Vernal for a long-awaited visit before the elk season ended. Once they arrived, I would not have much time for hunting. Fat commiserated, and on a Sunday morning shortly before my family was due he suggested that we ride out together and look for my elk. It was a pleasant morning, fairly warm now that the storm and cold of the opening days had gone. We looked around in some aspen-shrouded glades on the slopes of Diamond Mountain, but no game appeared. I was getting a case of the "what-did-I-do-to-deserve-such-rotten-luck?" blues, and I was about to add "after-all-this-work" to my lament when we spotted the ears and back of a cow elk loping along just below the next rise. I jumped from the truck and ran ahead a few steps to where I could see a whole band of cows and calves all running ahead of a fine bull elk.

Fat said, "There's your bull."

I was that sure myself. The elk was rocking along about a hundred and twenty-five yards away. He must have stood nearly five feet at the shoulder and weighed almost seven hundred pounds. I swung the rifle on him and pulled the trigger. Nothing happened. I had forgotten to release the safety. I hurriedly pushed it off and banged away the contents of the magazine. I walked back to where Fat was waiting. He said, "For a minute there, I thought you was going to git him."

He said it more to cheer than to chide me. But after all those years of hoping and the weeks and days of anticipation and effort, my failure left me with an enormous sense of loss and emptiness.

It still rode with me two hours later as I drove through Steinaker Draw, just north of Vernal. My folks had sent a message via the police radio-dispatcher, and I was on my way to meet them.

In a little waste area outside of town, I notiched a parked car with a man standing beside it. As I came nearer, I was pleased to see that the man was my father. Mother was sitting in the car, but neither of them was looking for me. They were intent upon a spike-tailed little black puppy that was sniffing a bush.

XII / MY DOG JILL

"Your father cried when he had to have
Gunner put to sleep."

—MY MOTHER

MY FATHER WAS NEVER A DOG LOVER. IN FACT, HE WAS SOME-what afraid of them, although his aversion didn't keep him from owning a long series of retrievers. Among all the breeds, they were his favorites. The worst of them were at least good companions, while the best were enthusiastic professors of bird hunting.

The Labrador he drove a thousand miles to deliver in Vernal came from Carnation Farms, proving grounds for fancy dogs and Friskies dog food. Her pedigree was impeccable and her purchase price had equaled the redoubtable Pig's. And, like an American tourist venturing abroad with his sacred supply of pills and portions, the puppy arrived with bags of scientifically balanced dog food. (It filled her with gas, so I changed to the plebian "Parooney" in the old checkerboard bag.) There was also a list of the shots she'd had and those she would need to get from the local vet. This young man had to be approached respectfully, for he had a very proud mother, and if you wanted an appointment you had better ask for "the Doctor."

Along with the pup's pedigree, I received a copy of *Training Your Retriever*, a champion-endorsed training whistle, and two small boat fenders, to be used as retrieving dummies. The pup was ignorant of all her trappings, and she reminded me of the rich kid meeting the hoodlums in *Dead End*. Because, heretofore in Uintah County, most dogs could be considered well off if they were alone when they found a dead sheep—and rich if the carcass weren't laced with poison.

After our meeting on the outskirts of Vernal, I loaded my curious pup into the pickup's cab and led the way to the old house that squatted over my basement apartment. Mother began picking up and cleaning it as soon as she came down the creaking stairs. The door had no lock, and opened into a dark hallway that led to the pink-walled living room. Under the pervading glare of the ceiling's unshaded light fixture, the place resembled a sitting room furnished by the eccentric, acquisitive Collier Brothers. All along one wall were stacked cartons of college lecture-notes, plus bales of raw data that eventually went into my master's thesis. None of it had been dusted in over a year.

Except for a pine do-it-yourself bookcase, all the remaining furniture was rented; pieces of dark, splitting veneer reflected in a wavy, yellowed mirror. I tried to overcome my parents' protests by explaining, "It's all right. I only sleep here."

"It may be all right for you," said my father, "but I'm not sure I want to leave that pup here. Where's she going to sleep?"

My bedroom was pinched in behind the furnace room on the far side of the basement. I explained that the pup could sleep in the big cardboard carton beside by bed. Later, she preferred bedding on the pile of dirty laundry in the closet, but she did sleep in the box that first night. I remember how the somewhat aloof little twirp curled up in the cereal box with a rubber mouse between her paws. The last thing I heard before falling asleep was the toy's plaintive squeaks. In the morning nothing remained of it but some shards of rubber and the metal squeaker.

The puppy was standing in her box when I awoke the next morning. I am sure it was the intensity of her stare that had awakened me in the first place. When I reached out and sleepily stroked her head, she immediately sprang from the box and began sniffing enthusiastically around the room. "Wait a minute!" I jumped up, threw on my clothes, and rushed her outside to the parking strip.

After the pup was emptied, then refilled with Friskies, I met my folks for breakfast at Fat Belcher's western-style restaurant. After I had assured them that the pup had spent a comfortable first night, they asked if I had chosen a name. When I said I hadn't, Mother suggested Jill. It was a good dog's name, short and distinct, and in our family, it had already been worn with honor by a sweet Golden Retriever now many years dead.

Old Jill had come into our home as a result of my wish for a big dog and my father's hopes for one that could retrieve ducks and geese, set pheasants, flush quail, and, very important, not cost too much. The dog remained an amorphous notion until we met a man named Snell. He was a friendly chap who, over his store counter, affirmed that such all-purpose dogs truly did exist; they were called Golden Retrievers, and he just happened to raise them. A Golden, we learned in the next minutes, was the delightsome issue of an old cross between a bloodhound and a Russian tracker. Mr. Snell filled us with tales of the Golden's vigor and sagacity, and just as we left gave us his card with a little map drawn on the back.

My father used it to find the field-trial grounds the following Saturday. We had also found a new world of leather-faced trousers, jodhpurs, bird-shooter boots, tweed, down, or deerskin coats, and snapbrim hats with badges in their bands. It was a land of whiskey in leather-covered flasks and martinis poured from steel vacuum bottles. Mr. Snell was there with several of his shiny dogs, and while I stroked their lustrous coats he told my father, "Field trials are a poor man's horse racing." After pricing the dogs, their training costs, and numerous accouterments, my father snorted, "What d'you mean 'poor man's' horse racing?"

When the dogs began going to the line they immediately broke down a lot of our sales resistance. There were big, rough Chesapeakes that could stand any weather that a man or duck could. More stubborn and bellicose than the other retrieving breeds, the Chesapeakes were also better-equipped physically for lugging in ten-pound geese. Nevertheless, they were outnumbered by the surging black Labradors who struck the water with the speed and determination of aerial torpedoes. The Labs had style, and they consistently won the prizes. Some people confuse the yellow Labrador with a Golden Retriever. But the Golden has longer, finer fur than the Lab, and I have always felt the Goldens were a better choice for the man who wanted a yellow dog. The Golden has a sweet nature, a soft mouth (they will retrieve a raw egg without cracking the shell), and hunts upland birds as well as waterfowl.

We watched almost in disbelief that day as representatives of all these breeds completed retrieves of up to a mile. In some events the dogs were not even allowed to see the birds fall. To complete these blind retrieves, the dogs were given a line of direction by their handlers and all further directions were by whistle-punctuated hand signals. Some of the dogs stopped in mid-lake, rose up, and looked back for more complete direction. When they got them, they churned ahead to find the duck. They retrieved the pinioned birds unharmed, with a flourish and flick of the tail. In the uplands, game-farm pheasants were shot and the dogs brought them in easily and quickly. Generally, two birds were killed for each dog, and he was judged on his memory of the lie, style, and speed. When the day ended, we would have been delighted to claim the last-place competitor for our own. The dogs were wonders and we were on our way to owning one.

Between trials and visits with Mr. Snell, my father sent me to study dog books in the library. Simultaneously, he was sending inquiries, laced with library-acquired expertise about shots, papers, worming, and accepted shipping methods, to breeders of Golden Retrievers. These breeders ranged from crusty railroad magnates to dirt farmers who bred dogs on the side down to obvious crooks who should never have been allowed to raise dogs at all.

Letters began arriving from glorious, virile-sounding kennels with pictures of magnificent dogs and one-hundred-year-old oaks on their letterheads. They offered "started" dogs, untrained yearlings, and forlorn old pelters that were described as "experienced." None had the pup we sought at the price my father could afford.

While waiting for that, I thumbed through *Dog World* and read all the Judy books on dog raising and care. I learned to identify every breed the American Kennel Club recognized, but I began to feel that I would never have one. Then a bright yellow letter with a purple representation of a Golden Retriever arrived from South Dakota. It was from the Larson Farm Kennels and Mr. Larson, in his huge, sprawling hand, wrote that he had a female pup for fifty dollars. He enclosed a sample pedigree, which was good though not outstanding.

My father has always been prudent with his money and he weighed the purchase of this pup against a young started dog from a glib-sounding kennel owner. I wanted a puppy, and finally Mr. Larson got our order. But the pup didn't arrive. Instead, there was another yellow letter—our pup was sick. He wrote, "The pup's head swole up as big as a watermelon then all the hair come off." Mr. Larson offered either a refund or to keep the pup until he was sure it had fully recovered. My father agreed to wait.

We waited and waited. The summer wore on and the copies of *Dog World* in my room grew into a sizable stack. When there seemed no hope at all, the express man called. "Got a dog for ya." My father was working, so mother and I went after the pup. Getting a new puppy more than makes up for learning the truth about Santa Claus—in fact, getting a new pup can make up for a lot of worldly lacks in an adult life. At the freight depot I looked along the loading dock until I saw a small, slatted crate. I hurried to it and, reaching through the rough slats, stroked the woebegone creature hunched inside. Her matted tail twitched tentatively in a sodden, smelly mass that had once been straw. I patted her some more and talked to her, and she moved the few inches nearer that the crate permitted. When she moved some well-flattened droppings were revealed. I wasn't sure whether the dog smelled like them or if they smelled like the dog.

After the papers had been signed and the shipping bill paid, the expressman shrugged us into custody of the dog. He did this with the same show of relief his colleagues displayed when handing over my father's malodorous geese. The crate was to be returned to South Dakota, so I reached through its slats and fastened a new collar and leash on the pup before we released her. As we walked to the car she stopped, wagged her tail apologetically, and then squatted. The water spread out from around her until I was holding the leash at arm's length to avoid soaking my shoes. A man passed by and grinned derisively.

My Dog Jill

When my father came home and saw this self-effacing, gangly pup with the tiny bald spot on the end of her muzzle, he was visibly disappointed. He had inspection privileges, and his first inclination was to ship her back to Mr. Larson's Farm Kennels. To me, she was beautiful; why, her name, Jill, had been ready and waiting even before we bought her collar, leash, and feeding pan. Only a few pups are attractive at six months, and Jill was not one of them. She had a pointy, hound head and accentuated it by habitually looking down. But she could retrieve, and I threw a tennis ball down the lawn to prove it. She went bounding after and returned it to my hand with the docile eagerness that was to become her life-style. My father tried her on another retrieve and she easily accomplished that and several more. In his mind's eye my father was transforming the ball into a broken-winged, running pheasant. "Do you really like her?" he asked. "Sure!" I said with a big, kid grin, and Jill was home.

She was never a handsome dog, but she was so good and so eager to please us that we couldn't help loving her. A hard word was all the punishment she ever needed on those rare occasions when she needed punishing at all. Training her was proof that the dog is often wiser than its master, because we made every conceivable mistake. We even made her gun-shy, but Jill hung on, to eventually become a good all-around bird dog.

We took her good manners for granted. Even when she was in season, the attendant problems were not so much with her as they were with the incessantly urinating dogs that slunk around the house. During one of these sessions, my mother had to go to the store. A number of dogs were hanging around, so mother, to be safe, decided to take Jill with her on a leash. Outside the store she told Jill, "Sit. Now you stay." Jill sat and mother went into the store. A few minutes later she looked out to see our trustworthy Jill standing in the middle of the street, being mounted by one of the local mutts. Mother rushed out, drove off the dog, and reeled in her straying bitch. "Why Jill," she said, "I told you to sit!"

This new, black Jill disobeyed with far more verve than her

predecessor ever had. But she made up for it by adding spark to everything she did. She learned to go swimming with a happy splash. She bounded up the stairs on the way out in the morning and sashayed down them eagerly again at night. Jill loved to play in the meadows around Stewart Lake, and when she was a safe distance off I fired my .22 revolver. In only a few days she had accepted the shotgun's roar, and regarded it as another part of the fun. She sat fascinated in the front seat of the pickup while I shot a deer. Uintah County, if not the world, became her oyster.

Her home, for terribly long hours, was the cab of the pickup. She slept and played there, and to pass the time chewed up anything I left on the seat or dashboard. I cashed paychecks with tooth marks in them, I puzzled over half-eaten letters from girl friends, despaired of ever repairing my gummy, ruined revolver holster. One day I returned to the truck to find several brass shotshell bases lying on the seat. I had carelessly left some live shells in the truck and in minutes Jill had eaten them, lead shot, powder, and wads. Another time I missed four big fishing sinkers that I used to anchor duck decoys. I couldn't believe a dog would eat more than one of the thumb-sized weights, and assumed they had been lost. Then, driving one day, Jill put her head into my lap in a way that I mistook for canine affection. Suddenly she shuddered convulsively and four sinkers were deposited in my lap, along with some much less savory material.

Despite her blue blood and diet-kitchen meals, Jill was a glutton. She doted on stuff the local dogs spurned, and I dreaded the time when she might find a poisoned bait.

One morning I met Fat for coffee and was puzzled by his distracted manner. He finally told me, "Poke got a magpie bait." Fat's bird dog had eaten a bait made from a chunk of pork belly that had been loaded with strychnine. At the onset of cold weather these poisonous morsels were nailed to the tops of fence posts. They killed the first magpie to peck at them, but all the squawking onlookers took the hint and thereafter avoided the baits. Fat told me his dog had come staggering home and collapsed, twitching, in the yard. "I split her tail an' she's still alive, so maybe she'll git better."

Splitting a dog's tail, Fat explained, means slitting the skin over the tailbone until blood flows freely. The poison-laden blood thus escaped and the dog recovered. I withheld comment; Fat had done what he thought best, and at that late hour there was no point in telling him about emetics and veterinarians. But, in spite of my misgivings, Poke recovered.

Like Poke, Jill was a short-haired dog and didn't come out of the fields covered with burrs and beggar ticks. A big cockle burr will stick to a Lab's coat, but the dog can usually nip it out and toss it away himself. So when Jill acquired some big burrs during a walk, I stopped to give her time to nip them out of her fur. She grabbed the burrs quickly enough, but instead of flipping them away, she ate them! Before I could reach her, the burrs were caught in her throat. The vomiting she attempted offered no relief and I could not reach far enough down her throat to get the burrs. So I hurried the retching, miserable pup to the truck and drove to a country store, where I bought a tin of lard and a loaf of soft bread. I coated the slices with lard and fed them to the still gluttonous pup. She carefully gulped them down, and eventually the burrs were carried on down into her stomach. A day later Jill had forgotten her ordeal, though she never again ate burrs.

This happened during the few days of relative calm between the close of elk season and the opening of deer season. I used the days to bait chukars out of, of all places, a potato patch, and to make a final assault on some beaver dams that were flooding private property. But the evenings were mostly my own, and I spent them at home. After feeding myself and the dog, I would drop into the old rocker with the new tooth marks on its arms and try to catch up with deliveries from the Book-of-the-Month Club. It was little use, because Jill immediately began thrusting her toys into my lap, then snatching them away again. If that didn't get noticed, she would nibble along my shirt-sleeve. Sooner or later she would get a pinch of me between her teeth, and that always provoked my undivided attention. I would get down on the thread-bare carpet and play with her until she was tired and ready for sleep.

But despite this and our lengthening, close association, I had always felt a certain reserve in Jill's manner. I was reasonably sure she would fall in with the first dog thief who came along with a biscuit. Then, one evening, Jill suddenly came over to my chair and put her head on my knee. She was a wiggler, and I assumed that once I had given her head a pat she would toss it and begin on another tack for more attention. But this time Jill didn't move. She kept her head on my knee and looked steadily into my face. "Are you my dog now, Jill?" I asked. She still didn't move and I stroked her head for a long time. Finally she curled up at my feet, and I never again sensed the peculiar reserve in her manner. Much later I decided that this act was what students of animal behavior call "imprinting." It is a strange yet warming experience that will bond you to your dog as tightly as he attaches himself to you.

That fall, as I sat with my books and dog, listening to the radio's screech, I decided to buy one of the new stereo-record players. Next evening I walked over to the furniture store (the proprietor also embalmed and provided coffins for his less ambulatory patrons) and bought a portable stereo set. To seal the bargain, the store-keeper threw in a recording of Strauss waltzes. At home I put the record on the machine, and as the orchestra loped into the *Emperor Waltz*, Jill burst into howling accompaniment. She made an eerie *wuuuu-ing* sound that rose and fell independently of the music. When the last grand notes died away, Jill lowered her up-turned muzzle and rather sheepishly resumed her normal expression. *Vienna Blood* and one or two others waltzed away unnoticed into the ether, and then the conductor went plunging into *Tales from the Vienna Woods* and Jill plunged in after him. It was nearly ten years before she let me hear that selection without her accompaniment.

The minister who lived upstairs never objected to Jill's caco-phanous howls. He frequently imported "Little Jimmy, the Sing-ing Cowboy Evangelist" to perk up his revivals, and must have been inured to howling. Nevertheless, I tried to lift the stereo's needle before they reached the howl-inspiring cuts on the Strauss record. The other upstairs tenants didn't seem as accepting as the preacher, and I didn't want them complaining to the landlord about the dog. One evening, however, the *Emperor Waltz* went spinning under the needle before I could lift it. As the music burst forth in all its Teutonic majesty, Jill began to howl. No sooner had she begun than a tremendous pounding thundered angrily through the ceil-ing. For an instant I was embarrassed, but then I stopped in my haste to reject the record. I looked up at the pulpy, reverberating ceiling and yelled, "Go to hell!" The banging stopped abruptly.

Somehow, answering back alleviated that cold truism in my law-enforcement manual, "The good officer has many friends but few close associates." I decided my closest associate could damn well sing if she wanted to.

Still, I couldn't develop too many fond illusions about Jill. I loved her, but I had lived around other retrievers long enough to know that mine wasn't perfect. Jill was never as wise as Ginger, the female Lab Clay Paulhamus had on his stump ranch.

Once I had taken Ginger and her grown son, King, on a catch-as-catch-can hunting trip out the logging road that ran between Deep Creek and the Humptulips River. King was eighty-five pounds of happy, boisterous muscle, and was always leaping off the road to follow some scent through the dense brush. Ginger stayed beside me; not even a deer or elk crossing the road ahead could lure her away. But this day, as we were returning home Ginger suddenly sprang off into the brush. I had chores waiting and called her back, but she didn't obey. I stood there impatiently for some minutes before I heard rustling in the brush. I assumed it was Ginger re-turning. As I waited the noise increased, and finally there was a leafy explosion at the road's edge. A huge bobcat was standing in the road before me. King charged it, and when the two came shoulder to shoulder the wildcat looked taller than the dog. At that instant Ginger burst out onto the road and the bobcat fled. I was too startled to do more than stare. Since then I have always felt that Ginger caught the cat's scent and drove him to me.

Our Gunner was another smart dog. He was a Golden Retriever that my father bought when old Jill began to age. Gunner came as a surprise; the first I knew of him was when my father called, asking mother and me to meet him at the old Salt Lake Airport. (We had moved to Utah shortly after acquiring old Jill.) The new pup was due in from Billings, Montana, on Frontier Airline's morning freight plane. We met my father and Frank Fletcher at the airport just as an old war-surplus DC-3 landed, then rolled down the runway to the terminal. As the pilot gunned an engine and turned the plane around for unloading, its big cargo doors swung back. There sat Gunner.

It was a sunny June morning, and the sunbeams rested on him like a golden spotlight. He plainly hadn't come like Jill, years before, as miserable animal freight. Gunner came like Caesar beginning an occupation. He was three months old and although he was too small to be imperious, he was big enough to have all the self-possession of Douglas MacArthur. He was solidly round like a cub bear and his light-golden fur shone in dazzling contrast to his yellow bedding straw. He was interested but not cowed by all the activity around him. When he came through the gate, riding serenely on a freight truck, he was almost regal—just a shade too appealing for the purple. And he plainly didn't miss home or mother one damn bit.

Gunner promptly made his home in our tree-shaded yard and began chewing on old Jill until she adopted him. She loved Gunner, and let him suck industriously at her dry old dugs. He was the golden boy of dogdom, and very soon we all loved him. He grew from a husky puppy into a powerful dog without ever seeming to pass through a gangly stage. His lustrous coat darkened to the color of old gold and was full of enough highlights to make him the handsomest thing you could have on a deep green lawn.

It was Gunner's intelligence, though, that welded him into our hearts. He breezed through lessons that old Jill had patiently pondered. Gunner seemed to know a lot of things automatically; he never had to be housebroken, he didn't tear up the paper when the kid tossed it on the porch, and he always relieved himself in a weedy, unused part of our large lot. The big dog seemed to share my moods and would sit pensive and still beside me if I was reflective. He wasn't a clown but he could always chase the blues with a touch of his paw and a cavalier sweep of his magnificent tail. When Gunner pranced in to rout me out of bed every morning, he always took a slipper or sock back to prove he had done the job.

My father had an associate who was afraid of dogs. It was months before he would accept an invitation to our house, and he came then only on the condition that Gunner would be locked in his run. But when the man walked toward the kennel, Gunner stood on his hind legs at the gate and put out a big, smooth paw. Naturally, our guest shook it. Gunner was a friendly dog and treated visitors as equals, even if they were not. We let him out of the kennel and the man patted Gunner. In a few minutes they were friends, and in a few days the man was bringing his grandchildren to visit Gunner.

Duck hunting was the thing that Gunner loved best. In a blind we always sat facing each other. A beetling of his wide brow meant ducks were coming in from behind me. And I could judge their range by the intensity of his expression. He seemed to understand if you had a bad day and missed most of the shots. Of course, a gun wasn't necessary for hunting ducks with Gunner. He could always pick up a limit of other men's cripples while walking back to the car. When he brought in a duck and delivered it to hand, Gunner made a prideful ceremony of the occasion. He imparted the feeling that he had given you the duck, and that is quite different from your having shot the duck for the dog. At day's end, when the birds were on the duck strap, Gunner guarded them. Woe unto the strange dog that came sniffing around!

When Gunner was entering his prime, ducks were abundant and limits generous. I shot a fearful number of birds in those years, and Gunner retrieved them all. It didn't matter where a crippled duck fell, Gunner found it. A cripple, falling in deep water, will dive and swim under water to elude the dog. Gunner was on to this and either went right under after the duck or herded it ashore, where he grabbed it easily.

One bitter-cold day, we were sitting in a blind together while intermittent rain and snow slowly coated us both with ice. Only a few duck were flying, and virtually none would so much as tip a wing toward our decoys. Then, suddenly, from out of a gray squall a small bird swirled into the deeks (decoys) and I shot it. Gunner ran out and when he returned with the bird I realized it was like no duck I had ever shot before. It had fierce red eyes and a murderous, rapier-like beak. The creature was still alive, and had it not been for Gunner's deft grip that angry beak would have been imbedded in his eyes. Gunner brought this bird in more slowly than usual, and instead of putting it into my hand, dumped it at my feet. It was a grebe.

I was embarrassed by my error but dispatched the wounded bird and then examined it more closely. On its feet were great, fleshy, lobed toes. In the spring, when they are displaying, grebes are tremendously interesting birds and they are also fun to watch all year round, when they dive for fish. But dead, they are awful; the deadest duck is not so miserably moribund as a dead grebe. Gunner would hardly recognize me the rest of the afternoon. And Gunner was a most communicative dog.

When I came home he used to meet me by jumping up and placing his paws on one of my outstretched forearms. Then he would arch his neck and put the back of his head on the other arm. Thus braced, I was expected to lift him off the ground. When I came home after a year's absence in the Navy, he knew me and was in my arms and braced the instant the kennel gate flew open.

Gunner wasn't perfect. He was a finicky eater and during his lifetime must have sampled every available brand of dog food. None of it held his fancy too long and he let us know when he was tired of a certain brand by giving it a sniff and then lifting his leg on it.

Neither would he hunt pheasants. He would never allow himself to be left behind when the car was packed for a hunting trip. But once in the uplands Gunner stayed at heel. Oh, he would hie obediently into any bramble patch where he was directed, only to make a quick U turn and be out and beside me again. His expression said very clearly, "No pheasants in there, heh, heh." Even when he malingered, I loved Gunner.

He correctly anticipated that his kennel mate, Bang, would struggle through the brambles and flush out the roosters. Bang was a fairly good pheasant dog. But he could never rip free from the briar patch soon enough to get the pheasants he flushed for us to shoot. Gunner retrieved them all.

One day my father noticed a peculiar swelling between Gunner's eyes. The vet operated and found a malignancy in the bone. For a time the operation seemed successful, but then the swelling reappeared and Gunner was embarked on a long, painful series of treatments. They were only partially successful, and toward the end his pain seldom abated. As soon as the car stopped at the vet's, Gunner would leap out, dash in through the waiting room, and spring up on the examining-room table. Finally, the pain could not be stopped even there.

When Gunner died, we all wept.

My new Labrador pup, Jill, had a lot of Gunner's verve. She was eager to accompany me on every job, and one of the first was the removal of a series of beaver dams on Brush Creek. I hoped to remove these dams just before the arrival of the fall freeze. If I timed my destruction right, the beaver would not be able to rebuild their dams that winter and, hopefully, they might move away. Accordingly I filled a feed sack with sticks of extra-strength ditching powder, slipped in a coil of fuse, and knotted the bag's top. Then, disregarding the rule about carrying caps and dynamite together, I slipped a can of blasting caps into my shirt pocket.

I began at the dam farthest downstream and blasted my way upstream until, by mid-afternoon, Jill and I stood below a monster edifice. It was the patient work of many years. I estimated that it was over fifty feet wide and almost seven feet high at its center. I had twenty sticks of powder left, barely enough to crack this giant. I began mining the dam's center so that the pent-up waters in the beaver pond would finish what the blast started. When all but the last stick was placed in the interlaced branches and muck, I made a detonator of it by piercing it and then threading a capped length of fuse through it. The concussion as this stick exploded would detonate all the others. It should be an awsome display, I thought, as I lit the four-foot fuse, then hurried off the dam.

"Foot-a-minute" fuse is only approximate in its burning rate, but I had ample time to call Jill and trot off with her to a safe vantage point. Halfway there, I looked around to be sure the dog was still following. She was not! She had run back to get a stick from beside the dam. I called for her to come but she ignored me and lay down to chew the stick.

Guessing that I had a couple of minutes, I ran back after the pup. When she saw me pounding down upon her she shied away. "Oh! Jilly! Come on!" I stopped chasing her and she trotted over to where I stood—stood very shakily. I ran my hand over her head then down the back until I could grab the scruff of her neck. There it was. In one motion I swung her off the ground and began running. I was still running with the dog in my arms when there was a heavy, thumping explosion that shook the ground. The black center of the dam blew out and pelted us with muddy but harmless shrapnel.

By the time Utah's pheasant season opened, I had made damned sure my pup came when called. This season typically opened on fall's very last pleasant weekend. In fact, the surrounding mountain tops might already be white with several coatings of snow on opening day. To be in the golden fields at this time is to breathe vintage air and bathe your cheeks in its crispness. With the radiant cock pheasants to lure you on, you can walk all day.

Unfortunately, this fine season has been going to hell for several years. Clean farming and urban sprawl combining with too many hunters on too few acres have made each opening day a little more unpleasant than the last. It has become a foot race among hunters to see who could get into a field first, and often one line of gunners would march down upon another file in an insane game of upland "chicken." NO TRESPASSING signs blossomed on more and more fence posts, and in many areas of the state finding a place to hunt was as difficult as finding a bird to shoot at. All the small staff of wardens could do on opening day was patrol the farm land and hope that being seen by the hunters would help keep them in line.

That year, the first barrage did not roll out until a gratifying minute or two before the legal shooting hour. Then there was a strong flurry of fire, which soon subsided into periodic pops. The pheasant is an extremely wary bird and he requires little warning on opening day. In no time some birds have escaped far out into the marshes, where they logroll on the rushes. Even more will fly to the foothills and hide in the sage. By the afternoon of a typical opening day, the birds have vanished so completely that many hunters quit in the belief that all the roosters have been killed. Nothing could be further from the truth!

As the hunting progressed through the first weekend, I set up temporary roadblocks along the farm roads. I would check hunters passing there for an hour or so and then move on to another spot. I soon found what we had half-suspected: a mediocre hatch was not filling too many game bags. I didn't have to issue a single citation for an overlimit.

Then a big sedan with pendulous fenders purred up to my sign and stopped. "How's hunting?" I asked the car's occupants. "Purty good," was audible from among several unintelligible grunts. One tired-acting fellow rolled out of his seat and scuffed around behind the car to open its trunk and show me their bag. When he lifted the trunk lid I nearly gasped. The big compartment was thickly layered with pheasant corpses. I counted them and found the men had come within a bird of two of bagging a legal two-day limit for each of them—almost forty roosters. But in counting them I noticed that many of the birds wore scarcely enough male plumage to identify them as legal cocks. The hatch had been late, and it would have taken extraordinary vision to single out and then shoot these drab young birds when they flushed. There was an easier alternative: the men could have killed every flushing bird, picked up the legal cocks, and left the illegal hens to rot. I double-checked their licenses, and looked under the seats and in the spare-tire well for hidden birds. The dusty hubcaps showed no signs of having been recently removed to conceal pheasants. "Okay, fellows, thanks," I said. The car's driver gave me a leering grin and spun away in a shower of dusty gravel.

I had no sympathy for a hen shooter. It may have been biologically possible during years of abundance to kill hens legally, but they were too different from the roosters to kill them by accident. I was thinking about this later in the week when I went out to hunt pheasants myself. A farmer friend had invited me to try his soil-banked property near the Green River. It was almost legal shooting time as I slipped myself and little Jill through his fence.

The dry grass and weeds lay there in twisted chaos following the first fall storms. The small pup had to bound over the tangle to keep up with me. I walked slowly and soon two hen pheasants flushed. Jill stopped bounding and watched with surprised attention as they sailed away. I took her over to where the hens had been and let her smell their hot scent in the frosty grass. Her bayonet of a tail began to wag excitedly, and I knew I had better cement this budding interest by bagging the first cock to flush.

Not two hundred yards farther on he appeared, jumping into the pink sky with a thumping whoosh. At the top of his rise he centered himself on the rising sun and flew straight at it. I fired and the bird's head jerked back as though it had struck some invisible obstacle. "That one's dead," I thought. The crumpled bird had no sooner landed than Jill ran over to it. I could see her tail wagging furiously as she worried the dead rooster. But as I walked toward the dog and her first pheasant, a tiny pea of apprehension began growing in my stomach. I, the infallible game warden, had just killed a hen pheasant. With my happy but questioning pup at heel, I slunk back to the truck. For me, the pheasant season was over.

It was all the same to Jill. She was my friend and perpetual companion. There were some moments when I have not liked her much. Like the time, early in the morning, when I smelled an unmistakable, fetid odor in the house. I sprang from my bed and went stomping barefoot through the dark, raving furiously at that black culprit. Suddenly there was a soft, squishy feeling under the sole of my bare foot. "Jill! *You son of a bitch!*"

But I have always loved Jill. She became a good partridge dog. And she is an enthusiastic duck hunter, although she has never equaled the non pareil, Gunner. But she excelled him on pheasants and, on moving to Wyoming, Jill became an excellent sage-grouse hunter.

But as the years piled on, she spent more days here beside my chair than she did hunting. While out driving, not long ago, we came upon a large flock of sage grouse treading through the sage with comically obvious stealth. The season was closed, but I stopped the car and unloaded the gray-chinned old girl. I could feel the arthritic grinding in her hindquarters. She was doubly stiff from riding and upwind of the birds, but at my urging she went on until the huge grouse began exploding all around her. For a moment she danced, then darted ahead, the way she had done when birds flushed half a decade before. After her first burst of enthusiasm, she remembered, stood quietly, and watched as the last of the dark silhouettes glided away to the even darker horizon. Then, with a characteristic little shrug, the old dog turned and came back to me, wagging her tail. I helped her into the car, and we drove on.

XIII / THE QUICKENING
WIND

*"We seen some deer, but they was too far away.
We had the fun of shooting at 'em, though."*

—WESTERN DEER HUNTER

W HEN THE GENERAL DEER SEASON BEGAN IN LATE OCTOBER, FAT
was only a distant and infrequent radio-signal away in the
Book Cliffs. Jill and I were in our old elk camp near the eastern tip
of the Uinta Mountains. I had restocked the camp with necessities
a couple of days before the opening Saturday. To pass the last hours
of the year-long truce, I spent some time walking with my pup
through the surrounding pine-edged mountain parks. Near the
clumps of timber, chickarees scampered just beyond Jill's avid
reach. If she got too close they skittered up the nearest tree trunk
and scolded from the safety of a limb. As we walked I gave the pup
lessons in "No!", "Sit," and "Come here." It was essential that she
learn them, because during hunting season my galloping pup
could become anything from a bear to a porcupine in the fertile
imagination of a deer hunter.

Although many hunting seasons opened throughout the fall,
the deer-hunting season was the big one. It was a last fling in the
mountains before winter came, and everyone seemed to take it.
The prospect was especially attractive in our area, because the
chances of getting a deer were excellent. At that time Utah was
still attracting lots of nonresident hunters, many of whom
spent substantial amounts just calling long distance to the game-
department offices in Salt Lake City. They were often connected,
and chatted happily, with office girls who had never hunted deer
in their lives. At the height of one season, one of the girls reported
that a hunter came into the busy office inquiring for his hunting
partner. He described him by saying, "He was wearing a red hat."

Hunting camps were set up at nearly every good site in the
mountains. These camps ranged from station wagons with rumpled
sleeping bags in their backs to sleek trailers with showers and flush
toilets. Mormons love group jollifications, and when some families
gathered their far-flung members for the fall hunt, the resultant
camps were huge. They often used surplus Army tents and cooked

small mountains of food on batteries of stoves. Some even hauled café-sized grills into the mountains, fitted them to butane bottles, and fried acres of steaks at a time.

Sometime before opening morning, after the potatoes were peeled for the morrow's brunch and the wood was ready and waiting for the evening fire, someone set up a target. Then, typically prefacing their target practice with "I don't do so good on paper but just give me some meat to shoot at," the hunters tried out their guns. Many do not fire their rifles from one season to the next; ammunition is expensive, and many hunters in suburbia find target practice inconvenient or impossible. So they come to the mountains and blast the remains of last fall's cartridges away at rocks, boxes, or blazes on trees. Any shot striking within six inches of the aiming point is taken as proof that "I got my sights lined up perfect."

Once I offered to help a family friend and his young son adjust the sights on their war-surplus rifle. He was a small man who, until his beard became too noticeable, had been a featured child player in a popular film series. He brought little away from his Hollywood experience except the experience. At the range we walked back and forth between the firing points and the hundred-yard target butts a few times and the man began protesting. "I was out on a party till two this morning. This goddam walking is killing me."

By that time, however, their rifle was sighted in, and what father and son obviously needed now was lots of practice. I suggested that they use the rest of their shells, and offered to mark the target for them. They agreed and began shooting.

Parallel with the rifle range was a shorter pistol range. It had been terraced to prevent wild shots from crossing into the adjoining range, and trees had been planted between them. The trees also shaded the range caretaker's cottage and backyard. Nevertheless, several pistol targets could be seen from our firing point.

"Denny," said the father to his son, "shoot at that bullseye over there." He was pointing to the partially obscured pistol target.

Immediately, the kid swung his rifle and bored loose cross range. I fully expected to hear the *whock!* of a bullet striking flesh, and while I was protesting the boy slammed across another shot. He was reloading when I made them stop and realize what an inexcusably dangerous thing they were doing. When I had finished the father regarded me the way W. C. Fields used to regard a street urchin. "It's all right," he said, "I know the commissioner."

Until they see what a bullet can do to flesh, many hunters never fully understand how destructive their guns are. The effect on human flesh is the worst, possibly because there is no layer of hair or feathers to sponge up the blood. I saw a boy shot in the thigh with a .25 caliber pistol—regarded as an almost impotent firearm. Actually, I saw the boy after he had been shot, after he had run up a flight of stairs with blood from a torn artery spurting out over the cream-colored walls and clotting in dark-red pools on the stairs. He was down and nearly unconscious when I arrived. His bloody pants were pulled half down and his ashen skin was smeared with blood. I understand it is common to wonder at such times how one body can bleed so much. I did not wonder; my senses were too ripped apart by the shock of what I was seeing.

As a rule, Utah wardens didn't wear sidearms, because the law prohibited their use in enforcing the game code. Also, going unarmed among thousands of heavily armed hunters gave us a psychological advantage over those few who might resort to violence.

That possibility, though remote, existed. Fat had once leaped into a ditch to avoid being run down by a poacher's car. And Fred Reynolds reported that someone had shot out his red spotlight when he turned it on a car one night. It was also an unwritten rule that we helped the local peace officers in emergencies. Fat helped them recapture some escaped prisoners, and I assisted in checking out a suspected bank robber. In those cases we carried guns.

The nearest I ever came to using mine was down at Santa Clara, in southern Utah. The game department operated a twenty-four-hour checking station there throughout the deer season. With thousands of Californians coming through to hunt each fall, the station collected valuable kill data and also had law-enforcement value.

I was sent there one October to run the station for a few days. Several other wardens had been assigned there, in addition to about a dozen college boys hired to collect data from hunters. Shifts were set up for the students and the wardens, although the latter were on call and sometimes on duty twenty-four hours a day. At peak periods there were perhaps fifty cars waiting in the big turn-out beside the highway.

During these rush hours, which lasted from about four to ten P.M., everyone was on duty. If the crush became too great, one of us would flag the cars of non-hunters through without stopping them. We guessed at these on the basis of the cars' licenses and the occupants' clothing. One afternoon, just before the rush, the highway patrol called, asking us to watch for a dark-blue Nash Rambler with Idaho plates. A piece of cardboard had been used to replace the missing glass in the left rear window. We were to hold the car's two male occupants, men in their forties, who had beaten and robbed a hitchhiker and then thrown him out of their speeding car.

I didn't really expect the pair to get as far as our station, but I posted a description of the Nash and gave orders that all the college boys should immediately leave the parking area if the car did arrive. There had been an incident in northern Utah in which a wanted murderer had nearly gunned down the students manning a game-checking station.

I had a .357 magnum revolver and strapped it on that evening, just in case. The rush that night became too great, and I went out with my red-lensed flashlight and began waving through what I guessed to be general traffic. When a car approached the well-lit area bearing Kansas plates, I began waving it through, past the checkers. It came all right: the driver sent it leaping forward at a dangerous speed. The posted speed limit was fifteen miles, and this driver was doing twice that. When he reached me I slapped the side of his car.

"Hold it!" The car stopped, and I walked down to it; its driver had been too anxious to get past us. He was a sandy-haired young fellow sitting alone in the front seat. In the back was a tough-looking woman of about forty and a man of about the same age, wearing a white shirt. Someone had given him a beating, and one eye was purple.

"You're way too fast," I said to the driver. He didn't reply. "Let's see your driver's license." The young man pulled out a thin wallet and slowly began removing its contents. I saw what appeared to be armed-forces identification cards, but he mumbled something about having lost his driver's license. I pointed to our station house. "Pull over there, please, so you won't hold up traffic while you're finding it." As the car pulled off the road, I yelled for Art Kinsky, a department employee, to finish checking the car. In a few minutes Art and Dean Doell, another warden, called to me. "This guy hasn't any license. The registration's missing."

"Call the highway patrol," I said. "Tell 'em to get someone here quick!" We were getting in way over our heads.

A patrolman arrived promptly and escorted the car and its occupants back to court in Saint George. In a couple of hours the patrol called to tell us that the suspects' car had been stolen; its driver was an Air Force deserter, and the couple was wanted in the east for felonies. They were all in jail.

The other fellows were thoroughly satisfied with the evening's work, and I was too, although it had also put me a little on edge. Our station was on a main line from the east to Las Vegas and Los Angeles, and we never really knew who was waiting in that next car. I wondered where the two guys in the Nash were, and hoped they were somewhere in jail. The hours passed and they didn't appear. "Somebody must have taken those guys," I said, and put my gun back in the desk drawer.

The midnight lull began and the parking strip loomed empty under the arc lights. The graveyard shift began to arrive. Bud Camp, the warden from Kanab, was there along with Dean Doell. I was sitting wearily in the office while a commercial fisherman from Monterey told me about his last dozen deer hunts. I pretended to listen. In the midst of my guest's greatest hunt, the dark-blue Nash pulled into the empty parking lot. *"There they are!"* someone almost shouted. There was no mistaking that missing window and its cardboard replacement. I jerked open the desk drawer, grabbed my revolver, and crammed it down into my hip pocket. I vaguely remember the fisherman sitting there with his mouth open. "Call the patrol," I said to Dean. "Quick!"

Dean was placing the call when Bud and I walked out to the waiting car. "Wait'll the driver starts talking to me, then kind of ease up along the other side of the car. We've got to get 'em out of the car." Bud was carrying his holstered revolver out of sight beside his leg.

"Hello," I said, walking up to the driver's open window. I approached him from the rear of the car and stood slightly behind the front seat, so that he had to twist around to talk to me. If he held a gun it would be more difficult for him to use it that way. My own right hand was resting on my hip, just hovering over the butt of my gun. "You boys been doin' any hunting?" I asked.

The driver was wearing striped bib overalls, an engineer's cap, and a clean T shirt. He laughed. "Oh, we like to hunt, but we ain't had a chance this fall."

"Oh. Actually, we've got to check all cars comin' through here, it's our orders. Would you mind opening your trunk for us?"

My hand moved to my gun butt, while the driver opened his door and started to get out. If he was going to start trouble, this was his chance. But all he did was grin and saunter back to the trunk. I was relieved to see his partner get out, too; a man of medium build in blue jeans and a black, western shirt. The driver lifted the trunk lid. Inside were heavy tools, the kind bulldozer mechanics use. Lying on some rags were a couple of heavy power tools. I would have bet the stuff was stolen, but I ignored it.

"Okay, thanks," I said. "I've got to tell you that we have a hold on you fellows from the state patrol." To the driver, "Put your hands on top of the car, that's right. Now step back and straddle your legs." My heart was beating wildly but the fellow obeyed, and I decided he had been searched before. Bud stood behind the other man while I checked the driver. I did it with one hand; the other was on my gun in my hip pocket. The driver had grown careful and quiet. His thin body was rigid as I patted along his legs and around his front, feeling for a gun or knife. He knew he was in grave danger. He had no weapon.

"Okay. You move up the car, keep your hands on the top." I turned to the other man; his face was sullen. "Now you come up to the car. Put your hands on top like your partner, step back, farther. Okay." I had just started to frisk the second man when Dean Doell came up.

"I got the patrol. They don't want these men anymore. Said to let 'em go."

"For Chrissakes!" I said.

The two men didn't move. "I'm sorry, fellows. No hard feelings?"

Their eyes were hard, but they smiled. "Naw, no hard feelings." They jumped into their car and sped away into the night.

"That damn patrol should have called us. I was ready to shoot those guys." I drove back to my motel, took a drink, and fell asleep until late the next morning.

Actually, the carelessly handled sportsman's gun was a more consistent danger than the outlaw's weapon. Many hunters believed that a cartridge in the chamber of their rifle gave them an advantage over game they spotted from their cars. But it was so lethal to hunters that the legislature finally banned it.

One afternoon, during my first deer season, I checked a sedan in which a man, his wife, and their teen-aged son were riding. The first thing I noticed in the car was a fully cocked Winchester rifle. It was leaning against the front seat between the adults and pointing straight at their son in the back seat.

"Is that rifle loaded?" I asked. In response the man flipped its level, and a live shell popped out of the chamber. I said, "It's against the law to have a loaded gun in your car."

"Huh?"

"You can have shells in the magazine," I said, "but not in the barrel. The law's for your own protection. That rifle was pointed at your boy." I went on to explain in more detail the danger of carrying a loaded rifle, while the man began to nod his head in apparent agreement. I concluded, "I have to issue you a citation for this."

"Well," said the man, "if you think so . . ." He seemed to accept being ticketed with unusual good grace. I got the citation pad from my truck and began filling in the necessary information as he cheerfully dictated it. Then, half-way through the form, he suddenly stopped, "Hey!" he cried, "you're givin' me a ticket!" Apparently, he had assumed that being issued a "citation" was like getting a medal.

I regularly carried a loaded .22 Smith and Wesson revolver in my pickup. It was too lethal a weapon to be considered a tool, but it was very useful. Stray cats fell to it whenever I found them too far from barnyards. I tried to shoot cats with a minimum of show, however, because some farmers maintained that the strays ate enough field mice to justify themselves.

One day I left the deer ranges to make a quick check of the farming areas. It proved an uneventful trip, although as I was about to return to the mountains I saw a big cat stalking a hen pheasant. I was near the intersection of two farm roads, and after driving onto the shoulder I looked up and down both roads carefully. No cars were in sight, so I quickly aimed my revolver at the cat creeping through the weeds. It dropped at my shot and the pheasant flushed in terror. Suddenly a car appeared on the road ahead and then another zoomed down the crossroad behind me, to meet a third car coming from the other direction. Naturally, the occupants of all the cars began peering intently at me in my marked truck, for rural people are always interested in the game warden's activities.

With so much instant traffic passing, I couldn't drive back on the road myself, so I just sat there and let the cars pass. Suddenly that damned cat began leaping wildly into the air. It must have made three or four arcing springs, going higher each time, before the last car had driven slowly by. I sat there crimson-faced, trying to make believe that the astounding behavior thirty yards to my left wasn't really happening at all. When the cars had finally gone, the cat promptly succumbed.

A few days later one of the police radio dispatchers called and asked me to drop by the office. When I did he told me he had been hunting in a remote area and found an old cabin filled with untagged deer. He said, "I think most of the deer were sneaked out that night. The way their camp's fixed, though, I'll bet they'll be back this weekend."

I drove up the jeep trail which led to the old cabin the following Sunday morning. There were fresh tire tracks in the ruts and I followed them. It was rough going. Just as the grinding, jolting truck seemed about to spin out on a steep grade, it burst over the top and into a secluded little dimple in the mountainside. On one edge of the grassy clearing, matching the dispatcher's description, were the remains of an old log cabin. The roof had fallen in, but the walls were intact and lying beside one of them was a buck deer's carcass.

In the middle of the basin stood a large tent with a jeep parked in front of it. As I stopped, a ruddy-faced little man in his early forties came bustling out of the tent. "Well, well! Utah Fish and Game, huh? We're just havin' a cup of coffee, want one? We don't know you, do we?"

As I was explaining the reason for my visit, a whey-faced woman came out of the tent. "What's your name?" she asked. "We don't know you, do we?"

I repeated my name without success while the couple caromed it back to me as Hawkins, Scroggins, and Coggins. I broke it off by asking to check their deer.

"We ain't had much luck," said the man.

I walked to where the buck lay. It was a prime four-pointer. And beside it lay the hindquarters of a fawn plus a large bobcat. "That ain't my deer," said the man. "It belongs to my buddy. You musta' passed him. He just left."

"I didn't see him," I said. "Did he leave a donor's slip for this buck with you?" There was a tag on the buck's hock, but the regulations required that a signed and dated note accompany any deer that didn't belong to the person in possession. It was a measure aimed at preventing hunters from using someone else's tag. There was no donor's slip.

"All we're doin' is takin' his buck home fer 'em. Hell's sake, we're not tryin' to pull anything."

While the man talked and protested his ignorance of the donor's-slip requirement, I turned over the untagged hindquarters of a fawn that were lying beside the buck. "Who do these belong to?"

"I dunno," replied the man. "They ain't ours." He switched the subject to the dead bobcat that was also lying near the buck. "What's the bounty on that bobcat?"

"See the county agent," I said, walking over to look in the old cabin. Except for the lower legs of some deer, it was empty. "We got a report of a lot of untagged deer being in this cabin last weekend."

The man shot me an angry look. "So what, there was a big crowd in here last week. I didn't pay no attention to what they done with their deer."

I told the man I was citing him for illegal possession of the buck.

"God damn it!" he blurted. "How can you write a ticket for this?" I continued writing, and the man's wife began yelling at me. I finally had to shut her up by warning that I would sign a complaint against her for interfering with an officer. The man refused to sign the ticket, and his wife urged him to demand an immediate hearing. So I loaded up the deer, including the abandoned hindquarters, and put a radio call in for the judge to meet us at his office in about ninety minutes.

In Vernal we only had to wait a few minutes before the judge came in, hung his hat and coat on the corner tree, then sat down and read the ticket I had placed on his desk. When he finished he looked at the defendant. "How do you plead to this charge of illegal possession of a buck deer?"

"Guilty—but only technically. See, judge, the deer belongs to my buddy. I was takin' it home for him."

I hoped the judge would put the fellow in jail, but instead he ruled, "I'll release you on your own recognizance. You come back tomorrow and get the matter of the deer's ownership straightened out at the same time." The man took his wife's hand and they strutted past me and out of the office.

"Well, that's a lot of goddamn bullshit!" I said. The judge looked startled but allowed me to explain the details of the case. In the end, however, my case came to nothing, and I had the embarrassing task of explaining my actions to a commissioner. After that session I drove out to the game farm, got the fawn's hindquarters, and threw them into a gulley.

Deer hunting can be such a deeply satisfying activity that I have never fully understood why people wanted to buck the game by cheating. I guess it's for the same reason that men with nice wives will still go to a whorehouse.

One year I drove out across the Burr Desert for a deer hunt of my own. I drove fifty miles, maybe more, without seeing anyone. My route out of Escalante followed a section of the Outlaw Trail; in that almost unspoiled, empty wilderness, I would have accepted even Butch Cassidy's appearing around the next bend. Finally, the Henry Mountains loomed out of the dry wastes like a mountainous desert island rising from the sea.

The Henry's are a series of laccoliths rising above the desert to peaks ten thousand feet high. They are so remote that even the mammals living there have developed special characteristics all their own. The game department built some access roads high on the mountains' steep flanks. They are mostly one-laned and best suited to jeeps and trucks with good clearance. Even in the early 1960's a detailed map of these mountains was not generally available. (This delightful situation may have drastically changed with the completion of Glen Canyon dam and its recreational facilities somewhat south on the Colorado River.)

I made my camp on the edge of a high, piñon-ringed basin. Mule deer came there, before dawn and at dusk, to browse in the sage. A doe always appeared first. She would stand in the edge of the trees for a long time, watching, listening, keening the wind before venturing into the open. Walking cautiously, she stepped as if the ground could give way. One hoof was firmly down before another was lifted. Her head bobbed rhythmically with each step, but she was not mechanically methodical; she was almost painfully attentive to her surroundings. She was watching, always watching. Great ears that could hear a twig crack a half-mile away framed the doe's eyes and were ready to catch any nuance of danger that her eyes might miss. Finally, like a gambler checking his hole cards one last time, the doe looked, then walked out into the sage.

She checked her surroundings again and was satisfied. Her ears relaxed and she lowered her head to eat. It could have been a signal, for other deer began appearing in the basin. Most of them came timidly, but an exuberant fawn or two bounded joyously into the basin.

I didn't see the deer the first night I intruded in their basin. But I saw them before dawn the next morning; they were hugging the piñons and watching hungrily. When I stepped away from my tent the deer sprang for cover, their rumps bouncing like kernels of popping corn. I tried not to disturb them, and as the days passed they began using the basin more freely. I suppose they merely became accustomed to my presence there, but it was pleasant to imagine that we had a covenant, a sort of nonaggression pact.

After a week of mountain solitude, which was broken only once, by two hunters who quickly moved on when they saw the game department device on my coat sleeve, I had to remind myself that there were only two days of the hunting season remaining. On the next to last morning, I walked east across the sage basin toward Ragged Mountain. The mountain was well named, for its top seemed to have been ripped from stone of the wildest shapes and jammed there in the sky. Below the mountain's jagged battlements, the country broke off into steep, piñon-filled canyons. A careful hunter might catch a buck at the head of one of the draws that widened as they went to become canyons at the mountain's foot. I wasn't always careful. I often moved too fast or let the shifting wind catch me going in the wrong direction. I blundered into little openings that held deer and sent the animals slipping off unseen. The deer would circle me and then come back to their clearings after I had gone.

On a brushy point that pushed out between two rough draws, I found fresh, warm droppings. A look at the wide hoof mark with its blunted toes made me guess it was left by a buck. I knelt on the point where I could command part of each draw and waited. I waited until one of my knees began to ache with increasing authority, but the buck didn't try to sneak down either of the draws. I moved my protesting knee slightly and waited a final twenty minutes, to confirm my new theory that the buck had crept back up the ridge behind me. Then I stood, turned my back on the draws, and took a step. The patient buck sprang and went clattering safely down a draw.

If he's so inclined, a mule deer can turn himself to stone and out-wait the most patient of men. It seemed ingrained in the behavior of these deer to stop for a last look before fleeing from danger. The habit has been fatal for thousands of these animals, but some of the big bucks don't pause. When they move, either the hunter is ready or the buck is gone.

Half the fun of hunting is the hindsight and remembering the what-might-have-beens. The other part is involved with seeing what's beyond the next ridge. I headed for the narrow meadow where Gibbon Spring rises. The matted grass there was fall-yellow and dying with the season. I walked around it, trying not to reveal myself to watching deer, staying close to the brush that bordered it on one side. Soon I was climbing up the ridge behind the spring and toward a glowering sentinel of dark and rough-cut rock called the Horn. This sentinel dominated the end of the ridge; you cannot go to the Henry's and see the Horn and ever forget it. It is not a Grand Canyon or an Old Faithful but it is unique, and it awed me.

A cool wind eddied and spread across the slope, blowing in one direction along the ground and in the other through the tops of the surrounding ponderosas. I saw some does and fawns fidgeting along the ridge. They were more inclined to run than to stand and stare. As I climbed higher there were more signs of deer. I thought they must be shading up in the breaks and only coming out on the ridge at dusk and again at daybreak.

Ancient piñons dotted the ridge top. I sat down under one of the larger trees to watch. The ground was dry under the drifts of needles. They crackled if stepped on and jabbed when sat on. I could see the meadow around Gibbon Spring from where I was sitting, and as I looked something moved there. I pulled my binoculars from the front of my coat and focused them. From out of the blur of glass and mind a wild turkey slowly materialized. It was dark and very large. It was the first wild turkey I had ever seen, and I watched it intently. The bird had a rolling gait as it went along pecking at the dry grass. I followed the bird with my glasses until it melted into the oak brush and was gone. I never saw it again.

Then it was time for me to leave, too. The quickening wind made me shiver in my down coat, and I hurried along, undoubtedly warning all the deer around of my presence. I had decided to let that day go; the buck in the morning and the turkey in the afternoon were enough. As I rattled rocks in descending the ridge, I caught glimpses of my tiny green miner's tent, two miles off in the sage basin. I was tired when I reached camp, but I took a few minutes to build a fire in the pit before the tent. Then I built a drink and sat down by the fire to enjoy them both.

When the last amber drop had been drained from my enamelware cup, I got up and cooked supper. I ate it hurriedly, because the night was cold and the fried meat and potatoes were congealing in the bacon grease left in the pan from early morning. The wind was blowing, and that made it colder. The sky was clear and no snowstorm could be seen lurking beyond Waterpocket Fold or drumming itself into violence in the solitude of the far-off Sinbad.

I decided to try south of the Horn in the morning. A great, rolling sage basin lay between the Horn and Mt. Pennell. A few deer used that plain steadily. I made my hunting plans after I went to bed. After several days in the open, a tiny tent with starlight glimmering through its walls becomes a special sort of haven. It is a place to hide and re-arm for the morrow.

I was awakened by a night wind whipping the tent. I lay there for awhile, imagining great, wet snowflakes plastering the tent and sealing off the road down the mountain. When I had thoroughly alarmed myself, I sat up and peeked out at the sky. It was clear and perforated by a billion stars. I wiggled back down into my sleeping bag and alternated between dozing and waking until there was an almost imperceptible lightening on the east wall of my tent. The wind was still whistling; then it suddenly popped my tent one last time and hurried west after the night. I knew the deer would be moving, but they might feed a bit longer this morning—deer are spooky in a wind but sometimes become less wary after it is calm again.

The first minutes of arising are the worst ones of a hunter's day. There is no fire and no hot coffee simmering on the Coleman stove. In fact, the dregs of last night's coffee have become a frozen conglomerate. My boots were so stiff that I could scarcely pull them on; even the rawhide laces were stiff and resisted lacing. I let them drag while I clumped around, starting the truck's engine and collecting a breakfast. I settled for some fruit juice with bread and jam. I wasn't hungry but I was anxious to go, on this last day of the hunting season. The juice tasted of tin can and had ice in it. But I got it down, then ate some clammy bread heavily coated with jam. Augie Diehl would have braced himself for such a morning with half a tumbler of bourbon. He drank it slowly while he shaved with a straight-edge razor and gave sage hunting advice to a wide-eyed boy, who, in those almost forgotten years, was me.

I doubt that I thought of Augie that morning. It was cold and my thoughts were of the necessities, like the can of Vienna sausages and the candy bars I dug out from the grub box, then tossed onto the truck seat. I tied my boot laces and patted my bulky clothing in the appropriate spots to make sure my equipment was in place.

In the truck I turned the heater on full and luxuriated in the suggestion of warmth that poured forth. Then I switched on the headlights, it was still dark. I let in the clutch and drove slowly away from camp. I watched for my turn, not hurrying. It appeared and I drove up it, a bumpy pair of wheel tracks that climbed for a while and then abruptly ended beside a barbed-wire fence.

When I switched off the truck lights, the fence blurred into the early morning grayness. Behind the fence the Bureau of Land Management had disked out the sagebrush and planted grass. It was another act of obeisance to the stockmen. The grass failed, and later a big buck deer had become entangled in the sagging barbed wire. He died there, and now his eyeless skull and bleached antlers were still held erect by the wire, while the skeleton wasted away into the soil.

As I stood shivering there that morning, my next thought was to check my rifle sight to see if I had shooting light. I also checked my pockets for deer tags, shells, knife, matches, and tobacco. They were all there, and I thought, "Get going." I would need two or three hours to hunt across the lower part of the rolling sage plain. Then, if I found nothing, I would circle up toward the aspen belt that clung to Mt. Pennel.

I found nothing in the first draw. I paused there to recall the terrain. There was a patch of aspen below the next rise. I thought a buck might be in there, so when I topped the rise I was ready to shoot. But only a doe deer and her fawns were there, watching me curiously. While I was growing up, it was against the law to kill a doe. I still have that memory to keep me from shooting a doe, but there is also the fact, that for me anyway, buck hunting is better than deer hunting. I can't say why, exactly, but I feel better hunting bucks. The does and her fawns went off on stiff, springing legs.

Sometimes a morning breaks bright and you almost squint; then the light dims for a time, and you either roll over and go back to sleep or you scuff along, tripping on unseen rocks and letting the sage scratch noisily across your boot tops. I was doing this when a movement, vaguely seen, stopped me. I turned to see a great buck flying across and over the skyline, his heavy antlers briefly silhouetted against the gray sky.

I walked over to where the buck had been. It did no good, and standing there beside the great tracks was like visiting a historical landmark a hundred years after the fact. I went on to the edge of the plain, where it fell away into a deep, angry-looking canyon, without seeing any more deer. This was nearly the end of the hunt and the days of doing as I pleased. Tomorrow the deer could begin to shed their caution and prepare for winter.

By the time I reached the plain's abrupt edge, the light was strong, the day well established. But my plans from that point on had not been well established. I decided to walk along the canyon rim. Before me a bare ridge split as it flowed smoothly down from the mountain. Its right branch spread into the flat, while its left broke, then fell away into a small basin at the head of the canyon

I had been following. In the basin, twining among the sage and aspen, were a couple of game trails; their tails hung over into the canyon.

I heard a *click*, like fingers snapping suddenly in the dark. Then there was a raspy, rattling sound, the sound a deer makes running across shale. There were two of them, bouncing toward me on the bare ridge ahead. I knew they were bucks without seeing their antlers. The deer were four hundred yards off, and I had time to run forward to a rocky knoll commanding the ridge. I flopped down there, puffing and struggling into a sitting, shooting position.

The bucks started down the ridge toward the basin. I knew the larger one would be behind. The range was still too great, but it was closing fast. I ran a cartridge into the barrel and closed the rifle's bolt, but didn't flip on the safety. An errant wind must have fooled these fleeing bucks into our collision course. It has happened to me before. One time, hunting in eastern Oregon, a misguided doe ran right through the spot where several of us had stopped to boil coffee and have our lunch. Once a mule deer decides to run in a certain direction, he seems to have difficulty changing his mind.

I thought, "Can't let the first one get across the basin or he'll be gone down the canyon. But shoot too soon, and the larger one will turn and cut back over the ridge. Time this right!" The oncoming deer weren't bounding now, they were running hard with their heads held low. Jesus! Those were big bucks! The kind all hunters may miss because they can't take their eyes off the antlers.

The leading buck was almost off the ridge and into the basin. I aimed a trifle low and lead him; the buck staggered at the shot, then came on. My next shot missed. At the third shot the buck stopped, sat down, and slowly collapsed, dying. I swung on the other one. He saw me and veered away toward the canyon, his hooves spewing shale. In the morning sunlight his great antlers had a golden cast. I missed him, and he surged forward, running even faster. I flipped the rifle's bolt, caught the deer in the sight, and fired. He didn't falter, and I was out of shells. But as he came nearer, I could see a foreleg pinwheeling. "Oh! Goddammit!"

I groped in my coat pocket for another cartridge and single-loaded it, but the deer disappeared before I could shoot. Half sick, I ran across the knoll, jamming shells into the rifle's magazine. But I knew that my haste and the reloading were useless: the wounded buck would be gone over the canyon's rim.

I stopped and absently dropped the shells back into my pocket. The great buck lay still in the sage below me. I hadn't broken the leg but the shoulder. He had let it all out, he had run as far as he could. I walked up to him and looked down—the hunt was over, and the mountains were very quiet.

That trip to the Henry Mountains has always had a special, satisfying significance to me. I can never have a "bad" hunting trip now, because I always have that one to remember, and it is enough for me. All my subsequent deer-hunting trips have never been more than well-rehearsed encores. I think I have been very lucky. After every hunting season in Utah several hunters who have killed or wounded someone are asked to appear before the game commission. The commission's only power in cases of negligence is to suspend the shooter's license-buying privileges for a few years. They can't even require an accused to appear at his hearing.

Under these conditions, few accused hunters ever appear. But I happened to meet one who did. He had that open-faced and healthy look of the well-fed American. A bit of fleshiness was beginning to soften the line of his jaw, although it did not seriously detract from his over-all appearance. He was very neat. His sandy hair had been trimmed and combed into a modest pompadour. There was a sharp crease in his gray slacks, and his loafers were shined. His sport shirt was of a pleasant but subdued check and was open at the throat. He wore a new gray windbreaker, of the kind millions of American men wear to the supermarket on Saturday mornings. He was an average lower-middle-income citizen, and he looked me straight in the eye when he said, "I killed that kid. I don't say I didn't and I probably won't go hunting again, even if they don't revoke my license. But I'm not negligent."

It is probably fair to say that "negligent" was a new word in the man's vocabulary and that he had looked it up and been embarrassed by the definition he found in the dictionary. He continued his explanation.

"We were hunting pheasant, see? After lunch we decided to ride the county roads and look for birds. Pretty soon this here rooster ran out in a field an' we shot it. But it wasn't dead. It was gettin' away.

"The kid and me, we was sittin' next to each other in the back seat. He was on the side next to the field. I figured he'd sit still. So I jumped out an' pulled down on the pheasant. Just as I shot, the kid jumped out on the other side of the car. He was a tall kid. I'm actually glad he didn't suffer or anything.

"But what I say is this: I didn't kill that kid negligently. Why, he was just as negligent as me for standin' up when I shot."

In that, as well as in all other cases of firearms accidents or law violation, we wardens duly recorded the make, serial number, and gauge or caliber of the firearm involved. This registered every gun carelessly or illegally used, together with the name of the person using it. I could never see that this had the slightest effect on crime or accident-prevention.

On the other hand, we are past the point of tolerating crimes and accidents involving guns. Some people should not own guns. Who they are might be determined through an expansion of the hunter-safety courses now taught in most states. These courses have produced more responsible young hunters—tens of thousands of them.

I recall a rather intense young towhead who enrolled in one of my gun safety courses. He found the sessions on firearms nomenclature and types fascinating. But he plainly was impatient with safety drills, and when I spent an evening equating responsible gun owner-ship with observance of the law, the boy dropped out. I was disap-pointed because the young man had proven himself an amazingly good rifle shot, but I did not issue him a certificate of competence—without this he could not legally purchase a hunting license. Later on I unknowingly nearly ran over this boy with my truck as he lay beside the carcass of a poached deer. Perhaps, in addition to denying him a hunting license we should also have denied him the privilege of owning a gun and ammunition.

XIV | WINTER WARMTH

"We didn't get much snow last winter. So, if you're going to plant fish down here this summer, send their water with 'em."

—SOUTHERN UTAH GAME WARDEN

A HEAVY SNOWFALL IS ALMOST TRADITIONAL DURING THE SECOND weekend of a Utah deer season. The roads spilling out of canyons along the rugged Wasatch Front become glazed and as wheel-rutted as the pioneer trails of a hundred years before. The snow can fall so abundantly that the state snow plows, often wedged behind hunters' slewing cars, never get it under control. The roads fill until each vehicle leaves three ruts, two for its wheels and a third between them for the transmission.

Driving at any other time would be an icy nightmare, but on the final Sunday of deer season, it is more often a snow carnival. No one seems to mind the delay; drivers don't exchange curses and try to blind one another with their lights. Everyone is out there bucking the storm together and if a car slides off the road, a dozen others stop to help it. I have seen squads of husky men swarm over a ditched car and joyously heave it back onto the road again.

We didn't get the customary snow in the Uintah Basin on my first close-of-season weekend. But the northern cold drifted in slowly until, just before Thanksgiving, there was more ice than water at Stewart Lake Refuge. Up at the game farm, pheasants by the score were feeding under Clif Greenhalgh's Russian-olive trees. And the good old Pig was warm and fat under a thick, shaggy coat. Horse hair is such good insulation that the rime of frost forming on horses' backs during a cold night never disappears until the morning sun melts it away.

Until the mid-1950s the warden force had been left to outfit for cold weather as each man wanted to. Then a governor told them they looked like bums and ordered uniforms all around. After their initial outfitting, the wardens received a small uniform allowance. No one ever explained why a job paying three hundred fifty dollars a month required twenty-dollar Stetsons and eight-dollar shirts. The coat, however, was worth every penny of the fifty dollars it cost. It was down-filled, and I wore mine until the down leaked out,

[234

leaving a miniature snowdrift wherever I paused. We could also order heavy insulated boots that kept our feet warm and dry in any weather. The weighty clodhoppers were especially good, someone remarked, "for standin' still in." We also had water-repellent woolen trousers and matching Eisenhower-style jackets, which made us look like bread salesmen.

Our field equipment was issued with winter in mind. I had a surprisingly warm Dacron-filled sleeping bag, which I kept rolled inside a heavy duck bed tarp. A bed tarp not only helps to keep camp bedding clean, but also makes the sleeping bag much warmer. It is an old stockman's accessory, and not generally found in sporting goods stores. Most wardens also had small tepee tents that could be made comfortable in winter by putting lighted gas lanterns inside.

This equipment, plus a big battery-powered spotlight, hip boots, guns and ammunition, traps, fire extinguishers and fire crackers, first-aid kits, suitcase, and, in my instance, dog food, was packed inside a large, tin-topped box in the back of our pickups. In addition to the box, Fat and I also carried big grub boxes. Mine had once housed an Army field transmitter; it was waterproof and held a two-week supply of food plus utensils. For dry ranges like the Book Cliffs, we added ten-gallon milk cans filled with water.

Our pickups had "no-spin" differentials that were almost as good as four-wheel drive for taking us where we had to go. If there was a heavy-duty equipment option, the department wisely put it on our trucks. But the fine points of equipage were left to the driver. I began carrying two spare tires after being stranded on Blue Mountain with two flat tires. I also had an extra fan belt, a fifteen-gallon gas barrel, hand tools, heavy-duty tire chains, a wonderfully useful Handyman jack, tow chain, ax, shovel, and several yards of baling wire. The wire was wrapped in flattened coils and stowed behind my equipment box.

With baling wire and the necessary amount of desperation, you can repair almost anything. I have used baling wire to fix pack saddles, broken trailer axles, and tire chains, as well as to successfully splice a fan belt that broke during a snow storm in desolate Clay Basin.

In most seasons, but particularly in late fall, there was a fifth of bourbon snug in its niche behind my truck seat.

I was prepared, then, when Fat asked me to work a post-season deer hunt in the Book Cliffs during Thanksgiving week. I was glad to have somewhere to go on the holiday.

On the morning I planned to leave, I was delayed by a farmer complaining about ducks raiding his pit silo. It was after noon when I got that taken care of and began the long drive out to Willow Creek. Fat had been staying at a ranch there, and I hoped to camp with him that night. As I drove south toward Ouray, a lowering overcast that had been oozing down from the northwest finally reached and overlapped the southern horizon. Outside a gentle breeze was blowing, but when I stopped for gas at Ouray I could feel that it carried splinters of ice.

Beyond Ouray little gray-brown wisps of dust followed me, toppling gently into ditches when the breeze hit them. The big golden eagles, perched on the tips of the open ridges, seemed to have hunched their shoulders against the cold. "Hard hunting" was their way of life. Jill was curled next to me on the seat, company and warmth in one black package.

Driving up Willow Creek Canyon and past the Stevens's Ranch, the swollen gray clouds were like opaque skylights curving over the cliff tops. Every few seconds a lonely snowflake tumbled out of them and came drifting to earth. The thought of being snowed-in, even in this wilderness, wasn't particularly unpleasant; it might even be an adventure. (Once you actually have been snowed-in, you feel more like the old warden I once paused with on the top of a snowy mountain pass. "Goddamn," he said, "I hate this."

(What?" I asked.

("It bein' me, instead of you, that has to shit.")

It was dark when I drove into the forlorn yard of the ranch

where Fat was staying. His truck wasn't there, but I went to the house to inquire for him. An old man came to the door. In the yellow lamplight he resembled an old N. C. Wyeth painting from an edition of *Kidnapped*. Fat, he said, had gone home. Then the man smiled painfully and shut the door.

I had little choice but to go on and stay in the BLM cabin at Three Pines. The road to it, up Bull Canyon, was really a rock-studded jeep trail, but it was the only direct route. There was no sign at the junction, although I remembered a big boulder near it. I drove along with Jill's head on my lap, looking in this rocky land for one particular rock. For entertainment I turned up the volume on my two-way radio and listened to the woes and foibles of men in a half-dozen different towns. Sporadic flurries of snowflakes zipped out of the surrounding blackness to flash briefly in my head-lights.

I wasn't sure of the distance to Bull Canyon. Places always seem farther apart at night, so I drove on, expecting at any time to see the rock. No car passed and no firelight shone from a hunter's camp to reassure me. When the road began climbing, which it was not supposed to do, my little nugget of doubt became a lode. I kept hoping there would be a road sign.

Finally there was. A big white sign loomed in my headlights. OURAY EXTENTION, UTE INDIAN RESERVATION, TRIBAL HUNTING LICENSE REQUIRED.

"Son of a bitch!" No, I wasn't really lost, because I could turn around. But there was no place here to stay and I half remembered a road out that might bring me back around to Steer Ridge, from where I could eventually reach Three Pines. I looked at my watch. It was almost ten P.M.

The road climbed steadily. I was apparently driving up a very long dugway on the side of a ridge. I came to a sign that pointed to Moonwater, and proclaimed that it was a preposterous number of miles off in another direction. I continued on in the direction I had chosen. It grew colder, and I pushed the heater controls full on.

Snow had been inching out from the road edges, until the whole surface was covered. The white mantle was untracked. I am all for wilderness but on nights like that one I long to see a freshly discarded beer can or, better, a few garish swirls of neon—which at that moment would have looked like garlands on the throne of God.

The snow deepened and my back wheels began to slip occasionally before they re-gripped the road. Going on like this was insane, but now there was no place on the mountain road to turn around. I was driving very slowly, so when the truck skidded into a ditch there was no damage.

I whipped the shift lever quickly through the gears, rocking the truck. The wheels spun, the engine revved, small rocks pelted the fenders' undersides, and in less than five minutes I had buried the back wheels down to the differential.

Jill sat in the truck, watching me while I got out my gas lantern, lit it, and began the tedious process of jacking up and shoveling out. I left the truck's engine running to ensure Jill's comfort and to power the parking lights, which I left burning for their additional light. I also left the radio on, for no other reason than its occasional emission of a human voice.

By eleven o'clock I had filled in the ruts under the truck and had it again resting on its wheels. There was still a steep though short climb between the ditch and the road. I trimmed the front wheels, aligning them in the direction the truck was facing, to prevent them from causing a drag at the instant of starting. All of my laborious preparations paid off. The pickup bounded out of the ditch and onto the road. For an elated instant I was moving—and then the truck slewed and I was back in the ditch again. This time it was bad: both left wheels had slid in, leaving the cab tipped so tightly against the mountainside that I could not open the left-hand door. I had to clamber out over Jill on the passenger side.

At least it had stopped snowing. A star peeped icily here and there through the rolling overcast. But, as a mountain man had carved on an aspen one hundred years before, I thought, "This is a

[238

hell of a place to camp." I had little choice but to go back to work. It would be more difficult this time, because of the way the pickup had cozied up against the hillside. I dug and jacked until I was perspiring freely despite the cold. In the midst of my efforts the truck's slowly purring engine suddenly stopped. I opened the door and received a friendly lick across the face from Jill, while I turned off the electrical switches. I could work in silence by lantern light, and Jill could stay warm by running around.

By one A.M. everything was jacked up, shoveled out, and ready. I slid into the truck seat and turned the ignition key to "start." There was a languorous whine, followed by tsk, tsk, click from the starter solenoid. The battery was dead.

THE GODDAMN BATTERY WAS DEAD! And my truck, my green foam-cushioned womb in the wilderness, was useless. The cold and the long idling with the electrical accessories running had overdrawn the generator's electrical output.

Fortunately, the truck was on a grade. I could chivvy it backward onto the road and then coast downhill in reverse until the engine cranked itself. While I worked at the jack I periodically looked out over the void beyond me, hoping to see a light. There was none. I continued jacking. A Handyman jack is similar to a standard bumper jack except that it has Mr. America muscles. One man can move a ton of dead weight with this jack, although he moves it slowly. Once, as I looked out over the surrounding limbo, I thought I saw a light. "Couldn't be," I decided. Then the light reappeared and was nearer. Surely no one would be driving around out here at night. Maybe it was a car-load of celebrating Utes. Some of them could travel long and unpredictable distances on a few quarts of muscatel. I hoped it wasn't Indians. They would be of no help and, worse, they would find my predicament hilarious. The stoicism of the Indian invariably collapses under the weight of a white man's folly. I began working harder.

The lights came nearer and nearer until I was dazzled by their brilliance. Then they came abreast of me. A pleasant voice called down from what I now could see was a big stake-bodied truck. "What in hell you doin' out here?" The driver climbed down from his truck, slamming the door as he walked over to me. "Looks like you really got into it," he said.

He was a sturdy man, of medium height. I guessed that he was in his mid-forties. In the lantern light I could see the deeply weathered lines of a stockman's face. He examined my preparations for moving the truck, then said, "Why, I believe we can hook onto you and jerk you right out."

We fastened my tow chain between the two machines and he "hit 'er." The pickup lunged forward, but its dead weight was too much for the big truck. The truck's wheels began spinning. The stockman stopped, and we tried fastening the chain in a new position to get the utmost from the tow. When he tried again, it was like snow sliding slowly on a roof and then suddenly flashing off the eaves with a floury, pounding roar. The tow chain jerked loose and in a twinkling the big truck shot across the road and plunged over the other side.

Hurrying to where the truck had disappeared, I was relieved to see it still upright on the slope below. The driver made several attempts at driving back up on the road, but each one resulted only in his skidding farther down the mountain side. He shut off the engine and the headlights.

"I'm sure sorry. You probably could shoot me," I said.

"Well, it can't be helped now, I guess. I got a herd of sheep up here a few miles. Let's git your outfit going, we can't stay here all night."

The jack clattered mechanically as the locking bolts shot in and out of their notches, and inch by inch we forced the truck back onto the road. I fell under the wheel. "Now," I said to myself. My benefactor gave a shove, and the truck began rolling. I was looking over my shoulder through the back window and steering one-handed; when the truck was coasting fast enough, I let in the clutch. There was a surprised, clattering wail from the engine and gear train. But there was no discreet cough from the engine. Halfway down the hill, I realized that a car can't be started by coasting down a hill backwards. I put on the brakes.

The sheepman walked wearily down to where I stood surveying the dead truck. "Bastard," he said, while I accused it of being a pervert.

"We'll have to turn it around."

"Jack up one side, then push the sonofabitch over."

"Take all night."

"Probably."

I don't remember who said what, but I well remember the Oriental patience required to turn a truck completely around by hand. We jacked the pickup as high as possible, and then we shoved it sideways off the jack. Each time the truck came down, it was turned a few inches. Each pump on the jack handle and each shove became a major effort. At one point, I said, "I've got a bottle of whiskey. When we get this truck running, you're welcome to a drink, or all of it."

"Don't ordinarily use it," said the shadowy figure toiling beside me, "but tonight I sure do."

When the truck finally showed signs of pointing headfirst downhill, we were numbed to everything but our weariness. Jack up, push over, jack up, push, jack, push.

"What time is it?"

"Two-thirty."

"Oh, Christ!"

"My turn to jack."

By three A.M. the great dead whale of a truck stood heading downhill. I got in, arranged the gears, and turned on the ignition, and the sheepman pushed with all his strength. The truck began to roll, and as it moved the man walked and then ran after it, pushing it, leaning into it with all his might. Finally, he could not keep up, and I let in the clutch. The engine gave a sucking cough and started, vibrantly. I pulled out the hand throttle and let it roar.

We had our drinks, big ones, on the way to the sheepman's camp. Then, in his tent, we had another while I fried some thick venison steaks. We ate them sitting on the edge of his heavily quilted double bed. When we had finished, the man shucked his outer garments, and jackknifed under the covers. "Turn off the lantern when you're ready," he said.

"Ready for what?" I thought. I'd heard all these stories about lonely sheep herders. I suddenly knew how a tremulous virgin feels on her wedding night. But I was too tired to give a damn.

When I awoke it was daylight, and I was unsullied. I dressed hurriedly in a fog of my own frozen breath. Outside the previous day's overcast had broken into big, fast-sailing clouds, and below them the sage and squawbush sparkled under thick, crystalline frost. I looked around more carefully. I hadn't an idea in the world where I was. The sheep camp seemed to be perched atop the highest ridge in the Book Cliffs. As far as I could see, there was nothing but cold shards of blue sky looming over deep canyons and snowy vermiculated ridges. The single thread of road leading into the camp was the only attachment to civilization—wherever that was.

We had hotcakes in the sheep wagon with the sheepman's young herder and his wife. His previous job had been that of a taxi driver. I don't know what his unkempt but well-padded wife had done before, but I'm sure it wasn't cooking.

As the sheepman and I drove down to his truck he said, "Whoo-ee! Isn't she a lousy cook? I don't know how she ever got so fat on such rotten food."

We had no trouble pulling his big truck back up onto the road. We left it there for the herder, and I drove the sheepman home to his ranch on the Uinta slope.

"Can I pay you for all your trouble last night?"

"Hell, no, that could happen to anyone."

"Well," I said as we were shaking hands, "thanks until you're better paid."

"Okay."

I never saw him again.

The cabin at Three Pines was a big one-roomed frame building with a high-peaked roof covered with pinkish-red roofing paper. When I unlocked and opened the door, I was greeted by the smell of musty, frozen old air. In one corner stood a rusty Monarch range with a chipped ironware kettle sitting on its warped top. Across the range, next to the wall, was a low bench and washstand. I carried in my ten-gallon water can and put it down beside the stand. On the same side of the room was a big wooden table with benches attached on either side. The top was covered with linoleum and cigarette burns. Along the wall opposite the table was a counter with cupboards above and below. At the end of the room, against the back wall, were two iron-framed double-deck bunks. I tossed my sleeping bag down on one of the bottom ones. Then I went outside and brought in my grub box, and then my lantern, gas stove, suitcase, and a bag full of dog food for Jill. Enroute to the cabin I had stopped to gather wood. I threw the logs down near a scarred chopping block and cut enough juniper to fill the woodbox beside the stove.

Jill gaily retrieved the flying chips, and I got her to bring in a billet of wood each time I carried in an armload.

I had set a pot of coffee to boil on my gas stove, and it was ready by the time the wood was cut. I had a cup and then drove out in the truck for a look around.

The few existing roads in the Book Cliffs run mostly along the ridge tops. The floors of many of the canyons have a verdant look, in contrast with the roughness of the ridge-top vegetation, but some hunters who tried driving into one of them eventually had to climb out and abandon their jeep at the bottom. Driving south, the ridges continue to rise, as they had been doing ever since I left Ouray, and I had the eerie feeling out there that I was very near the edge of the world.

It was the day before Thanksgiving, and I found few hunters' camps. However, in one a middle-aged hunter and his grown son entered a foot race with me in an attempt to tag their deer before I reached them. The men lost. They were from California, and the violation seemed more an oversight than a deliberate attempt to evade the law. After giving them a lecture, I let them tag the deer.

Farther on I met a party of trophy hunters, also from California. There was one excellent buck in their camp. They said they had hunted Arizona's Kiabab and areas in southern Utah known for trophy bucks, and were now trying the Book Cliffs. Before I left them, I promised to keep an eye out for exceptional bucks.

I was also watching the wooly cloud bank beating down toward us from the Avintaquin. A few flakes of snow were again fluttering by. People would say during such spells of indecisive weather, "Well, if it don't snow today, it sure will miss a hell of a good chance."

Back at the cabin I lit the lantern and built a fire in the range. I put a pot of coffee on and fried some hamburger and potatoes.

After dinner Jill and I played. She would rush me and I would catch her in my hands and wrestle with her. She loved it, and if I tried to break off the struggle by patting her, she would take hold of my hand or arm in her mouth and squeeze just a shade too hard. Once a raspy howling in the stovepipe caused her to pause in mid-charge and look questioningly at the stove.

"It's just the wind," I said, "Come on."

But it had an eerie sound, and as it rose to a pounding gale, the fire's warmth seemed to be sucked straight up the stovepipe. The stove gobbled wood, and yet the room, and especially the floor, grew steadily colder. When Jill curled up beside the stove and closed her eyes, I propped my feet on the open oven door and began reading a paperback book. The wind hammered at the cabin, rattling windows in their sashes and twisting groans of protest from the wooden walls. Finally I stuck a match between the pages of my book and prepared for bed.

I filled the range's firebox and shut the dampers in the vain hope that the fire would last a few hours. Then I crawled into my warm sleeping bag and continued reading.

The wind continued to pound the cabin, sending tiny jets of pulverized snow squirting through the walls. I turned the lantern out and lay there in darkness, feeling the icy threads of snow stitching across my face. Drawing the bed tarp around my face, I soon fell asleep. Some time later I was awakened by a rustling, followed by something crawling across my feet. I snapped on the flashlight, and there was Jill. She was lying across the foot of the bed with her back feet still on the icy floor. She looked very guilty and very unhappy.

"Oh, all right, come on up." Jill wagged her tail and hopped up onto the foot of the bed.

Thanksgiving morning arrived, brilliant and crackling cold. The wind had died, and without it the old Monarch quickly heated the cabin. I ate a leisurely breakfast and then drove out along the ridge-top roads. There were few hunters abroad that morning, and here and there innocent-eyed deer stood by the roadsides, watching as I passed. As I drove around the head of a big, wild-looking draw, a mustang appeared at its lip, tossing his black head. He was a small, short-coupled horse, yet despite his ugliness there was an aura of unbroken freedom about him. As I drew nearer, he whirled on his back feet and went crashing back down into the draw. He was one of the last. The BLM had hired men to shoot these wild horses, and they had succeeded in virtually exterminating them.

The snowstorm of the night before had more bluster in it than substance. Snow lay now under the sage in serpentine little drifts of delicate whiteness. But there was little heat in the sunshine, and I was happy when, in the late afternoon, the Three Pines cabin came into sight. I picked up the radio microphone. "Four-fifty—Vernal."

"Four-fifty?" The radio dispatcher in Vernal replied to my radio call number.

"Ten-ten at Three Pines." I said, going out of service for the day.

"Ten-four. How's the weather out there?"

"Clear and cold."

"Ten-four. Got any turkey?"

"Negative, Vernal."

"Ten-four, four-fifty, K.O.B. two sixty-two." The dispatcher acknowledged me then, using his station's call letters, and signed off.

I replaced the microphone in its dashboard bracket and turned off the ignition. A great weight of sudden loneliness settled around my shoulders. Before leaving the truck, I reached behind the seat and pulled out the bottle of whiskey. It was half full, and I set it on the table while I built a fire and replenished the supply of fuel in the woodbox. That done, I sat down at the table and poured myself a substantial drink. Jill ambled over and placed her head on my knee. For some reason I thought of what Clay Paulhamus used to exclaim over some item of food or drink that particularly pleased him. "By God, there's no Norwegians and damn few Swedes that gets anything as good as this!"

I got up and threw open the lid of my grub box, and began preparing Thanksgiving dinner for one. I took out a can of French-style beans, opened it, and poured the contents into a pan. I found a can of new potatoes and opened it. In the meat safe were some deer and antelope steaks, and I took one of each, dredged them in flour, and placed them in the smoking-hot frying pan. When I turned the steaks, I put a pat of butter on top of each. My coffee had boiled, so I set that aside and slipped a small frying pan over the gas burner. I dropped in a chunk of butter and adjusted the heat. When the butter was bubbling hot I sliced the canned potatoes, letting them fall into the butter. While they were browning, I opened a jar of sweet gherkins and set them on the table. Then I took the loaf of home-made bread Ruth Jensen had given me. I cut off two thick, snowy slices and buttered them. When the meat was cooked, I scooped it onto my plate and added a couple of big spoonsful of string beans, to which I had also added butter. There was just barely room on my plate for the golden fried potatoes, so I heaped them up and garnished them with ketchup. I sat down at the table, tossed off the rest of my drink, and refilled the cup with fresh, hot coffee. Jill inched closer, until her chin was resting on my knee. I took a bite and looked down at her.

"By God," I said, "there no Norwegians and damn few Swedes..."

I stayed on at Three Pines until Sunday, then I started home via Willow Creek. A lot of hunters had come out over the weekend, and most had killed deer. I met Fat on the creek, and we decided to run a check station that evening on the road to Ouray. Enough vehicles were coming out to keep us pleasantly busy. One party drove up together in a pair of pickups. The men had a buck each, plus one superb stag, which a hunter claimed for his wife.

"Where is she?"

"She went home this afternoon. But I've got her license. It's in the suitcase." The man hauled a big tin-covered suitcase from out of the back of one of the trucks. Opening it, he began rummaging while I held a light for him. The contents, some soiled winter clothing, dirty handkerchiefs, and rectal ointment, appeared unusually masculine items to be in a woman's suitcase, but I withheld my opinion until the man unfurled a dirty old union suit. A license fell out of it.

"You're sure this is your wife's stuff?"

"Oh, sure."

"You know," I said, "we have had cases where a man takes his wife's license and kills a deer on it, while she stays home."

"You have?" The hunter was properly amazed.

"Yes. But we always check them out by calling on the radio and having the dispatcher ask the lady to describe the deer she shot. So if you'll just give me your telephone number..."

"Shit!" said the hunter. I began writing a citation for him.

Before Christmas, I began longing for an assignment like the Thanksgiving one in the Book Cliffs. My folks were far away on the Pacific Coast, and the prospect of the approaching holidays seemed bleak indeed. The preacher in the apartment above mine controlled and paid for the heat produced by the furnace in the basement. He probably never realized that my apartment also depended upon this heat. The tiny gas heater in my living room wasn't capable of heating the apartment by itself. When the preacher left on his trip, he turned down the heat. My bedroom was separated from the rest of the apartment, and the temperature there hovered around forty degrees above zero. I had to sleep in my sleeping bag with a blanket and a bed tarp thrown over the top. When I awoke on extra-cold mornings, there would be an eighth of an inch of solid ice on the window panes. In the evenings I sat humped beside the gas heater and read until I was half frozen. I began eating dinner in restaurants more often and lingering longer over my coffee and dessert. On other nights I went to the movies, taught gun-safety courses, rode with one of the highway patrolmen, or just drove out along the dark, wintry roads by myself. I became increasingly eager to go to work in the mornings. And when I complained about my cold apartment, my listener would say, "Oh, hell, the preacher's just makin' sure you won't have any women down there while he's gone."

One day Fat and I were looking for a place to trap magpies northeast of town. In winter pheasants congregated along the road running through the area, and we patrolled it often. On this particular day we heard a number of shots coming from the road. We hurried to the truck and quickly overhauled the suspect car. It was driven by a young man.

"What're you shooting at?"

"Nothing. This gun fires only blanks."

He produced a small handgun, which indeed only fired blanks. We looked through his car anyway, but found nothing. "Why were you shooting?" I asked.

"Pheasants," said the young man. "There are lots of them along the road now. I was trying to scare them back so the poachers wouldn't get them."

I was telling Dale Jensen about this one day when I had gone into his Basin Laundry to pick up my weekly parcel. Dale gave my story a big grin. He was a stocky, irrepressible fellow who had made good in his own home town and talked straight from the shoulder. "You let that damn dog of yours on the bed?" he asked.

"She gets on sometimes after I've had a couple of belts."

"I know, I can't get the hair off your sheets," Dale laughed. "Say," he asked, "What are you doing for Christmas?"

"Nothing much, guess I'll go out and make sure the kids don't try out their new guns on the pheasants."

"Oh, hell." Dale said, "Let it go for one day. Winnie and I would like you to come for dinner."

I was touched. As a game warden, I had come to accept being socially untouchable. Even the zealous Mormon missionaries avoided me, and I accepted Dale's invitation gratefully.

He and his wife, Winnie, lived in a very pleasant apartment over the laundry with their two sons, Rick and Jimmy. On Christmas Day Dale answered my knock. We shook hands and I said "Hi" to the two boys who were sitting by the big Christmas tree. Dale asked me if I'd like a drink. I accepted, and while it was being mixed the two boys showed me some of their presents. Then Winnie came in. She was a vivacious, thoroughly friendly little woman and, like myself, was not a native of the Uintah Basin. But she had learned to share Dale's love of upland bird-hunting, and with him she was developing in her sons a healthy set of values. I noticed that the boys' presents were mostly things that could be used outdoors, but there were books, too.

It had begun snowing lightly that morning, the first snow of the season in Vernal. Winnie looked out the window. "It's finally looking like Christmas." The drab little cow town was beginning to gleam under its layer of white.

"What do you say we go up to Doc's Beach and shoot some trap?" Dale asked.

Doc's Beach was a rustic and run-down dance hall north of town. The gun club had lately taken it over and was trying to make a recreation area of it. The installation of the trap was one of the first steps in that direction.

We all bundled up, stopped for my shotgun on the way out of

town, and in a half-hour's time had a fine fire burning in the old resort's big stone fireplace. Once everyone was warm, we took turns going out into the snow and banging at the orange-colored clay pigeons Dale sent spinning out of the trap.

It was an unusual way to spend a Christmas afternoon, and I enjoyed every minute of it.

Later, however, Jimmy drew his father aside, "You guys had a drink and then you went shooting. That's against the Ten Commandments of Shooting Safety."

"What did you tell him?" I asked Dale.

"Hell, the kid was right, and that's what I told him."

I haven't mixed alcohol and gunpowder since that day. Neither have I tasted any steak more delicious, or remembered hospitality more genuine or freely given. When I went home that evening, the snow was still drifting down, adding a special glow to the Christmas lights shining in every window. When I clumped down the darkened stairs to my room and flipped on the light, Jill met me, her tail wagging happily. Someone had turned on the furnace.

XV / THAT MEAN, ORNERY

SONOFABITCH WAS ME!

*"All right! Who put that picture of the boss
in the urinal?"*

—MAIN-OFFICE PANJANDRUM

THAT YEAR SPRINGTIME CAME TO THE ROCKIES ONE MURKY CHIL- ling day at a time. Sodden clouds drooped far down the mountain flanks and made the valley streams swirl high and muddy. When the chance came to spend a weekend at Hardware Ranch, I took it gratefully.

The Ranch, high in Blacksmith Fork Canyon, was the winter rendezvous for hundreds of northern Utah elk. It had been purchased from a hardware company (hence its name) after World War II. The purchase had proved a success in holding elk in the canyon and thus reducing their depredations downcountry in Cache Valley. Every day men riding horse-drawn bobsleighs distributed hay around the Ranch's snowy meadows for the hungry elk. The winter herd attracted crowds of tourists every weekend, and as a public-relations gesture they were loaded on board the sleighs and given a tour of the elk pastures. By late winter the elk scarcely noticed the sleighloads of people. Except, of course, when they were hungry, and then even the regal bulls sometimes came up and nibbled hay from excited fingers.

The weekend at the Ranch provided a needed change, and I especially enjoyed driving the teams. There were two of them, matched pairs of huge draft horses that easily pulled the crowded sleighs around and around the elk herd. We carried about fifteen passengers at a time. Once they were aboard and seated on the bales of hay, we went off across the meadows with a clink of tugs and the gaiety of sleigh bells. The weather turned mild that weekend and brought out a large crowd. As soon as one sleighload of passengers was unloaded, others clambered aboard all urging a faster, longer ride than the last group had enjoyed. By Sunday afternoon the work was telling on the horses. Muddy smears of turf gaped through the melting snow, and the big Belgians leaned into their collars for all they were worth.

While I was loading a group, a man tapped my arm.

[252

"Will you come and help my brother get on the sleigh?" he asked.

It seemed a rather thoughtless request; people were waiting, and I was busy with them and the horses. But seeing that the man had already lined up another warden, I tied the team and followed him. We stopped beside a sedan with a husky-looking young man sitting in the back seat. He certainly didn't appear to need help, but his brother interrupted my mental protest.

"You'll have to make a chair with your arms and carry him between you."

Hearing this, the young man flushed and began sliding crab-like across the seat toward us. The other warden and I linked arms and slid them under the young man's legs, while he put his arms around our shoulders. When we had him out of the car and hoisted between us he said "Thank you," still blushing.

But I hardly noticed, for I was more ashamed of my impatience. This kid didn't have any legs, just two dangling appendages that hung over our arms like limp rope.

He seemed to overcome his embarrassment as we approached the team and sleigh. His eyes were shining, and he was barely able to contain his excitement when we swung him aboard the sleigh and seated him on a bale of hay. I popped the reins and the team swung away with a swish of snow from the runners and a volley of ringing from the bells. We went all the way to the end of the snowy meadow and then turned back and stopped in the midst of the elk herd. The young man pulled a handful of hay from the bale on which he was sitting and offered it to an inquiring cow elk. She ate it and inquired impatiently for more. Soon there were elk bumming all around the sleigh, and the young man fed every one he could reach. Seldom have I seen a human being so happy and so consumed with simple pleasure. He had tears in his eyes when the ride ended and we carried him back to the car.

Before returning to Vernal on Monday, I stopped in Salt Lake City and took a couple of merit-system examinations. One test was for a coveted game manager's job, and the other for a position in the department's public-relations office—the hand-shakers and back-slappers. I took the latter test mainly to get my name on the register.

Back in Vernal, I was too busy preparing for range rides to spend much time in anticipating the test results. Island Park was the first area to be surveyed, and the road was a greasy track with no bottom where it crossed over the gumbo washes. We had to caravan out, sending the four-wheel-drives ahead so that they could turn and pull our pickups through the bog holes with their winches. The horses had to be unloaded at every wash, led across, and then tied while we fought the trucks and trailers through. We cut greasewood and piled it into the wheel ruts, and the gray mud clung to our boots and slowly inched up our trouser legs until we were muddy to the knees.

On the slopes the horses slipped, slithered, and slid downhill on their haunches. By evening their legs and heaving bellies were plastered with half-dried mud.

The old ranch house where we stayed was overcrowded and underheated. The chest cold I had brought with me blossomed into bronchitis, and lifting a saddle up on the patient Pig became a life's work. When the rides were finally over I went home sick, and also disappointed, because the worn range didn't look a bit better than it had the spring before. We had fought over hunting seasons with sportsmen, stockmen, and the federal land managers, and in my naïveté I had unconsciously expected to see an improved range this spring. I guess nature disposes of her impatience by giving it to young men.

Finding the bald eagle was an added misfortune. After the range rides, I took a drive through my district and saw the big bird squatting in a pen beside a house. It was a handsome specimen, with pure-white head and tail. And possessing it, even just one feather of it, was strictly against state and federal law. The owner of the adjacent house kept a little menagerie, which he opened each summer as an attraction for his highway hamburger stand. It was disgusting to realize that this majestic eagle, our national emblem, was going to be used to hustle hamburgers.

Nevertheless, I drove on without stopping, because I had no idea what to do with the eagle if I seized it. At home I called the office, and they in turn notified a U.S. game management agent, who arrived within a few days.

In Utah these officers are primarily involved with enforcing waterfowl regulations. They are also responsible in cases of illegal game transported across state lines. It was a revelation for me to see the steely efficiency with which the agent cited the eagle-napper. It made no difference to the officer when I explained that the fellow was a member of an influential family. Some of his ranching kin had been meaner than cat piss about deer on their property. And I hoped that the eagle affair could be handled quietly enough to avoid stirring up old deer troubles.

I also told the agent, "Nobody ever tried protecting eagles out here before." He looked at me as though I had offered him a bribe. But he did listen while the accused explained how he'd acquired the bird.

"My uncle found him last winter. The eagle was hopping around in some tall grass an' he just picked him up. We probably saved his life."

Possibly the bird had overloaded himself on carrion and then had been unable to take off, or he may have been sickened by a trapper's poisoned bat. However, he seemed healthy enough when we went out to take him out of the cage. He fixed us with a soulless eye and began an almost-impreceptible chewing motion with his vicious-looking beak. I hoped it wasn't in anticipation.

My apprehension mounted when I saw that all the agent had brought along for eagle catching were a pair of old gloves, a cardboard box, and some sash cord.

"You just gonna' grab him?" I asked, surprised.

"Sure." The man was all confidence, and ignored the accused, who was grinning wolfishly in the background.

When the agent opened the pen door, the eagle raised its great wings threateningly. I expected blood to fly, but the agent easily caught hold of the raised wings and pinned them gently but firmly behind the bird's back. Then, as I held the carton, he maneuvered the bird into it and closed the lid. The bird fought the box while the agent tied its top shut with the sash cord. The lashing was loose but, remembering his performance so far, I was almost afraid to ask.

"Won't he get out?"

"No," said the agent as we slid the quaking box onto his car's back seat. "It's dark in there, he'll go to sleep."

The eagle continued to jump around in the box, making it shudder ominously on the seat. I rode with one eye on it and the other on the road ahead. My surveillance was briefly distracted and when I looked back there stood the biggest goddamn eagle I have ever seen. His wings were partially spread, like Death coming in for a landing, and his fierce head was low and partially extended.

"Jesus!" I whispered.

"What?"

"That son of a bitch is loose!"

The agent immediately slowed the car, and as he did so I began opening the door.

"Don't do that," he said, "he'll get out."

"Exactly!" I thought. But I sat still while the agent with cautious confidence, reached back and recaptured the eagle.

The case wasn't heard until several days later. And the judge had obviously been brooding about it.

"Why do you always bring these things in here?" He was apparently still upset about my last deer case, so when the eagle-napper appeared, he was promptly released with a suspended fine. When we were alone, the judge growled. "Don't bring me any more eagles."

I resolved that my next case would be clear-cut, and preferably involving someone without relatives in the Uintah Basin. Then I was summoned to Salt Lake City. I had passed the merit examinations and was now to face a board of examiners. It wasn't a long confrontation; a more-senior employee was in line for the game manager's job. But they were optimistic about the public-relations position. "Here is an opportunity," one said, "to talk wildlife conservation with everyone in Utah." I didn't share his enthusiasm; I wanted to conserve wildlife, not talk about it. When the board dismissed me, I supposed that I would be in Vernal for some time to come.

My conviction was firm enough to justify buying a second-hand house trailer before I left the city. It was a ponderous, pink-sided thing, forty-five feet long. But after freezing in my gloomy basement apartment all winter, I thought my new home was perfect. It did require some minor repairs, and trailer deliveries to eastern Utah were slow anyway, but in only a few weeks I would never again hear the woman upstairs taking a pee! I rented space on a pleasant little lot outside Vernal just before the regional pilot flew in to begin our antelope counts.

Bob Phillips had not been flying long for the department, but he was a veteran mountain pilot. "Did you order this?" he asked, waving at the stormfront approaching from the northwest. We pushed the little Cessna into a hangar and I drove Phillips to a motel in town.

The sky next morning was heavily overcast, and our flight was postponed. A grounded pilot becomes a nervous animal, and I asked Phillips if he would like to ride around with me that afternoon. He seemed delighted, so, with Jill riding behind the cab, I stopped by his motel soon after lunch. I took him for a drive through some of the farming areas.

We saw hundreds of pheasants feeding in the fields. The somber hens hunched low, like reclining numeral 9s, while the gaudy roosters stretched and made themselves as brassily obvious as possible. Every one was a beauty.

As we drove I told Phillips how motoring poachers watched carefully ahead and behind but often neglected to check the adjacent crossroads. A warden could sometimes spot them by looking carefully to his right and left at each intersection. As luck had it, we looked left at the very next crossroads and there was a chubby guy running along with a cock pheasant in his hand.

He looked easy. "We got a pheasant hunter!" I exclaimed, jamming down on the pickup's accelerator. As I did so, the poacher, who was crawling through a fence, looked up and saw us. He dropped the bird and ran for the station wagon waiting on the road. My pickup was a logy machine, and I flipped the shift lever into second gear, trying for a burst of speed that would intercept the poacher. It was no use—he outran us to his car by thirty yards. Then, just as we reached his back bumper, the poacher sent his car breaking away in a burst of V-8 speed.

He ignored my red light and blaring horn. The road was narrow and unpaved. Almost immediately, my speedometer needle was bouncing on sixty. When we left Vernal I had chained Jill to my equipment box in the back of the truck. Now I glimpsed her in the mirror: her ears were planing in the wind, and she was riding like a vengeful Valkyrie. I didn't look back again; the road ahead ran straight for a while, then began bobbing over and around some low hills.

"Bob!" I yelled, "Call Vernal. Ask if they can get a car at the east end of the Oil Field Road."

I took a curve, slewing around it, then straightening the wheel and throwing showers of gravel through a towering veil of dust. Over the roar we heard the police dispatcher's laconic voice. "Negative, four-fifty. No cars your area. Keep your suspect in sight. I'm sending a car."

There was a hill ahead, and the station wagon disappeared over its crest. Every second he was getting farther away. We shot up the grade. I never eased up on the gas pedal, and the truck almost flew over the hilltop. The road swam to the left, I spun the wheel, and in the same instant I saw the station wagon. It was lying upside-down in the shallow ravine ahead. The road jerked back to the right, I turned the steering wheel—gravel flew away from the skidding tires like machine-gun bullets—and I touched the brake.

Instantly the road reared up wildly to my left and then shot into the sky. "Ohh, *shit!* We're going over!" The right front wheel ripped loose, and dust billowed into the cab. Simultaneously, there was a rending crash that rose and fell but never stopped as we began rolling. Everything was whirling dust and flying chaos. I held to the steering wheel. We started over again, and I was jammed head-first into the windshield. A gout of blood spattered down. I bounced backward, then lost my grip on the wheel and plummeted heavily down on top of Phillips. He didn't know it then, but his back was broken.

Silence. The truck had come to rest on its right side.

"Are you hurt?" I asked.

"I don't think so. Can you get off me?"

The door was jammed, so I crawled out through the window. Blood was streaming down my face and over my shirt from the cut in my scalp. I mopped it away, then looked at the truck. It was twisted and squashed like an old beer can.

"Jill."

She was gone. Her chain hung broken from the ring on my smashed equipment box. The box's contents were scattered wildly out through the sage. I walked down to the overturned station wagon and met the dazed-looking poacher, a young man in his early twenties. His pale face was scratched, and one of his trouser legs was ripped and dark with blood.

"You're under arrest."

"I know it."

I walked past him to two young women half-lying beside their overturned car. "Anybody hurt?"

"Don't think so." They looked at me vacantly, and then I noticed that both girls were monumentally pregnant. I could visualize miscarriages exploding all up and down the ravine. To the poacher I said, "Keep them still."

He said something, and I answered, "We're okay but my dog's gone. I think my dog's been killed."

Phillips was out of the truck now. He was very pale, and I thought he was in shock. "Your radio still works," he said.

I reached through the gaping windshield and pulled out the microphone, "Four-fifty—Vernal."

"Go ahead, four-fifty."

"Better send an ambulance out here. We've got some people hurt. Both cars went over.

"Ten-four, four-fifty. Take it easy, boy, you'll have some help right away."

There were two rifles in the poacher's car, a .22 with a fired shell in the chamber and a .300 Savage. Mentally, I began listing his violations. This one would go to jail for sure. Then Sam Hatch barreled up in his blue highway-patrol sedan. Sam was an old-timer, chewing gum and calmly cleaning up the ragged cut on my head.

"Can I get him for resisting arrest, Sam?"

"Might. But why don't you take this guy on all the game counts an' let us handle the accident?"

It was good advice, and I took it. Vernal's combination hearse-ambulance drove up, and Phillips, the two women, and the poacher were helped in and hurried away to the doctor. Sam waited with me. He had offered to drive me back along the road so I could look for Jill and the pheasant.

We found the bird lying where it had been dropped. Already it had dried and faded into a stiff lump of inconsequence. But we could not find Jill, and I began to fear that she was lying crushed under the wreck. On the way to the doctor's Sam said that Jill might have been thrown clear, and that he would have his men watch for her.

Dr. Christian worked with practiced skill on my laceration. I could feel his needle punch through the loose flaps of scalp, and a drawing sensation as the gut drew tight.

"How are those women?" I asked.

"They seem to be all right. The young man had a bad gash on his knee, and I've sent your partner to the hospital for the night.